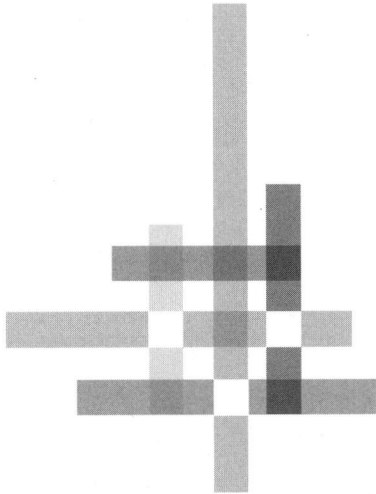

Frontiers in Development Policy

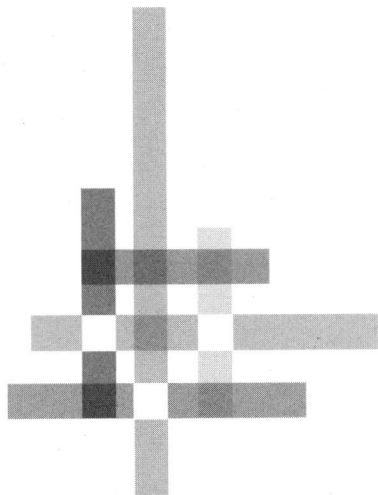

Frontiers in Development Policy

A Primer on Emerging Issues

Raj Nallari, Shahid Yusuf, Breda Griffith,
and Rwitwika Bhattacharya

THE WORLD BANK
Washington, D.C.

ISBN: 978-0-8213-8785-6
eISBN: 978-0-8213-8786-3
DOI: 10.1596/978-0-8213-8785-6

Library of Congress Cataloging-in-Publication Data
Nallari, Raj, 1955-
  Frontiers in development policy / by Raj Nallari, Shahid Yusuf, Breda Griffith, and Rwitwika Bhattacharya.
    p. cm.
  Includes bibliographical references and index.
  ISBN 978-0-8213-8785-6 — ISBN 978-0-8213-8786-3 (electronic) 1. Global Financial Crisis, 2008-2009. 2. Developing countries—Economic policy. 3. Free enterprise—Developing countries. 4. Economic development—Environmental aspects—Developing countries. I. Nallari, Raj, 1955–II. Title.
  HB37172008 .N35 2011
  338.9—dc23

                                                                    2011025640

Cover: Naylor Design, Inc.

CONTENTS

Tables

PREFACE

This primer was compiled for the Frontiers in Development Policy course that took place in April 2011 at the World Bank. The goal of the book is to bring home the interlinkages in various parts of the economy and the need for practical policy making to reach development goals while being aware of the instabilities, complexities, and risks inherent in an economy operating in a globalized world. The book is targeted toward change agents and policy makers.

The book was written in light of the global crisis of 2008–09, which brought to the forefront a plethora of economic and policy issues. There was a reopening of discussion concerning basic economic concepts (such as the definition of development), discussion about appropriate framework for analysis (for example, the roles of political economy and institutions), analysis of the balance between private and public sectors in the economy, evaluation of how best to achieve structural transformation of economies while ensuring human development, and exploration on managing growing risks and crises (for example, financial and food crises) in a rapidly changing world.

The criteria for topics to be included in this book were (1) whether the policy issue is of importance to promote strong, sustainable, and inclusive growth in low-income and middle-income developing countries and (2) whether the policy issue is "new and emerging" and necessitates a discussion and debate among policy makers and practitioners.

The book has been divided into five parts. Part 1 focuses on clarifying the basic concepts (that is, what are the appropriate goals of economic policy?), the challenges of low- and middle-income developing countries, and suggested frameworks for analysis.

Part 2 moves from the macroeconomic to the microeconomic; it focuses on the private sector as the engine for growth and is balanced with "softer" issues of the need for trust, accountability, and corporate social responsibility.

Part 3 examines the growing consensus on the need to balance the public and private sectors' roles in the structural transformation of an economy. The discussion centers on newer thinking on industrial policy and public-private partnerships in infrastructure.

Part 4 focuses on human development policies in emerging topics, such as investment in early childhood development, health and nutrition, and quality of education. The discussion recognizes the roles of the state and the private sector.

Finally, part 5 is dedicated to issues of global shocks and risks (including climate change and financial crisis), as well as systems and institutions that need to be in place to manage such risks, and the new thinking on social protection and insurance to mitigate adverse shocks.

The first draft of the book was used for the face-to-face and e-learning course based in Washington, DC. After feedback from the course participants, the manuscript was revised to include additional topics pertinent to development.

The authors would like to thank the participants of the face-to-face and e-learning course for their feedback on the book; the Korean Development Institute for helping to organize this course and, indirectly, contributing to this book; and Dulce Afzal for her commitment and hard work.

ABOUT THE AUTHORS

Raj Nallari manages the Growth and Competitiveness Practice at the World Bank Institute. He holds a doctorate in economics from the University of Texas at Austin and has been with the World Bank since 1992. He is the coauthor of several books on macroeconomic stabilization, growth and poverty, and gender issues. Mr. Nallari has also written monographs for the World Bank and published articles in economic journals. He can be reached at rnallari@worldbank.org.

Shahid Yusuf holds a doctorate in economics from Harvard University and a bachelor of arts degree in economics from Cambridge University. He joined the World Bank in 1974 as a Young Professional and while at the Bank spent more than 35 years tackling issues confronting developing countries. He has written extensively on development issues, with a focus on East Asia, and has published widely in various academic journals. He is currently chief economist for the Growth Dialogue at the School of Business, George Washington University. He can be reached at syusuf@worldbank.org.

Breda Griffith has worked as a consultant with the World Bank Institute since 2005, mainly in the areas of growth, poverty, and gender. She holds a doctorate in economics from Trinity College Dublin and a master of arts degree in economics from National University of Ireland. She can be reached at breda_griffith@yahoo.com.

Rwitwika Bhattacharya is a Junior Professional Associate at the World Bank. She holds a master's degree in public policy from the Harvard Kennedy School. She has worked at the World Bank since 2010 and can be reached at rbhattacharya@worldbank.org.

ABBREVIATIONS

BRIC	Brazil, the Russian Federation, India, and China
CSR	corporate social responsibility
FDI	foreign direct investment
GDP	gross domestic product
GHG	greenhouse gas
GNDI	gross national disposable income
GNI	gross national income
GNP	gross national product
GPI	genuine progress indicator
HIV/AIDS	human immunodeficiency virus/acquired immune deficiency syndrome
IAH	inequality-adjusted happiness
ILO	International Labour Organization
ISEW	Index of Sustainable Economic Welfare
LFPR	labor force participation rate
MDG	Millennium Development Goal
MILES	World Bank framework for analyzing five main factors affecting employment: macroeconomic performance, investment climate, labor market policies and institutions, education, and skills and social protection for workers
NNDI	net national disposable income
NNI	net national income
OECD	Organisation for Economic Co-operation and Development
PPI	private participation in infrastructure
R&D	research and development
TFP	total factor productivity
USPTO	U.S. Patent and Trademark Office

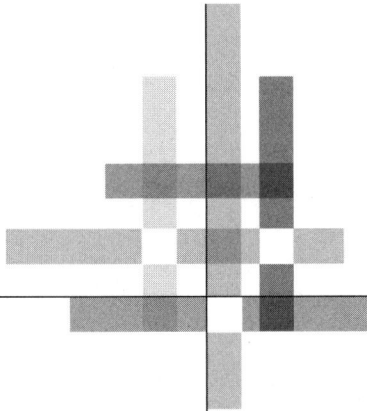

Part I

DEVELOPMENT CHALLENGES IN A POSTCRISIS WORLD

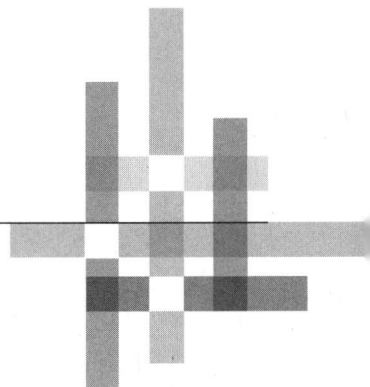

Overview

Raj Nallari

Genesis of the Crisis

The recent financial and economic crisis that hit the world economy had all the markings of a "perfect storm." As we examine the debris and isolate the development challenges, it is instructive to look at the crisis in this light.

The ex ante global saving glut that resulted from the emergence of Brazil, the Russian Federation, India, and China (the BRIC countries) and the redistribution of global wealth and income toward the Gulf states because of the rise in oil and gas prices depressed long-term global real interest rates to unprecedentedly low levels (see Bernanke 2005). The supply of safe financial assets did not meet the demand. Western banks and investors began to scout around for alternative, higher-yielding financial investment opportunities. Brazil, China, India, Vietnam, and other labor-rich but capital-scarce countries raised the return to physical capital formation everywhere. The unsustainable current account deficit of the United States was made to appear sustainable through the willingness of China and many other emerging markets to accumulate large stocks of U.S. dollars, both as official foreign exchange reserves and for portfolio investment purposes.

The excess liquidity in the world went primarily into credit growth and resulted in speculative bubbles in housing, stocks, and commodities (and not into consumer price inflation). The exact time when the home mortgage problems surfaced can now be pinpointed to mid-2006, even though government and market players did not fully acknowledge the housing problem until almost the summer of 2007. By mid-2006, there was enough evidence of housing prices beginning to decrease significantly, and default rates were increasing in some U.S. states, such as Arizona and California.

Economic Situation in the Developing World

The developing world had experienced unprecedented growth in the run-up to the crisis. Most countries achieved per capita growth rates of more than 2 percent in the period 2003–07, which facilitated progress in reducing poverty rates. Emerging market economies in Europe, Latin America, and Southeast Asia led by almost doubling their 1990s per capita growth rates. Some fragile states also experienced an acceleration in growth—reflecting, in Sierra Leone's case, the transition from conflict, and in Angola, Chad, and Sudan, the effect of higher oil and gas exports during the period (World Bank 2008).

Table 1.1 examines global output for advanced and developing economies from 2007, with projections to 2013. Global output that fell heavily in 2008

Table 1.1   Global Output
percentage change

| Region | 2007 | 2008 | 2009 | Projection | |
				2010	2011–13
World output	**5.2**	**3.0**	**–0.6**	**4.2**	**4.4**
Advanced economies	2.8	0.5	–3.2	2.3	2.4
Emerging and developing economies	8.3	6.1	2.4	6.3	6.6
Central and Eastern Europe	5.5	3.0	–3.7	2.8	3.8
Commonwealth of Independent States	8.6	5.5	–6.6	4.0	4.1
Developing Asia	10.6	7.9	6.6	8.7	8.6
Middle East and North Africa	5.6	5.1	2.4	4.5	4.8
Sub-Saharan Africa	6.9	5.5	2.1	4.7	5.7
Western Hemisphere	5.8	4.3	–1.8	4.0	4.2

Source: World Bank 2010b, 70.

worsened further in 2009 across all country income groups. Global output began to recover in 2010 on the back of improved financial conditions and rising world trade (World Bank 2010b, 70). Commodity prices declined sharply in 2008, but rebounded again in 2009 and maintained their position in 2010, bringing good news for commodity exporters. The continuing high food prices are not good for the poor, however. Growth in emerging and developing economies is expected to reach 6.3 percent in 2010 (from 2.4 percent in 2009), and the outlook for the short and medium terms is positive. The longer-run scenario is less predictable as we cannot know if there are longer-term implications of the recent crisis that may divert the growth path of the developing economies. This question is especially important for low-income economies, where poverty is much more of an issue.

The favorable macroeconomic performance among low- and middle-income countries in terms of inflation, current account balance, external debt, and fiscal balance in the years preceding the crisis is expected to help these countries better weather the storm. Moreover, the financial sector in low-income countries was less affected by the crisis than in the emerging market and advanced economies.

Prior to the financial crisis, the combination of economic growth and good macroeconomic performance helped developing countries attract significant capital flows. Private flows became more important than official sources.[1] Official financing has not been very important in the emerging market economies in recent years—even becoming negative, on average, as many countries prepaid their debt to the official creditors.[2] The improved macroeconomic environment and high growth rates spurred the demand for bonds and private equity. Debt-generating financing (both official and private) became less important in emerging markets as foreign direct investment and workers' remittances increased considerably.[3] (See table 1.2.)

Private financial flows to developing and emerging market economies suffered greatly in the wake of the crisis and have not yet recovered to the precrisis levels. Bank financing and foreign direct investment declined sharply and account for the weak recovery in financial flows. Official capital flows and transfers have increased. Worker remittances are expected to increase by 2 percent in 2010, from a fall of 6 percent in 2009 (World Bank 2010b, 74).

In Conclusion

The preceding discussion suggests that parts of the developing world were in a relatively good position going into the crisis. However, the downturn

Table 1.2   Net Financial Flows, 2007–10
percentage of GDP

Flows	2007	2008	2009	2010
Emerging market economies	12.6	11.4	8.7	8.2
Private capital flows, net	8.0	7.0	3.2	3.1
Private direct investment	5.4	5.1	3.3	3.3
Private portfolio flows	0.8	−0.5	−0.3	0.1
Private current transfers	4.1	3.7	3.8	3.6
Official capital flows and transfers, net	0.4	0.7	1.7	1.6
Memorandum item				
Reserve assets	−3.9	−1.6	−2.5	−1.9
Developing countries	14.0	17.7	13.9	13.9
Private capital flows, net	6.6	7.7	5.2	5.3
Private direct investment	6.6	6.2	4.8	4.7
Private portfolio flows	−0.7	−0.6	−0.4	−0.2
Private current transfers	5.6	5.8	5.2	5.1
Official capital flows and transfers, net	1.8	4.2	3.6	3.5
Memorandum item				
Reserve assets	−4.0	−2.3	−1.6	1.0

Source: World Bank 2010b, 74.

affected all developing regions (table 1.1), particularly the emerging market economies in Europe and Central and South Asia.

Official creditors increased their support to low- and middle-income countries. In particular, the International Monetary Fund and the World Bank increased their funding, especially to those countries adversely affected by the crisis. "Official grants (excluding technical cooperation grants) rose by 13 percent in 2008, reflecting donors' commitment to a substantial increase in official development assistance to help developing countries, especially those of Sub-Saharan Africa" (World Bank 2010a, 3).

The challenge for development is to sustain the good performance that the emerging economies had achieved prior to the crisis and maintain the strong position they are experiencing at the moment. At the same time, economic growth in the low-income economies and the fragile states must be pursued—not least for the achievement of the Millennium Development Goals (MDGs) in which the human development priorities depend on economic growth.

The following sections examine development policy in the wake of the financial crisis, beginning with an explanation of what is development and then moving to a discussion of poverty traps, followed by the progress made on the MDGs. The book then turns to looking at middle-income traps and pathways to development, followed by an analysis of why development is blocked, of precrisis challenges, and of the political economy.

Notes

1. During the 1990s, about half (as a proportion of gross domestic product) of total external financing came from private sources, increasing to two thirds in 2007.
2. Net liabilities to official creditors have decreased because of shifts in the composition of external financing and debt reduction operations.
3. Most of the foreign direct investment was in infrastructure projects, but the success of the macroeconomic stabilization policies also prompted investment in other sectors (World Bank 2008).

References

Bernanke, B. 2005. "The Global Saving Glut and the U.S. Current Account Deficit." Sandridge Lecture, Virginia Association of Economists, Richmond, VA. http://www.federalreserve.gov/boarddocs/speeches/2005/200503102/.

World Bank. 2008. *Global Monitoring Report 2008: MDGs and the Environment— Agenda for Inclusive and Sustainable Development*. Washington, DC: World Bank.

———. 2010a. *Global Development Finance: External Debt of Developing Countries*. Washington, DC: World Bank.

———. 2010b. *Global Monitoring Report: The MDGs after the Crisis*. Washington, DC: World Bank.

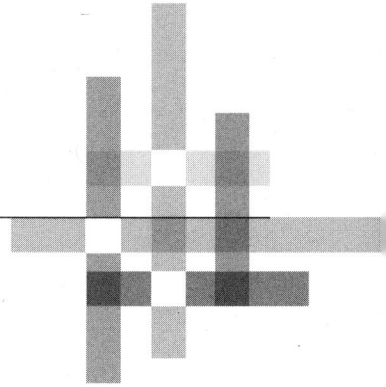

What Is Development?

Breda Griffith

Development is a normative concept and is therefore subject to value judgments. Development, according to Seers, is the "realization of human personality," the absolute necessity of which is adequate nutrition (1972, 21). Given that prices are involved, income is required to purchase food and have some income left over for other basic physical necessities (Seers 1972, 23). Unsurprisingly, then, national income, gross domestic product (GDP), or its derivatives—GDP per capita, GDP growth rates—have long been viewed as convenient indicators of development. Furthermore, the view that increasing economic growth would bring about development through reductions in poverty has been all pervasive.[1] Yet, it has been and continues to be obvious to those working in development that focusing on a single, aggregative measure of income as an indicator of development is inadequate. Thus, the past 50 years have seen many attempts at providing a more encompassing measure or measures that would target the many facets of development necessary to "realize the human personality." Seers notes that once "undernourishment, unemployment and inequality dwindle," educational and political participation become important, followed by freedom from repressive sexual codes, noise, and pollution (1972, 24). The following paragraphs examine the criticisms of GDP as a measure of development and the progress that has been made in arriving at less aggregative measures that describe development.

Why GDP Is a Convenient But Inadequate Measure of Development

GDP is a measure beloved by many—economists, business owners, politicians—and it is a satisfactory measure for what it is intended, that is, to measure whether output in an economy is expanding or contracting. How satisfactory GDP is depends on time and place. For example, the structural makeup of an economy changes over time—witness today's modern service-led economy where many of the increases in output stem from quality improvements rather than increases in quantity of output. Moreover, many of the services provided by government in today's developed economy—education, public health, public housing—are inadequately measured in GDP[2] and the data do not reflect productivity improvements in these services (Stiglitz, Sen, and Fitoussi 2009).[3] In a developing economy, there are other issues[4]—not least the availability of data.

Criticisms of GDP have waxed and waned over the period from when it was first created by Simon Kuznets in 1934. GDP has often been used as a measure of well-being, although Kuznets himself cautioned against this (Kuznets 1934). Two of the major weaknesses long associated with GDP are "(a) being a monetary aggregate, it pays little or no attention to distributional issues and to elements of human activity or well-being for which no direct or indirect market valuation is available; (b) it is measuring productive flows and, as such, ignores the impact of productive activities on stocks, including stocks of natural resources" (Afsa et al. 2009, 1).

GDP is but one of a number of measures contained in the system of national accounts. Other measures—gross national income (GNI), gross national disposable income (GNDI),[5] net national income (NNI), net national disposable income (NNDI)[6] are but four measures that provide better measures of standards of living than GDP alone. However, these indicators do not capture all aspects of well-being; and a number of alternative measures that have at their cores an attempt to garner a better measure of well-being and, by extension,[7] a better measure of development are available.

First, there are indicators that have been developed at the national and international levels in an attempt to provide a more extensive description of living conditions and social progress and are referred to as a "dashboard of indicators" (Stiglitz, Sen, and Fitoussi 2009, 8). Other measures have been developed that "correct" GDP, while a third set of indexes measure well-being directly. Finally, there are composite indexes that combine approaches (Costanza et al. 2009). Table 2.1 presents a few indicators from each of the four identified groups. Further information and measures are available at Afsa et al. (2009).

Table 2.1 Alternative Measures of GDP

Type of index	Indicator		Objective	Scope/ dimension	Initiated	Geographic coverage
	Name	Measure(s)				
Dashboard of indicators	Alternative measures of well-being	1. GDP, NDP, NNI 2. GDP per capita adjusted for leisure time 3. Synthetic index of well-being focused on 16 social indicators—self-sufficiency, equity, health, social cohesion 4. Survey measures of happiness and satisfaction of life from various surveys	To assess whether GDP per capita is an adequate proxy of well-being, or whether other indicators used as complements or substitutes for GDP are more suitable	Compares evidence based on four measures of well-being	One-off publication in 2006 and 2007	OECD countries
	Calvert-Henderson Quality of Life Indicators	1. Education 2. Employment 3. Energy 4. Environment 5. Health 6. Human rights 7. Income 8. Infrastructure 9. National security 10. Public safety 11. Recreation 12. Shelter	To develop statistics of national well-being that go beyond traditional macroeconomic indicators	Developed by citizen and research groups	2000	United States

(continued next page)

Table 2.1 *(continued)*

Type of index	Indicator		Objective	Scope/dimension	Initiated	Geographic coverage
	Name	Measure(s)				
	Millennium Development Goals	1. Poverty and nutrition 2. Universal primary education 3. Gender equality 4. Child mortality 5. Maternal health 6. HIV/AIDS, malaria, and other diseases 7. Environmental sustainability 8. Global partnership for development	To achieve these eight goals by 2015	Poverty, hunger, health, education, gender equality, environment, and development	2000	189 developing countries
Indexes that "correct" GDP	Index of Sustainable Economic Welfare (ISEW)/Genuine Progress Indicator (GPI)	ISEW = Consumer spending adjusted for inequality + Public expenditures excluding defensive expenditures + Growth in capital and net change in international position + Nonmonetized contributions to Welfare – Defensive private	To account for current environmental issues and long-term sustainable use of natural ecosystems and resources	Assesses whether an economy's growth has resulted in the improvement of welfare (by accounting for crime, environmental degradation, income inequality, benefits from volunteering, and household duties)	1989, with GPI replacing ISEW in 1995	Developed economies

Indicator	Description / components	Purpose	Notes	Status	Coverage
	expenditures – Costs of Environmental degradation – Depreciation of the environmental capital base				
Green GDP	Adjust net savings for depletion of or damage to environmental resources	To correct GDP for environmental degradation	n.a.	Numerous attempts at a country level[a]; World Bank has calculated "green data" since 2006	Developed and developing economies
Genuine savings	Monetized index that defines net savings as net gross savings – Consumption of fixed capital + Education expenditures – Consumption of natural resources (fossil fuels, mineral resources, and forest) and monetary evaluations of damages from CO_2 emissions	To ascertain whether economies are enhancing or adding to their natural resource base and are thus on a longer-term sustainable development path	More in the spirit of sustainability than welfare[b]	1999	Developed and developing economies
Index of Living Standards	GDP corrected for 1. Leisure (hours worked) 2. Employment uncertainty (unemployment insurance)	To make an international comparison of living standards, adjusting for criticisms of GDP	Net national income per capita adjusted for elements of well-being, both individual and collective in terms	One-off research published in 2006; data for 2004	24 OECD countries

(continued next page)

Table 2.1 (continued)

| Type of index | Indicator | | Objective | Scope/ dimension | Initiated | Geographic coverage |
	Name	Measure(s)				
		of equivalent incomes				
		3. Healthy life years (additional one year of healthy life)				
		4. Household size				
		5. Inequalities: overweighting the poor (average income —Kolm-Atkinson index)				
		6. Sustainability: cost of natural resources depletion, weighted by share of national consumption in total consumption + cost of greenhouse gas emissions				
Well-being measures	Ecological Footprint	A measure of the surface of habitable land needed to support the current standards of living of various countries	To measure human demand on earth's ecosystem	More in the spirit of sustainability than welfare	1995	Developed and developing economies

	World Database of Happiness	Database devoted to studies and surveys of happiness and satisfaction	n.a.	n.a.	2005	Developed and developing economies
	Gross National Happiness	Gross national happiness	To provide guidance for the inhabitants of Bhutan, cognizant of their spiritual and cultural values	No specific methodology available	1980	Bhutan
	Inequality-Adjusted Happiness (IAH)	Index combining level and dispersion of happiness; data derived from population surveys on "how happy one is" and combined into a formula to arrive at measures of IAH	To make an international comparison of "societal performance"	Strives to combine the principles of average happiness and equality in happiness	2005	95 developed economies
Composite measures	Human Development Index	Index combining GDP per capita in purchasing power parity US$ with 1. Life expectancy at birth 2. Adult literacy 3. Combined gross enrollment in primary-, secondary-, and tertiary-level education	To provide a global assessment of country achievements in different areas of human development	Longevity, knowledge, and standard of living	1990	175 developing and developed economies

(*continued next page*)

Table 2.1 *(continued)*

Type of index	Indicator		Objective	Scope/dimension	Initiated	Geographic coverage
	Name	Measure(s)				
	Happy Planet Index	Index mixing subjective and quantitative data	To assess the ability of a country to combine the objectives of good and long lives while respecting the environmental resource limits	Satisfaction, life expectancy, and environmental sustainability	2006	All countries (179)

Sources: Compiled from Afsa et al. 2009; Stiglitz, Sen, and Fitoussi 2009; Costanza et al. 2009; and European Commission 2009.

Note: n.a. = not applicable; NDP = net domestic product; OECD = Organisation for Economic Co-operation and Development.

a. Costanza et al. (2009) refer to Japan in the 1980s and Australia, Canada, China, Cost Rica, Indonesia, Mexico, Papua New Guinea, and the United States as all having developed measures of green GDP at one time or another.

b. Afsa et al. (2009, 12) examine briefly the link between sustainability and well-being. They summarize that a higher level of current well-being is associated with a lower level of sustainability, and vice versa. Furthermore, they reference Neumayer (2004), who argues in favor of presenting well-being and sustainability indexes separately to ascertain whether a certain level of well-being is sustainable. Combining the indexes leads to a significant loss of information and therefore should be avoided.

Dashboard of Indicators

A set of indicators can provide a more encompassing description of standards of living and well-being than can just one indicator. During the 1970s, the Organisation for Economic Co-operation and Development (OECD) maintained a set of social indicators aimed at measuring social progress. Appetite for a dashboard of indicators abated in the 1980s and was revived in the 1990s. Among the indicators considered here are alternative measures of well-being, Calvert-Henderson Quality of Life Indicators, and the Millennium Development Goals. These indexes have in common a range of indicators that are designed to better capture progress on economic well-being. In particular, the Millennium Development Goals capture human development outcomes and help monitor the progress being made on these indicators of development.

Indexes That Correct GDP

A further set of alternative measures uses the national accounts and GDP as a foundation. Then by adding or subtracting various indexes pertaining, for example, to environmental issues (ISEW/GPI [Index of Sustainable Economic Welfare/Genuine Progress Indicators] and Green GDP), sustainability issues (genuine savings), and leisure (Index of Living Standards), arrive at a more comprehensive measure of well-being. These indicators are often subject to the same criticisms as GDP, however (Costanza et al. 2009, 11).

Well-Being Measures

The well-being indexes do not include GDP in their measures and therefore represent an alternative to GDP. Chief among these alternative approaches to GDP is the *economics of happiness*. The economics of happiness combines techniques used by economists and psychologists to ascertain the extent to which the Benthamite view of society prevails—that is, a society "where people were as happy as possible and the best policy is the one that made the most happiness" (Layard 2005, 5). The economics of happiness goes beyond the economist's view of happiness that concentrated on "revealed preference" and the supposition that the more voluntary choices an individual had, the happier he or she would be.

The findings from happiness surveys indicate that involuntary choices also matter, as do a person's relative income in society and the percentile rank of that income. In fact, beyond an income of $20,000 a year per capita, absolute income does not matter for happiness (figure 2.1). This finding concurs with what has been termed the Easterlin Paradox. Easterlin (1973, 1995, 2005a, 2005b) found no statistically significant relationship between well-being and GDP. Yet he and others (Layard 1980, 2003, 2005, for example) find that richer people are happier. One of the ways in which this finding is explained is in relation to relative income. Layard (2003, 2005) finds that after a certain level of income, happiness does not increase (figure 2.1).

Figure 2.1   Income and Happiness, 1980s and 1990s

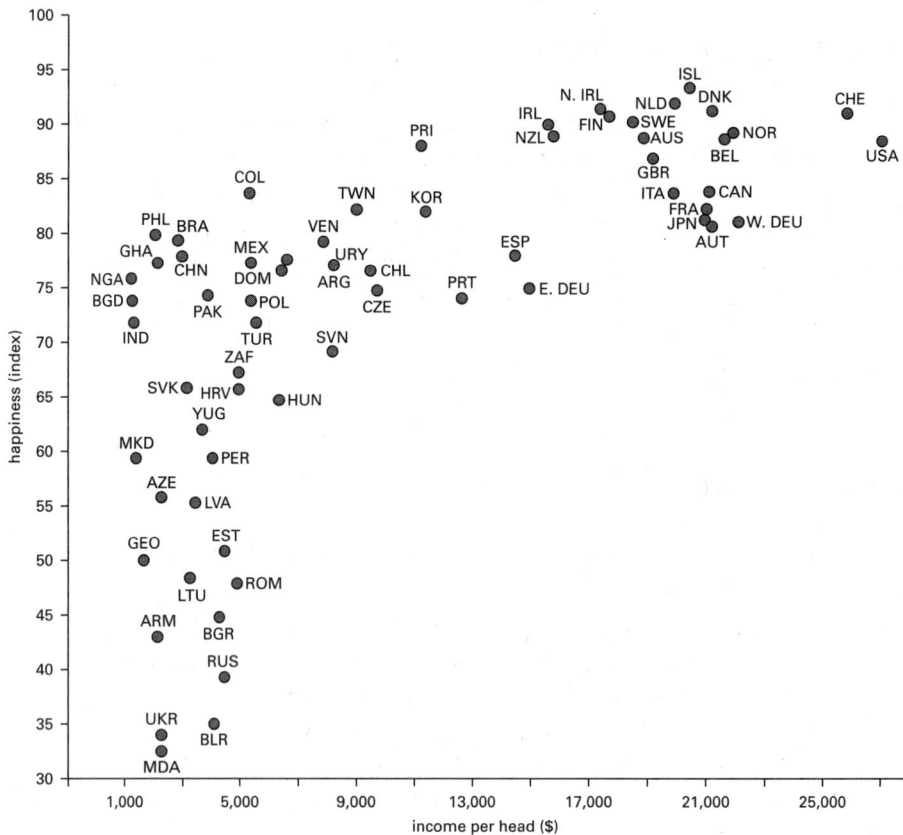

Source: Layard 2003, 18.

Poor countries are much less happy, on average, than are rich countries. Using data from the 1980s and 1990s, figure 2.1 suggests a curvilinear relationship that flattens once income per capita reaches around $15,000. As Layard (2003, 2005) notes, if one is near the breadline, then absolute income makes a big difference. We see the position of the poorer countries relative to happiness in figure 2.1.

Happiness has not been growing in the rich countries since 1980, despite unprecedented growth in income per capita and "opportunities of choice" (Layard 2005, 6). Rich countries with annual income above $20,000 per capita show no relationship between their average income and average level of happiness. Looking at the United States (figure 2.2), the proportion of people who said they were happy rose in the 1950s, fell in the 1960s, and has stabilized since then. Over the same period, GDP per capita increased rapidly.

Sacks, Stevenson, and Wolfers (2010) disagree with the conclusions of the research presented above. They conclude that "well being rises with absolute income, period. This evidence suggests that relative income, adaptation, and satiation are of only secondary importance" (p. 2), (figure 2.3). Based on evidence from 140 countries and several data sets, the authors find that richer people are more satisfied with

Figure 2.2 Income and Happiness in the United States

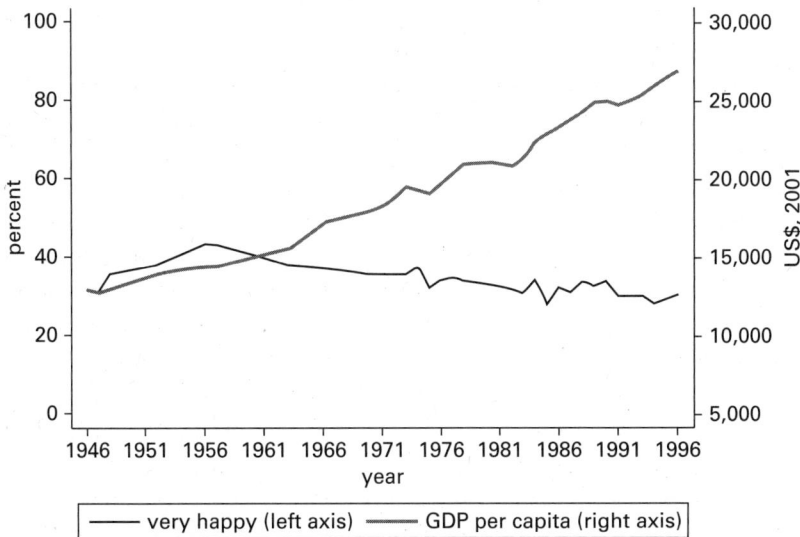

Source: Layard 2003, 15.

Figure 2.3   Relationship between Well-Being and Income within Individual Countries, Gallup World Poll, 2002

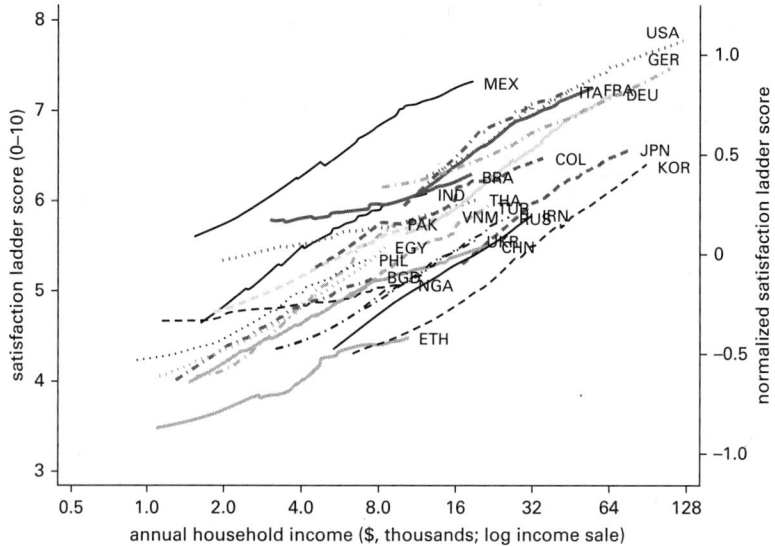

Source: Sacks, Stevenson, and Wolfers 2010, 38.

Note: The figure shows the central 90 percent of the income distribution for each country. A ladder score refers to an individual being shown a ladder that represents his or her life, with the top rung representing the best possible life and the bottom rung the worst possible life, and being asked to choose which rung he or she stands on. This figure shows, for the 25 largest countries, the lowest fit between individual satisfaction ladder scores and the log of household income, measured in the Gallup World Poll in 2002. The satisfaction data are shown both on their raw (0–10) scale on the left axis and as standardized variables on the right axis. We plot the lowest fit between the 10th and 90th percentiles of each country's income distribution. Satisfaction is assessed using the ladder of life question.

their lives and that this holds within countries (figure 2.3) and between countries and across time periods.[8] In all cases, subjective well-being rises with the log of income. They find no flattening of happiness at higher levels of income. Furthermore, the findings are consistent across other subjective measures of well-being—feeling love, not feeling pain (Sacks, Stevenson, and Wolfers 2010) and health (Deaton 2008).

These findings suggest that absolute income is critical in explaining subjective well-being. Sacks, Stevenson, and Wolfers examine the effect of economic growth on subjective well-being. Their findings, using GDP and life satisfaction scales, suggest a positive relationship between growth in happiness and growth in income that holds for developed and developing countries (figure 2.4).[9] The estimate of the relationship lies

Figure 2.4 Happiness and GDP, World Values Survey, 1999–2004

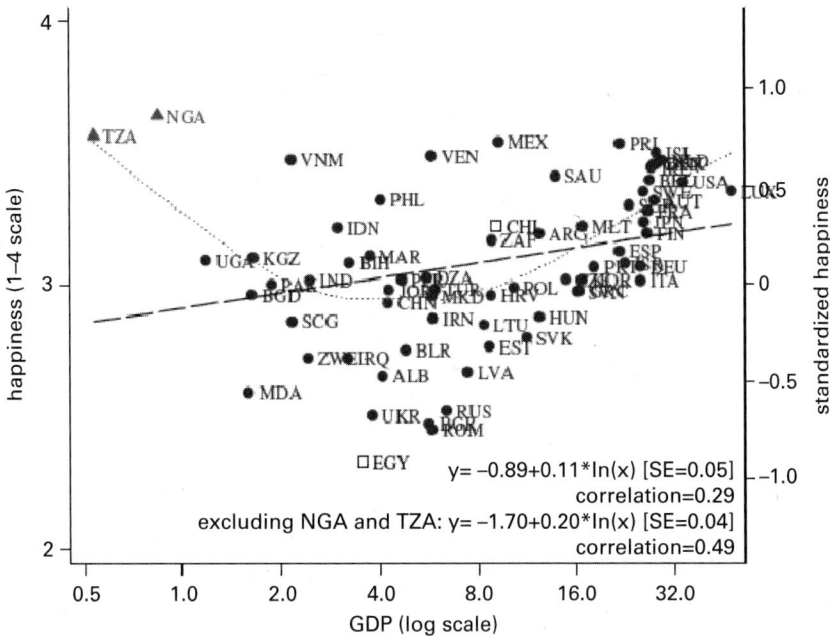

Figure 2.4 Happiness and GDP, World Values Survey, 1999–2004

$$y= -0.89+0.11*\ln(x) \; [SE=0.05]$$
correlation=0.29
excluding NGA and TZA: $y= -1.70+0.20*\ln(x) \; [SE=0.04]$
correlation=0.49

Sources: Sacks, Stevenson, and Wolfers 2010, 38; World Values Survey, 1999–2004; and author's regressions. Sources for GDP per capita are described in the text.

Note: The happiness question is, "Taking all things together, would you say you are: 'very happy,' 'quite happy,' 'not very happy,' [or] 'not at all happy'?" Data are aggregated into country averages by first standardizing individual-level data to have mean 0 and standard deviation 1, and then taking the within-country average of individual happiness. The dashed line plots fitted values from the reported ordinary least squares regression (including Nigeria and Tanzania); the dotted line gives fitted values from the lowest regressions. The regression coefficients are on the standardized scale. Both regressions are based on nationally representative samples. Squares represent observations from countries in which the World Values Survey is not nationally representative. Triangles represent the outliers (Nigeria and Tanzania) that do not conform to the regression. Circles represent countries that conform to the regression analysis. (See Stevenson and Walters 2008, appendix B for further details.) Sample includes 69 developed and developing countries.

between 0.3 and 0.4, similar to that which held for the static relationship within countries and between countries.

The conclusions from Sacks, Stevenson, and Wolfers have important implications for development economics. These are summarized by the authors as

1. Doubt is cast on the Easterlin Paradox and various theories suggesting that there is no long-term relationship between well-being and income growth.

2. Absolute income appears to play a central role in determining subjective well-being. This conclusion suggests that economists' traditional interest in economic growth has not been misplaced.

3. Differences in subjective well-being over time or across places likely reflect meaningful differences in actual well-being.

In summary, further work needs to be carried out on the measures of well-being and their relationship to GDP.

Composite Measures

The final category in table 2.1 examines composite measures of development. These measures combine several indexes to (better) measure what the researcher has in mind—that is, human development (as in the Human Development Index) or environmental sustainability (as in the Happy Planet Index). These measures capture a range of indicators. "The distinctive features of these indicators relate to the domains covered, the normalization methodology used, and the weights used for aggregation" (Stiglitz, Sen, and Fitoussi 2009, 13).

In Conclusion

GDP has been used as a measure of development since its creation. As a single, aggregative measure it has many shortcomings, yet it is critical for the growth and development story. It has been combined with other measures, it has been "corrected" for its shortcomings, and it has been used in synthesizing other measures. It shows a strong relationship with alternative measures of well-being, such as life satisfaction.

Notes

1. Sustained economic growth is the most critical factor in alleviating poverty, although the rate of poverty reduction differs from country to country and depends, among other things, on the initial level of income inequality, the growth of inequality over time, the pattern of growth, and where that growth is concentrated.

2. Government output is equated with government expenditure. The report by the Commission on the Measurement of Economic Performance and Social Progress, in an approximate measure, suggests that "government output

represents around 20 percent of GDP in many OECD countries and total government expenditure more than 40 percent for the OECD countries" (Stiglitz, Sen, and Fitoussi 2009, 12).

3. The national accounts provide a greater number of indicators that extend beyond GDP.

4. For example, the informal economy may account for anything between 30 and 50 percent of the developing country's economy.

5. GNI and GNDI take relations with the rest of the world into account by adjusting for taxes on production and imports; compensation of employees and property income to and from the rest of the world; current transfers to and from the rest of the world, including payments of taxes on property, income, social contributions, and social benefits.

6. NNI and NNDI take into account depreciation. Thus, NNI and NNDI represent GNI and GNDI adjusted for capital consumption.

7. We argue that the concept of well-being is central to Seer's definition of development—that is, "creating the conditions for the realization of human personality" (Seers 1972, 21).

8. Limited data mean that the findings for happiness and the log of GDP per capita over time are less precise than between-countries and within-country findings.

9. Note 7 holds.

References

Afsa, C., D. Blanchet, V. Marcus, P. A. Pionnier, L. Rioux, M. M. d'Ercole, G. Ranuzzi, and P. Schreyer. 2009. "Survey of Existing Approaches to Measuring Socio-Economic Progress." Commission on the Measurement of Economic Performance and Social Progress, Organisation for Economic Co-operation and Development, Paris. http://www.stiglitz-sen-fitoussi.fr/documents/Survey_of _Existing_Approaches_to_Measuring_Socio-Economic_Progress.pdf.

Costanza, R., M. Hart, S. Posner, and J. Talberth. 2009. "Beyond GDP: The Need for New Measures of Progress." The Pardee Papers Series, No. 4 (January). Boston University, Boston, MA.

Deaton, A. 2008. "Income, Health and Well-Being around the World: Evidence from the Gallup World Poll." *Journal of Economic Perspectives* 22 (2): 53–72.

Easterlin, R. A. 1973. "Does Money Buy Happiness?" *Public Interest* 30: 3–10.

———. 1995. "Will Raising the Incomes of All Increase the Happiness of All?" *Journal of Economic Behavior and Organization* 27 (1): 35–48.

———. 2005a. "Diminishing Marginal Utility of Income? Caveat Emptor." *Social Indicators Research* 70 (3): 243–55.

———. 2005b. "Feeding the Illusion of Growth and Happiness: A Reply to Hagerty and Veenhoven." *Social Indicators Research* 74 (3): 429–33.

European Commission. 2009. "GDP and Beyond. Measuring Progress in a Changing World." Brussels. http://eur-lex.europa.eu/Notice.do?checktexts=checkbox &val=499855.

Kuznets, S. 1934. "National Income 1929–1932." Report prepared for the U.S. Senate, 73rd Congress, 2nd Session. National Bureau of Economic Research, Cambridge, MA.

Layard, R. 1980. "Human Satisfaction and Public Policy." *Economic Journal* 90 (363): 737–50.

———. 2003. "Happiness: Has Social Science a Clue?" Lionel Robbins Memorial Lectures 2002/3, London School of Economics, March 3–5.

———. 2005. *Happiness: Lessons from a New Science.* London: Penguin.

Neumayer, E. 2004. "Sustainability and Well-Being Indicators." WIDER Research Paper 2004/23, United Nations University/World Institute for Development Economics Research, Helsinki.

Sacks, D., B. Stevenson, and J. Wolfers. 2010. "Subjective Well-Being, Income, Economic Development and Growth." Working Paper 16441, National Bureau of Economic Research, Cambridge, MA.

Seers, D. 1972. "What Are We Trying to Measure?" In *Measuring Development: The Role and Adequacy of Development Indicators,* ed. N. Baster, 21–36. London: Frank Cass and Company.

Stevenson, B., and J. Wolfers. 2008. "Economic Growth and Subjective Well-Being: Reassessing the Easterlin Paradox." *Brookings Papers on Economic Activity* 2008 (1): 1–87.

Stiglitz, J., A. Sen, and J.-P. Fitoussi. 2009. "Report by the Commission on the Measurement of Economic Performance and Social Progress." OECD, Paris. http://www.stiglitz-sen-fitoussi.fr/documents/rapport_anglais.pdf.

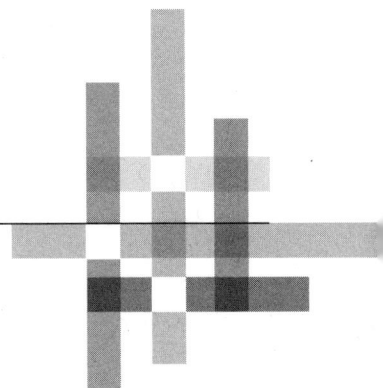

Poverty Traps and the MDGs

Breda Griffith

Poverty traps—situations whereby an individual, a group of households, a country, or a geographic region occupies a stable equilibrium at a low level of wealth and output—have long provided one of the main arguments for foreign aid. Poverty traps underpinned the classic approach to development policy[1] in the 1950s and have dominated the impetus for the United Nations Millennium Project[2] since the turn of the century. Theoretically, the concept of a poverty trap provides an appealing theme for greater aid. Under this view, chiefly associated currently with Jeffrey Sachs, a substantial level of foreign aid over an adequate time frame would raise the capital stock and contribute to growth while raising households out of poverty. Growth would become cumulative over time as households saved and public investments were facilitated by household taxation (Sachs 2005).

Research has shown, however, that aid has not generated the big growth effects anticipated by the existence of poverty traps.[3] In fact, Easterly notes that "(1) growth is lower in aid-intensive countries than in developing countries that get little aid, (2) aid has risen over time as a percent of income in Africa, but Africa's growth rate has fallen over time" (Easterly 2005, 9). The difference in growth rates between the poorest one fifth of countries in 1950 and the others, ranked by per capita income, over time to 2001 was not statistically significant. Countries that failed to grow within the poorest group—Chad, Zaire/Democratic Republic of Congo—were offset by those that did grow (for example, Botswana, Lesotho, China, and India).

Easterly (2005) finds no evidence for the poverty trap scenario based on the assumptions of a lower growth rate for the poorest countries and a per capita growth rate of zero in the poorest countries, (table 3.1). In fact, there was no statistical difference between the growth rate of the poorest 20 percent—1.9 percent per year—and the others over the 1950–75 period. A similar tale characterizes the 1975–2001 period and the 1980–2001 period. The data from 1985 suggest that the poor countries have fared worse, but this occurs in the period when "poorest countries were getting more in foreign aid as a percent of their income. . . . Foreign aid is supposed to be helping the poor countries escape from the poverty trap; hence the poorest countries in the recent decade should have been LESS likely to be stuck in poverty than the previous decades with lower foreign aid" (Easterly 2005, 11).

Poverty Trap or No Poverty Trap?

The evidence for poverty traps based on income criteria is easily refuted, as noted above. For example, using data from 1985 to 2005, Sachs notes that the poorest one fifth of countries (28 countries) had significantly lower per capita growth—1.1 percentage points lower, on average—compared with the other countries in the sample. However, if one subscribes to the definition of a poverty trap where a country remains stuck, this finding is inconclusive

Table 3.1 Testing the Poverty Trap for Long Periods

Per capita growth	1950–2001	1950–75	1975–2001	1980–2001	1985–2001
For poorest one fifth at beginning of period indicated (%)	1.6	1.9	0.8	0.5[a]	0.2[a]
For all others (%)	1.7	2.5[b]	1.1	0.9	1.3[b]
Rejects stationary income for poorest one fifth	Yes	Yes	Yes	Yes	Yes
Fails to reject nonstationary income for poorest one fifth	Yes	Yes	Yes	Yes	Yes

Source: Easterly 2005, 10.

Note: Sample size is 137 countries.

a. Poorest one fifth is not statistically distinguishable from zero.

b. All others' growth is statistically distinguishable from poorest one fifth.

Frontiers in Development Policy

based on the fact that 11 of the 28 poorest countries in 2001 were not in the lowest-income group in 1985; nor does it pass the "zero-income growth rate" test (Easterly 2005).

Yet there is no denying that some countries remain poor while others become ever richer. This scenario of a widening income disparity over time between poorer and richer countries is redolent of a poverty trap and is what Pritchett (1997) referred to as "divergence big time." The ratio of per capita income growth between the poorest and richest countries went "from about 6 to about 70" (Easterly 2005, 12) over the past two centuries.

What maintains this "inequality trap"? Is it insufficient savings and increasing returns to capital, as suggested by the poverty trap; or is it indicative of "an institutional poverty trap" (Easterly 2005, 13)? We know from the growth literature (Acemoglu, Johnson, and Robinson 2002) that countries with sound institutional frameworks—property rights are protected, the legal system facilitates private transactions—experience higher rates of growth compared with economies having weak institutions, and we know that growth is good for poverty reduction. Institutions—and not just economic ones but social, legal, and political institutions—develop at different speeds with varying consequences for growth and development.

Institutions are important for policy. The effectiveness of public policies designed to encourage capital accumulation, knowledge, and technological creation depend on the underlying institutions. The right institutions can provide incentives for economic growth. Acemoglu and Johnson (2007) provide an in-depth analysis of why some countries grow and others do not. Central to their analysis is the notion of a reward structure that provides incentives for individuals and corporations to undertake investments in new technology and human capital that are necessary for growth. The political system—authoritarian or participatory—creates different types of reward structures, with the latter found to provide a growth-promoting cluster of institutions. Governments that do not provide a reward structure—so-called bad government (Easterly 2005)—are often corrupt and oversee a system of weak institutions. Easterly attributes the unsatisfactory growth record of the poorest countries to having "more to do with awful government than with a poverty trap" (p. 18).

Current development policy as summarized by the Millennium Development Goals (MDGs) initiative aims to bridge the inequality gap between poor and rich countries. For example, MDG 2 and MDG 3 seek to promote a commitment by individuals and societies to education and gender equality that is linked to economic development (see table 3.2). Furthermore, MDG 8, in calling for a global partnership for development, focuses on other

Table 3.2 Selected MDGs

Goal 2	Achieve universal primary education
	Target 2.A: Ensure that, by 2015, children everywhere, boys and girls alike, will be able to complete a full course of primary schooling
Goal 3	Promote gender equality and empower women
	Target 3.A: Eliminate gender disparity in primary and secondary education, preferably by 2005, and at all levels of education no later than 2015
Goal 8	Develop a global partnership for development
	Target 8.A: Develop a further and open, rule-based, predictable, nondiscriminatory trading and financial system (including a commitment to good governance, development, and poverty reduction, nationally and internationally)
	Target 8.B: Address the special needs of the least-developed countries (including tariff- and quota-free access for exports of the least-developed countries, enhanced debt relief for heavily indebted poor countries, cancellation of official bilateral debt, and more generous official development assistance for countries committed to reducing poverty)
	Target 8.C: Address the special needs of landlocked countries and small island developing states (through the Programme of Action for the Sustainable Development of Small Island Developing States and the outcome of the 22nd special session of the General Assembly)
	Target 8.D: Deal comprehensively with the debt problems of developing countries through national and international measures to make debt sustainable in the long term
	Target 8.E: In cooperation with pharmaceutical companies, provide access to affordable, essential drugs in developing countries
	Target 8.F: In cooperation with the private sector, make available the benefits of new technologies, especially information and communications.

Source: Author's compilation.

growth-promoting factors. Technology adoption is a key factor in promoting growth, and target 8.F calls for making the benefits of new technologies available to developing countries. Most developing countries adopt or absorb new technologies from elsewhere, and a country's institutions will influence the rate of adoption and absorption.

MDGs and Lessons from MDG Implementation as We Near 2015

The wake of the financial crisis and the coming-due of the MDGs in four years make this a good time to examine the progress made and the challenges that lie ahead. First, the international nature of the recent financial crisis was unlike any other crises experienced in the past. Second, the countercyclical policy responses by advanced, emerging, and developing economies and the mobilization of resources by the international financial institutions ensured a softer landing. There are consequences for developing countries in meeting the MDGs and moving beyond them in an environment where advanced economies strive to meet fiscal commitments and engineer their economies to achieve growth and sustainability in the wake of the 2008 financial crisis.

The macroeconomic base from which each country begins will impact the level of progress achieved. Countries that begin from a low base, with high poverty rates and low growth, have a lot of catch-up and, although they may have made progress, they are still far from reaching the targets suggested. The surge in economic growth that saw most developing countries achieve per capita growth rates greater than 2 percent between 2003 and 2007 (figure 3.1) and the resultant improvements in poverty reduction were insufficient for low-income countries to reduce poverty by the amount suggested in MDG 1. In particular, Sub-Saharan Africa and South Asia are faring badly on the MDGs.

Precrisis Growth and the MDGs

Precrisis growth was sufficient in halving the 1990 poverty rate in most regions (an exception being Sub-Saharan Africa). The poverty rate in

Figure 3.1 Per Capita GDP Growth Rates, by Country Group, 2003–07

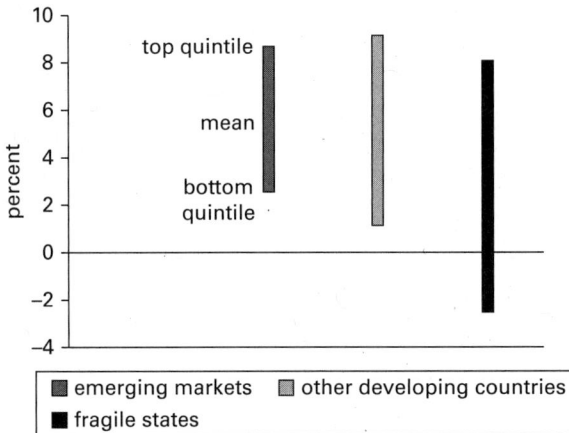

Source: World Bank 2008b.

Sub-Saharan Africa declined from 58 percent to 51 percent between 1990 and 2005, although the absolute number of poor people increased from 296 million to 388 million (figure 3.2). The number of poor people in developing countries, living on less than $1.25 a day, declined from 1.8 billion in 1990 to 1.4 billion in 2005—from 42 percent of the population to 25 percent (World Bank 2010, 14). Progress was largely attributable to East Asia, where poverty fell from 55 percent in 1990 to 17 percent in 2005, driven by the enormous reduction in poverty by China[4] and India.[5]

Significant progress has been made in achieving universal primary school completion, MDG 2, with fewer numbers out of school—even with growing populations.[6] Primary school completion reached 86 percent across developing countries as a whole, with rates of 93 percent for middle-income countries and 65 percent for low-income countries. Among the latter, Sub-Saharan Africa and South Asia are struggling to meet the target. Primary completion rates in Sub-Saharan Africa have increased from 51 percent in 2002 to 60 percent in 2007, and rates in South Asia increased from 62 percent to 80 percent. The number of children out of school in these countries is a barrier to reaching the MDG target.[7]

A further benefit of higher enrollments is gender parity in primary education. Almost two thirds of developing countries reached gender parity at the primary school level by 2005, ensuring that MDG 3—gender parity in

Figure 3.2   Poverty Rates in Sub-Saharan Africa, South Asia, and East Asia and Pacific, 1981–2005

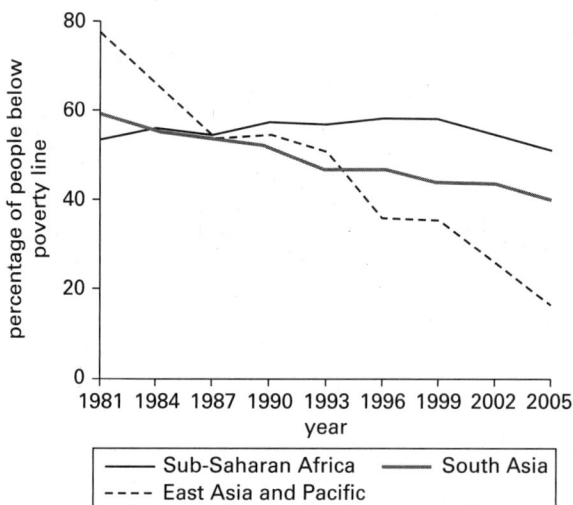

Source: World Bank 2010, 15.

primary and secondary education—is on track for 2015. Sub-Saharan Africa falls short of the global target (see figure 3.3).

Progress has been slow in other areas. In particular, the goal to halve the proportion of people who suffer from hunger (MDG 1.B) is not on track.[8] Progress in Sub-Saharan Arica and South Asia has been particularly slow, with 46 percent of children under 5 affected by stunting due to hunger and malnutrition (World Bank 2010, 18). Failure to achieve this goal has implications for several other MDGs—in particular, infant and maternal mortality

Figure 3.3   Gender Parity in Primary Education, 1991 and 2007

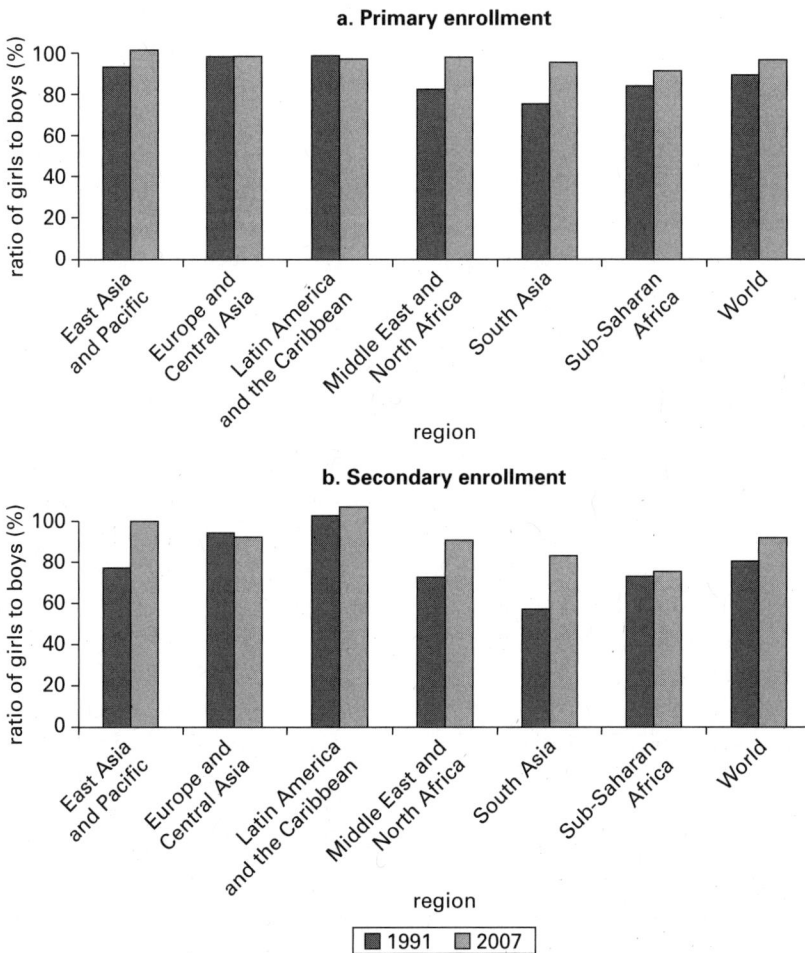

a. Primary enrollment

b. Secondary enrollment

Source: World Bank 2010, 17.

(MDG 4 and MDG 5). The 2010 *Global Monitoring Report* notes that child malnutrition accounts for more than a third of the disease burden of children under 5, and malnutrition during pregnancy accounts for more than 20 percent of maternal mortalities (World Bank 2010, 18).

Declines in infant mortality from 101 deaths per 1,000 live births in 1990 to 74 per 1,000 in 2007 are insufficient to achieve MDG 4—reducing child mortality under 5 by two thirds. Lack of progress on this goal is particularly evident in South Asia and Sub-Saharan Africa. The latter region's progress has been further hampered by HIV/AIDS and civil conflicts.[9]

Sub-Saharan Africa is the region most heavily affected by HIV/AIDS. Two thirds of all people living with HIV/AIDS reside in Sub-Saharan Africa, and the region accounted for three quarters of all deaths related to HIV/AIDS in 2008. There has been some progress in redressing these numbers, with antiretroviral treatment now reaching a third of all people living with HIV/AIDS in developing countries. However, the goal of universal access remains out of reach for most countries. Progress in halting the spread of tuberculosis and malaria has been mixed. Deaths from these major communicable diseases are still high in Sub-Saharan Africa, compared with other regions, and 80 percent of malaria-related deaths occur in children (World Bank 2010, 19). In general, progress on MDG 6 has been mixed, with progress in Sub-Saharan Africa difficult because it began from a high base and because of a failure to make progress.

Progress on MDG 1, target 1.b, full and productive employment (especially for women), is difficult to chart. It is difficult to account for the significant underemployment in informal and rural activities that characterize developing economies. Further, female employment ratios began from a low base (even before the financial crisis); and cultural considerations in the Middle East and North Africa determine a lower female employment ratio, compared with the male employment ratio in these regions. Nevertheless, some progress has been evident, with increasing female employment ratios in Latin America and the Caribbean (see figure 3.4).

In general, the 2010 *Global Monitoring Report* notes insufficient progress on MDG 7—environmental sustainability. Access to sanitation is inadequate in developing countries, with close to half the population lacking adequate sanitation. South Asia and Sub-Saharan Africa fare worst.[10] The report laments the lack of attention that has been given to achieving environmental goals and notes that it behooves the high-income countries, which produced most of the greenhouse gas emissions in the past, to provide financial and technical assistance help to the developing countries to move them onto a lower-carbon path.

Figure 3.4 Ratio of Employment to Population, Men and Women, 1991 and 2007

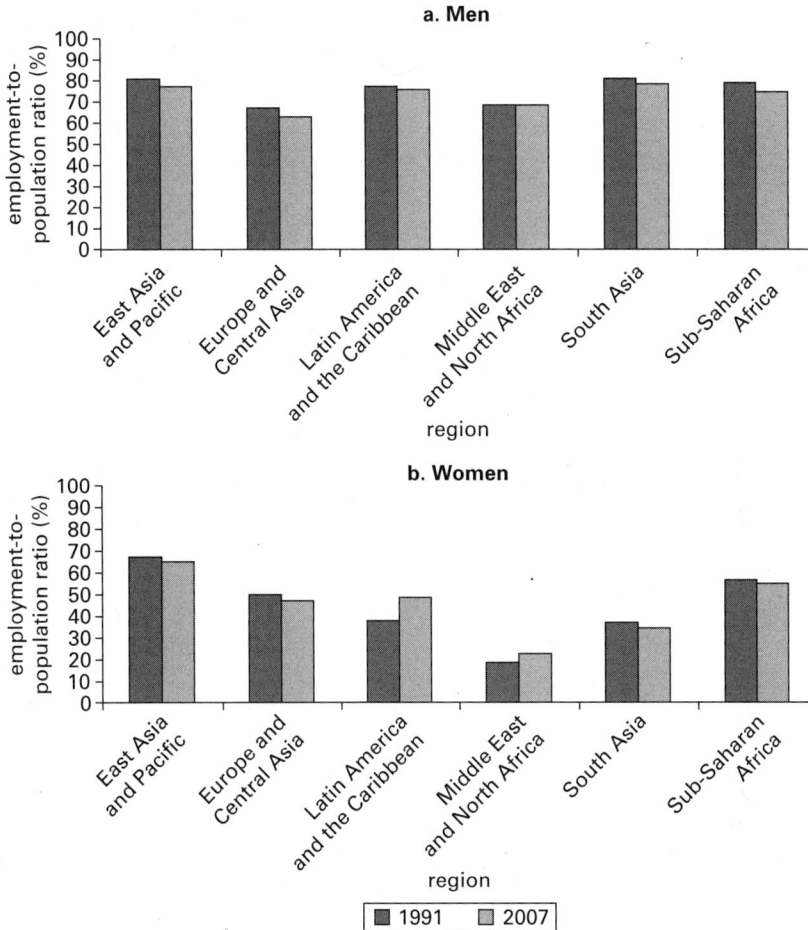

a. Men

b. Women

1991 2007

Source: World Bank 2010, 19.

Finally, MDG 8 and a global partnership for development needs further progress. MDG 8 covers cooperation in aid, trade, debt relief, and access to technology and essential drugs (World Bank 2010, 20). Global commitments to development aid are unsustained and fall short of the commitments at Monterrey.[11] Monitoring progress[12] on improving aid effectiveness is difficult, given the myriad of actors involved—more than 280 bilateral donor agencies, 242 multilateral programs, 24 development banks, and about 40 United Nations agencies, together with an increasing number of private foundations, nongovernmental organizations, and "an estimated 340,000 development projects around the world" (Deutscher and Fyson 2008, 16). Lack of aid predictability,[13] lack of coordination, and aid fragmentation further constrain aid effectiveness.[14] The failure to conclude the Doha Round of negotiations stymies progress on global cooperation on the trade component of MDG 8. Transfer of technology and access to essential drugs is hampered by the lack of specific targets. On the other hand, the Heavily Indebted Poor Countries Initiative and the Multilateral Debt Relief Initiative have proved very effective in providing debt relief to poor countries (World Bank 2010, 20).

In Conclusion

The concept of the poverty trap underlies the approach to development policy. This is readily seen in the United Nations Millennium Project, an international effort to improve social and economic indicators in developing countries that relies on a "big push" in international development aid. The static concept of the poverty trap does not hold up to the data. Instead, a more dynamic interpretation of countries moving in and out of poverty and a growing divergence between rich and poor countries characterize the data. The wide-ranging reach of the MDGs—eight goals comprising 18 targets—focuses on growth-retarding issues in developing countries and enlists the aid of the international community in so doing.

The MDGs define human development outcomes and represent a rallying call for the international community. They represent a commonly shared understanding of poverty reduction that can come about from targets and indicators to motivate policy decisions and accountability.

Notes

1. Greater aid and investment are required to move countries out of a poverty trap and onto a path of higher per capita income.
2. A "big push of basic investments between now and 2015 in public administration, human capital (nutrition, health, education), and key infrastructure (roads, electricity, ports, water and sanitation, accessible land for affordable housing, environmental management)" is required to escape the poverty trap (Easterly 2005, 3, quoting UN 2005, 19).
3. Easterly (2005) refers to Kraay and Raddatz (2005), Graham and Temple (2004), and Easterly (2003).

4. Poverty in China fell from 60 percent in 1990 to 16 percent in 2005. The absolute number of extremely poor persons fell from 683 million to 208 million.

5. The share of the population living in poverty in India fell from 51 percent to 42 percent between 1990 and 2005, although population growth over the same period made for an increase of 4 percent (from 436 million people to 456 million).

6. Over 90 percent of primary-school-age children are in school in more than 60 developing countries. The number of children out of school fell from 115 million in 2002 to 72 million in 2007. (World Bank 2010, 16).

7. Forty-one million primary-school-age children in Sub-Saharan Africa and 31.5 million in South Asia are out of school (World Bank 2010, 16).

8. "The proportion of children under 5 who are underweight declined from 31 percent in developing countries in 1990 to 26 percent in 2007" (World Bank 2010, 18).

9. Sub-Saharan Africa has 20 percent of the world's children under age 5 but 50 percent of all child deaths.

10. Just 31 percent of the population in Sub-Saharan Africa had access to adequate sanitation in 2006, up from 26 percent in 1990. The proportion in South Asia increased from 18 percent in 1990 to 33 percent in 2006 (World Bank 2010, 18).

11. "Net disbursements of official development assistance (ODA) from the Development Assistance Committee of the Organisation for Economic Co-operation and Development rose during 2003–05, but fell in both 2006 and 2007, dropping from 0.33 percent of donor gross national income (GNI) in 2005 to 0.28 percent in 2007. The ratio of ODA to GNI reached 0.31 percent in 2009" (World Bank 2010, 20).

12. A first round of monitoring took place in 2006, based on activities undertaken in 2005 in 34 countries where some progress was noted but significant efforts were still needed. A second round of monitoring in 56 countries in 2008 noted that, despite the progress made on reducing poverty, much more needs to be done if the MDGs are to be met. The Accra Agenda called for greater effort in (1) working toward country ownership, (2) building more effective and inclusive partnerships, and (3) achieving development results and openly accounting for them.

13. Celasun and Walliser (2008), using data in International Monetary Fund staff reports from 1992 to 2007 for a set of 13 countries, found that, on average, disbursed budget aid differed from the amount expected by about 30 percent.

14. For any average country, just 45 percent of aid arrives on time. In 2005–06, 38 developing countries received official development assistance from 25 or more Development Assistance Committee and multilateral donors; in 24 of these countries, 15 (or more) donors collectively provided less than 10 percent of the country's total aid budget. Furthermore, some countries are ignored by donors. Fragmentation of aid means that some countries receive a small amount of aid from a plethora of donors, all requiring adherence to different procedures and standards (OECD 2008).

Bibliography

Acemoglu, D., and S. Johnson. 2007. "Disease and Development: The Effect of Life Expectancy on Economic Growth." *Journal of Political Economy* 115 (6): 925–85.

Acemodlu, D., S. Johnson, and J. A. Robinson. 2002. "Reversal of Fortune: Geography and Institutions in the Making of the Modern World Income Distribution." *Quarterly Journal of Economics* 117 (4): 1231–94.

Acemoglu, D., and J. A. Robinson. 2000. "Political Losers as a Barrier to Economic Development." *American Economic Review* 90 (2): 126–30.

Azariadis, C., and J. Stachurski. 2005. "Poverty Traps." In vol. 1 of *Handbook of Economic Growth,* ed. P. Aghion and S. N. Durlauf. Amsterdam: Elsevier.

Bowles, S., S. N. Durlauf, and K. R. Hoff, eds. 2006. *Poverty Traps.* Princeton, NJ: Princeton University Press.

Brookins, C. L. 2008. "Maximizing Effectiveness of Development Finance Institutions: Dynamics for Engaging the Private Sector and NGOs." Second International Business Forum on Financing for Development, Doha, Qatar, November 28.

Celasun, O., and J. Walliser. 2008. "Managing Aid Surprises." *Finance and Development* 42 (3): 34–37.

Clemens, M., S. Radelet, and R. Bhavnani. 2004. "Counting Chickens When They Hatch: The Short-Term Effect of Aid on Growth." Working Paper 44, Center for Global Development, Washington, DC.

Collier, P. 2007. *The Bottom Billion: Why the Poorest Countries Are Failing and What Can Be Done About It.* New York: Oxford University Press.

Deutscher, E., and S. Fyson. 2008. "Improving the Effectiveness of Aid." *Finance and Development* 45 (3): 15–19.

Easterly, W. 2003. "Can Foreign Aid Buy Growth?" *Journal of Economic Perspectives* 17 (3): 23–48.

———. 2005. "Reliving the '50s: The Big Push, Poverty Traps, and Takoffs in Economic Development." Working Paper 65, Center for Global Development, Washington, DC.

———. 2006. *The White Man's Burden: Why the West's Efforts to Aid the Rest Have Done So Much Ill and So Little Good.* New York: Penguin Press.

Graham, B. S., and J. Temple. 2004. "Rich Nations, Poor Nations: How Much Can Multiple Equilibria Explain?" Unpublished manuscript, Harvard University, Cambridge, MA.

Kraay, A., and C. Raddatz. 2005. "Poverty Traps, Aid, and Growth." Unpublished manuscript, World Bank, Washington, DC.

OECD (Organisation for Economic Co-operation and Development). 2008. "Scaling Up: Aid Fragmentation, Aid Allocation, and Aid Predictability: Report of 2008 Survey of Aid Allocation Policies and Indicative Forward Spending Plans." OECD, Paris.

Pritchett, L. 1997. "Divergence, Big Time." *Journal of Economic Perspectives* 11 (3): 3–17.

Ravallion, M. 2009. "Poverty Traps." Knowledge in Development Notes. World Bank, Washington, DC. http://econ.worldbank.org/research/kindnotes.

Sachs, J. 2005. "Ending Poverty in Africa: We Are Not There Yet." *New Perspectives Quarterly* 22: 31–33.

UN (United Nations). 2005. "Millennium Project, Investing in Development: A Practical Plan to Achieve the Millennium Development Goals, Overview Report." UN, New York.

———. 2006. "Rethinking the Role of National Development Banks." Department of Economic and Social Affairs, UN, New York. http://www.un.org/esa/ffd/msc/ndb/index.htm.

World Bank. 2006. *Global Monitoring Report 2006. Millennium Development Goals: Strengthening Mutual Accountability, Aid, Trade, and Governance.* Washington, DC: World Bank.

———. 2007a. *Global Development Finance 2007: The Globalization of Corporate Finance in Developing Countries.* Washington, DC: World Bank.

———. 2007b. *Global Monitoring Report 2007. Millennium Development Goals: Confronting the Challenges of Gender Equality and Fragile States.* Washington, DC: World Bank.

———. 2008a. *Global Development Finance 2008: The Changing Role of International Banking in Development Finance.* Washington, DC: World Bank.

———. 2008b. *Global Monitoring Report 2008. MDGs and the Environment: Agenda for Inclusive and Sustainable Development.* Washington, DC: World Bank.

———. 2010. *Global Monitoring Report 2010: The MDGs after the Crisis.* Washington, DC: World Bank.

World Economic Forum. 2006. "Building on the Monterrey Consensus: The Untapped Potential of Development Finance Institutions to Catalyse Private Investment." World Economic Forum, Geneva.

SECTION 4

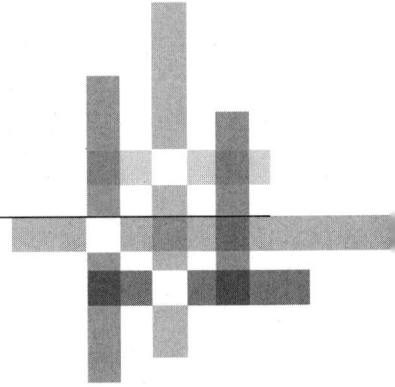

Middle-Income Trap

Breda Griffith

The middle-income trap refers to a situation whereby a middle-income country is failing to transition to a high-income economy due to rising costs and declining competitiveness. Few countries successfully manage the transition from low to middle to high income. Many economies in Latin America and the Middle East regions have been stuck in a middle-income trap, "struggling to remain competitive as high-volume, low-cost producers in the face of rising wage costs" (World Bank 2010, 27). The hallmarks of success become binding constraints for these middle-income countries. Recent evidence suggests that a number of countries in East Asia are in a similar position. The following paragraphs outline the economic environment necessary to facilitate a convergence to a higher-income status, with examples of countries managing the transition and countries that are failing to manage it.

Evidence to support the middle-income trap indicates a leveling-off of income per capita and a decline or stagnation in an economy's competitiveness. Figures 4.1 and 4.2 illustrate the middle-income trap for middle-income economies in the East Asia region. Figure 4.1 shows gross domestic product (GDP) per capita for the Republic of Korea, Brazil, the Philippines, and the Syrian Arab Republic from 1950 to 2006. All countries "took off" in growth from the mid-1970s. Korea continued to grow throughout the 1980s, achieving almost $8,000 income per capita in 2006. By contrast, the other economies leveled off over the period.

Figure 4.2 shows the competitiveness ranking for the middle-income economies of Malaysia, Thailand, Indonesia, and the Philippines beginning in 2000. All of the countries experienced stagnation in global competitiveness over the period to 2009.

Escaping from the Middle-Income Trap

At the minimum, a stable macroeconomic environment predicated on sensible fiscal, monetary, and regulatory policies is required. Furthermore, an economy with strong regional and global ties and with increasing urbanization is vital. Against this background, a number of ingredients are necessary to sustain the economy's growth and competitiveness and move it into the higher-income group. The World Bank (2010) identifies two key ingredients that comprise a number of others. These two overarching requirements are

1. high levels of investment that embody new technologies, and

2. innovation-conducive policies.

Figure 4.1   Middle-Income Trap

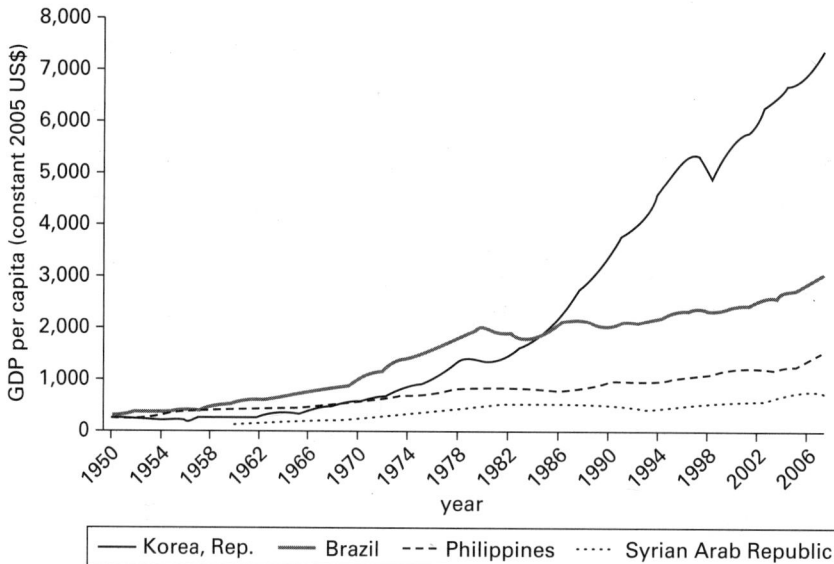

Source: World Bank 2010, 27.

Figure 4.2 Global Competitiveness Indexes

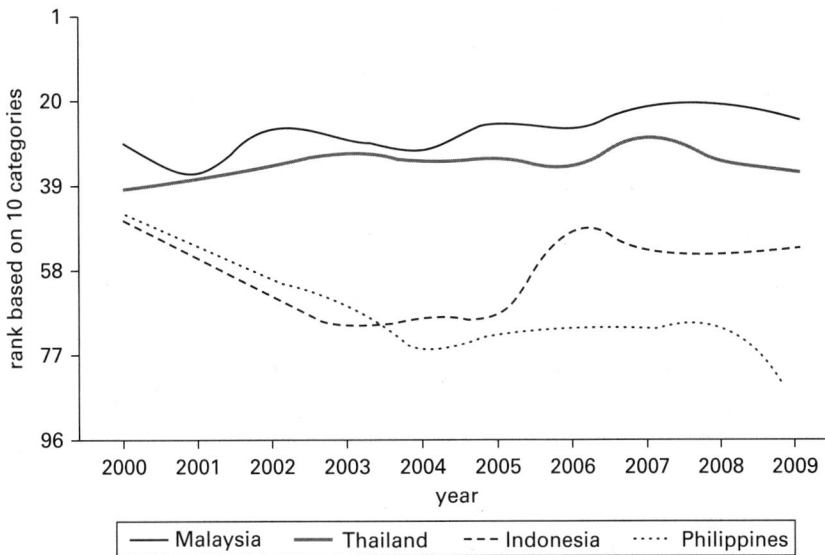

Source: World Bank 2010, 27.

Sustained higher investment is critical for long-term growth. The Growth Commission suggested investment levels of 25 percent of GDP or more to achieve strong growth. Investment rates in Korea and Japan have averaged 31 percent since their respective takeoffs in 1978 and 1950. Financial crises negatively impact investment, and the challenge is to build on the recovery by investing in both human and physical capital. Areas that may provide immediate opportunities for investment include

- infrastructure—roads, housing, energy, and information technology;
- green technology; and
- public-private partnerships.

Transitioning to a high-growth economy requires a move up the value chain.[1] Innovation in new products and processes both in adoption and development as well as in business operation is critical in this regard. While the middle-income economies in East Asia are beginning from a good base, having absorbed foreign knowledge and thereby improved their production capabilities, much more needs to be done (World Bank 2010). In summary, a good innovation policy requires

- creating incentives for productive entrepreneurship;

- providing adequate skills to the workforce;

- ensuring good transmission of information and ideas; and

- making sure that financing is available for start-ups, upgrades, and commercialization (World Bank 2010, 33).

In Conclusion

Investment and innovation are the two key ingredients to moving a middle-income economy into a high-income economy. It is necessary to understand the macroeconomic factors that affect investment in each middle-income economy. At the macroeconomic level, capital flows through foreign direct investment can have a large impact on an economy's growth potential. Growth in Vietnam has been dominated by foreign-owned firms, and economic liberalization has been successful in making Vietnam regionally and globally integrated (Ohno 2009). However, to sustain growth and move the country onto a higher growth trajectory, three policies are required: (1) generation of internal value, (2) coping with new social problems caused by rapid growth, and (3) effective macroeconomic management under financial integration (Ohno 2009, 26). Furthermore, Yusuf and Nabeshima (2009) note that, although Malaysia was successful in attracting foreign direct investment in the electronics industry, it failed to generate domestic capability. Very few domestic firms entered the industry, despite incentives by local and regional governments. Firms that are unable to reach a certain threshold of capacity will not be able to take advantage of opportunities offered by globalization (Paus 2009). Paus attributes the failure of many middle-income countries in Latin America to escape the middle-income trap to this reason. An innovation-conducive policy that meets the requirements noted above is critical for future sustainable growth and moving an economy toward a higher growth frontier.

Note

1. Wu (2010) examines the issue of intellectual property rights in moving an economy toward the (world) technology frontier. Adopting intellectual property rights early in an economy's industrial development prevents a middle-income trap.

References

Ohno, K. 2009. "Avoiding the Middle-Income Trap—Renovating Industrial Policy Formulation in Vietnam." *ASEAN Economic Bulletin* 26 (1): 25–43.

Paus, E. 2009. "Latin America's Middle Income Trap." *Americas Quarterly*. http://www.americasquarterly.org/node/2142.

World Bank. 2010. "Escaping the Middle-Income Trap." In vol. 2 of *World Bank East Asia and Pacific Economic Update: Robust Recovery, Rising Risks,* 27–43. Washington, DC: World Bank.

Wu, H. 2010. "Distance to Frontier, Intellectual Property Rights, and Economic Growth." *Economics of Innovation and New Technology* 19 (2): 165–83.

Yusuf, S., and K. Nabeshima. 2009. "Can Malaysia Escape the Middle-Income Trap? A Strategy for Penang." Policy Research Working Paper 4971, World Bank, Washington, DC.

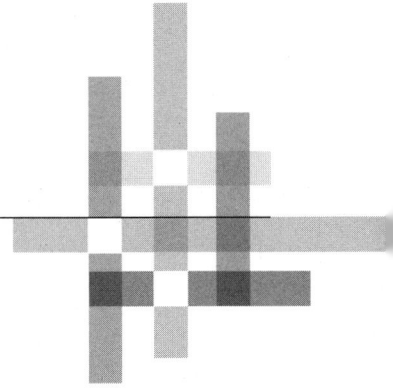

Pathways to Development

Shahid Yusuf

All pathways to development must first cover the difficult stretch called "growth," and the course of development is contingent on the momentum gained on this part of the journey. Sustaining this growth will depend on institutions and political will.

The Growth Paradigm

Almost every country in the world is struggling to raise potential growth rates and to squeeze a few additional percentage points of growth from the available resources. In the majority of cases, growth outcomes have fallen short of expectations.[1] Developed economies have averaged growth rates of 2.4 percent between 1990 and 2008, and some (such as Japan and Germany) have averaged rates of 1.5 and 1.9 percent, respectively. Developing economies have collectively increased their gross domestic product (GDP) by an average of 4.7 percent over the same period. A small number of emerging economies notched up growth rates of 6.0 percent per annum; but the majority of these have experienced a trend deceleration since 1997–98, leaving only three economies with annual growth rates exceeding 7.0 percent between 2000 and 2008: China (10.0 percent), India (7.1 percent), and Vietnam (7.5 percent).

It is unlikely that the high-income developed economies with slow-growing and aging populations will be able to improve on the growth performance of the past 20 years. It is also highly improbable that China, India, and Vietnam can grow at double-digit rates—although the two large economies could realistically aim for growth rates of 8–9 percent, given the momentum they have acquired, remaining cross-sectoral technology gaps, and the untapped potential of their domestic markets. The remaining one half of the world's population—3.5 billion people—is distributed among a heterogeneous group of middle- and lower-middle-income economies aiming for growth rates in the 6 percent range and of late-starting, low-income countries with youthful, rapidly increasing populations that need to grow at high single-digit rates to double per capita incomes in 10 years.

Efforts to accelerate growth and sustain higher trend rates must be tempered by three considerations. First, resource scarcities, rising energy prices, environmental factors, and the maturing of globalization are undermining policy-induced growth impulses. Second, the economies of the United States and the European Union, which served as the engines of global growth during the recent past, face strong headwinds—largely of their own creation, but undoubtedly problematic for late-starting countries that must export to accelerate growth. Third, development economics confronts a policy deficit. The advances in theory and the deepening of empirical analysis have yielded only a meager crop of ideas on how countries can accelerate growth in the face of multiple constraints, and only if policy interventions can be multiplied and effectively implemented are countries likely to realize their growth ambitions.[2]

The literature on growth empirics is now so rich that a brief recapitalization of the stylized facts can suffice.

- For low- and middle-income countries, capital is the principal determinant of growth, with labor and total factor productivity (TFP) trailing well behind. Since 1980, three quarters of growth can be explained by capital investment, with the bulk of this investment financed from domestic savings (see table 5.1). Thus, domestic investment and savings are intertwined with savings enabling investment but not "causing" it.

- Between 1913 and 1950, the world economy grew by an average of 1.82 percent per annum. During the second half of the 20th century, growth accelerated to 3.97 percent per annum. This led to a sharp reduction in poverty, in spite of much higher rates of population growth (Maddison 2003, 260). The $1-a-day poverty in developing countries declined from 40 percent of the population in 1981 to 18 percent in 2004 (Ferreira and Ravallion 2008, 9). The reduction in absolute poverty has

Table 5.1   Contribution to World Growth Percentage Share

Determinant of growth	1989–95	1995–2000	2000–06
Capital	54.1	46.4	40.7
ICT	12.8	15.6	11.7
Non-ICT	41.3	30.8	29.0
Labor	29.6	30.4	23.6
Hours	13.5	22.0	16.1
Quality	16.0	8.4	7.6
TFP	16.3	23.2	35.7

Source: Jorgenson and Vu 2009.

Note: ICT = information and communications technology.

been greatest in China and India, countries registering some of the fastest growth rates. But some of the growth benefits have been undercut by rising inequality. Although global inequality changed little between 1980 and the early 2000s, inequality rose in 30 of the 49 countries with data covering the 1990–2004 period (Ferreira and Ravallion 2008, 8; Firebaugh and Goesling 2007). Interestingly, changes in equality seem not to be systematically related to growth or to civic unrest and civil wars (de Dominicis, de Groot, and Florax 2006; Ferreira and Ravallion 2008; Voitchovsky 2009).

- Upper-middle- and high-income countries derive more of their growth from gains in TFP; and the consensus view among researchers is that, over the longer run, growth is a function of TFP (see figure 5.1) (Comin and Hobijn 2010).

- TFP has long been a catchall for other factors, the measurement and individual contributions of which have proved difficult to pin down. However, these various factors are the key policy targets, and the most interesting research on the sources of growth is precisely on these elusive "quarks." The list of quarks is long; but from among them, six are most amenable to policy action: human capital variously measured, and its quality; technological capability and innovation; managerial skills; organizational effectiveness; institutions affecting incentives, competition, allocative efficiency, and governance; and the characteristics of urbanization. Typically, all six affect the production and use of knowledge, resource allocation, and productive utilization.

- Growth has been spearheaded in the earlier stages of development by the industrial sector in almost all countries (UNIDO 2009); and though at

Figure 5.1   Sources of Economic Growth, by Region

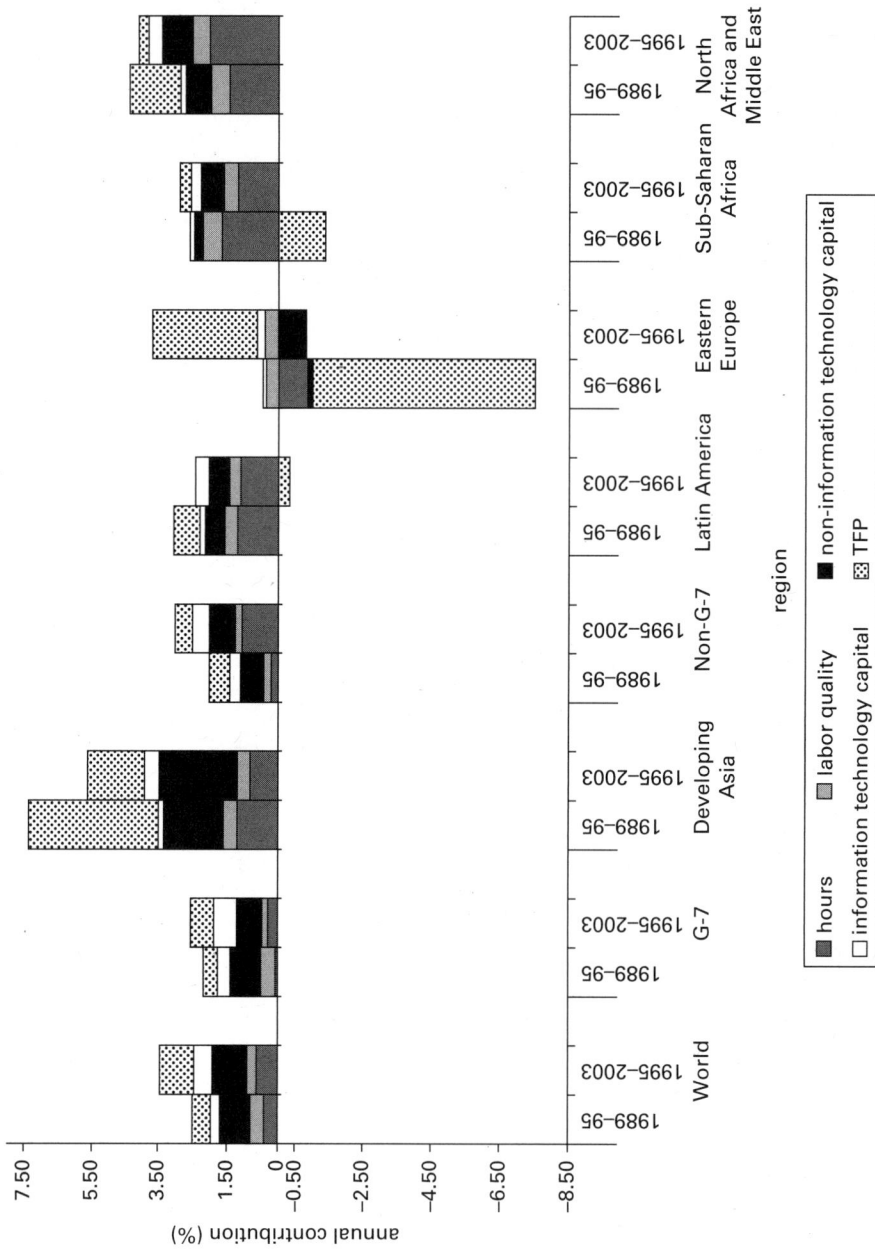

annual contribution (%)

region

Legend:
- ■ hours
- ▨ labor quality
- □ information technology capital
- ■ non-information technology capital
- ▨ TFP

Source: Jorgenson 2005.

later stages of development, services become the leading source of growth, industry remains the more productive and innovative of the two major sectors, with the share of agriculture in GDP everywhere shrinking into relative insignificance. The recent experience of India, Ireland, and some of the smaller East European countries points to the growth potential inherent in tradable impersonal services and in software. For small economies, services-led growth backstopped by investment in information technology and skills is a real possibility; for large economies, it can prove to be a valuable supplement to the impetus from other sectors.

• Some countries—many in Africa and the Middle East—have derived much of their growth from the development and export of natural resource–based products, whether minerals or agricultural commodities. In most instances, mineral (including energy) extraction has been paced by foreign investment, and it has created enclave sectors generating few spillovers and loosely linked to the rest of the economy. Although natural resources can boost economic performance and supplement other sources of growth (as, for instance, in Malaysia and Indonesia), large mineral resources have tended to inhibit industrialization, growth, and development more generally for a number of reasons that have been labeled the "resource curse."

• Although the bulk of demand derives from consumption followed by investment, most economies—small and large—have supplemented these with demand arising from trade. The smaller open and rapidly growing economies have relied (usually for brief periods) on net exports for as much as 40 percent of their growth, with 20 percent being closer to the norm. Imports have played an almost equally important role because they are vehicles for technology transfer and contribute to technological catch-up (Ding and Knight 2008; Lawrence and Weinstein 2001). Thus, tradable goods and services—mainly manufactures and resource-based products—have underpinned the rapid growth of economies that were able to create a production base of sufficient size through domestic investment financed in large part from national savings.

• Foreign direct investment in production facilities, infrastructure, and research and development has supplemented domestic investment, the technology transfer through trade, and the indigenous efforts at building innovation capacity. The contribution of foreign direct investment has rarely exceeded 3–5 percent of GDP, although in a number of the most successful economies, it has catalyzed industrialization, helped promote exports, and contributed to an upgrading of the product mix.

- For the past three decades, growth has been powerfully aided by the integration of the global economy. In particular, trade liberalization and measures that have eased the flow of capital, the circulation of skills, and the sharing of information have stimulated economic performance directly and through a variety of externalities.

- Last, but not least, the golden age of growth is indebted to the incentives, innovations, and productivity gains arising from a number of general-purpose technologies.[3] Two such technologies that have been at the forefront are the semiconductor or information technology and the Internet. These are the signature technologies of recent times, and each has spawned a host of productivity-enhancing innovations.

From the perspective of longer-term growth and its sustainability, capital, labor, and the factors influencing TFP are more relevant for policymaking purposes. Here the discourse on growth becomes intertwined with that of development, and one can see the growth pathway becoming one with the development pathway.

Successful developers have emphasized, to varying degrees, five objectives in their pursuit of growth—all of which relate to the drivers of TFP identified above. These objectives are

1. creating a "learning economy" so as to acquire skills, absorb ideas and technologies, and lay the foundations for domestic innovation;

2. stimulating entrepreneurship and organizational efficiency;

3. building institutions that promote competition and openness;

4. crafting the institutional infrastructure for a longer-term strategy in coordination with labor and the business community,[4] and enlarging the administrative capabilities of the state to frame and implement policies; and

5. internalizing these within an urban system that is conducive to spillovers and maximizes agglomeration economies.

Politics and Development

Each of those five determinants of growth—and of development—has an economic dimension and an overlapping political dimension. The fact is that politics can never be completely disassociated from economic activities and decision making. It introduces additional complexities, and political calculations mean that decisions can rarely be based purely on economic calculus. Hence, whether it is about the learning economy, strategy and coordination, or measures to raise urbanization economies, politics tempers economic decisions and can often dominate them. Policy makers must weigh the political costs and the demands of interest groups alongside economic costs and benefits, with the politics of decision making varying from one political system to another. There is plenty of theorizing on the political economy of development, but no simple recipes and plenty of scope for trial and error. As Acemoglu (2010) observes, "There is increasing recognition that institutional and political economy factors are central to economic development. Many problems of development result from barriers to the adoption of new technologies, lack of property rights over land, labor and businesses, and policies distorting prices and incentives. Typically policymakers introduce or maintain such policies to remain in power or to enrich themselves, or because politically powerful elites oppose the entry of rivals, the introduction of new technologies, or improvements in the property rights of their workers or competitors" (p. 18).

The pathways to development are few and narrow, and political factors all too often can constrain access and movement along these pathways. Successful development is predicated not just on a facilitating external environment and good policies, but also on domestic political dynamics that (at a minimum) are neutral toward development and ideally are highly supportive. Even weak states can develop if the politics are conducive and the business sector is powerfully motivated. By the same token, strong states have the power to hobble development if they are distracted by other objectives.

In Conclusion

The pathways to development are various; however, all require navigating the staircase to growth and using the insights provided by political economy to tackle the challenge of sustaining progress and improving the welfare not of some but of the vast majority.

Notes

1. Easterly (2009), relying on the findings of panel regressions of annual growth rates, observes that "only 8 percent of the variance is permanent cross-country differences, the other 92 percent is transitory deviations from a world mean of 1.8 percent per capita annual increase."

2. See Pritchett, Woolcock, and Andrews (2010) on policy implementation factures.

3. Most general-purpose technologies play the role of "enabling technologies opening up new opportunities rather than offering complete final solutions. For example, electric motors fostered the more efficient design of factories [and] users of microelectronics benefit from the surging power of silicon by wrapping around integrated circuits, their own technical advances" (Bresnahan and Trajtenberg 1995, 88).

4. Jagdish Bhagwati (2010) associates policy making with three Is: ideas, institutions, and interests or interest groups.

References

Acemoglu, D. 2010. "Theory, General Equilibrium, Political Economy, and Empirics in Development Economics." *Journal of Economic Perspectives* 24 (2): 17–32.

Bhagwati, J. 2010. "Running in Place on Trade." Project Syndicate, July 20. http://www.project-syndicate.org/commentary/bhagwati2/English.

Bresnahan, T., and M. Trajtenberg. 1995. "General Purpose Technologies 'Engines of Growth?'" *Journal of Econometrics* 65 (1): 83–108.

Comin, D., and B. Hobijn. 2010. "Technology Diffusion and Postwar Growth." In vol. 25 of *NBER Macroeconomics Annual 2010*, 1–84. Cambridge, MA: National Bureau of Economic Research.

de Dominicis, L., H. de Groot, and R. Florax. 2006. "Growth and Inequality: A Meta-Analysis." Discussion Paper 064/3, Tinbergen Institute, Amsterdam.

Ding, S., and J. Knight. 2008. "Why Has China Grown So Fast? The Role of Structural Change." Economic Series Working Paper 415, Department of Economics, Oxford University, Oxford, UK.

Easterly, W. 2009. "Economic Development Experts Versus Economics: The Example of Industrial Policy." PowerPoint presentation, World Bank, Washington, DC, September 14.

Ferreira, F.H.G., and M. Ravallion. 2008. "Global Poverty and Inequality: A Review of the Evidence." Policy Research Working Paper 4623, World Bank, Washington, DC.

Firebaugh, G., and B. Goesling. 2007. "Globalization and Global Inequalities: Recent Trends." In *The Blackwell Companion to Globalization*, ed. G. Ritzer, 549–64. Malden, MA: Blackwell.

Jorgenson, D. W., and K. Vu. 2005. "Information Technology and the World Economy." *Scandinavian Journal of Economics* 107 (4): 631–50.

———. 2009. "Growth Accounting within the International Comparison Program." *ICP Bulletin* 6 (1): 3–28.

Lawrence, R. Z., and D. E. Weinstein. 2001. "Trade and Growth: Import-Led or Export-Led? Evidence from Japan and Korea." In *Rethinking the East Asian Miracle*, ed. J. E. Stiglitz and S. Yusuf, 379–408. New York: Oxford University Press.

Maddison, A. 2003. *The World Economy: Historical Statistics*. Paris: Organisation for Economic Co-operation and Development Publishing.

Pritchett, L., M. Woolcock, and M. Andrews. 2010. "Capability Traps? The Mechanisms of Persistent Implementation Failure." Background paper for *World Development Report 2011: Conflict, Security, and Development*, World Bank, Washington, DC.

UNIDO (United Nations Industrial Development Organization). 2009. *Industrial Development Report 2009. Breaking In and Moving Up: New Industrial Challenges for the Bottom Billion and the Middle-Income Countries*. Vienna: UNIDO.

Voitchovsky, S. 2009. "Inequality Growth and Sectoral Change." In *The Oxford Handbook of Economics Inequality*, ed. W. Salverda, B. Nolan, and T. Smeeding, 549–74. Oxford, UK: Oxford University Press.

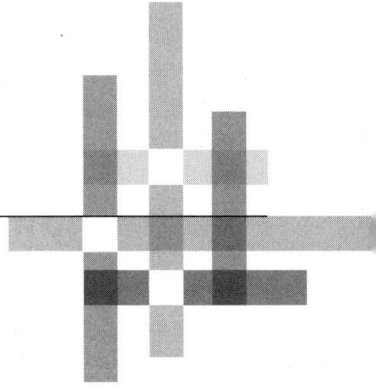

Why Is Development Blocked?

Raj Nallari

There are several reasons why growth and development have been uneven across countries and over time: high income inequality; state capture by elites and powerful groups; weak state and private institutions related to perennial problems of corruption, rule of law, property rights, and capacity to formulate and implement policies; and "lack of a regional growth pole." Several of these factors are interrelated. For example, high income inequality could coincide with higher state capture and higher levels of perceived corruption. These bottlenecks to development are detailed below.

Regional Growth Pole Helps Spur Development

Akamatsu (1962), the Japanese scholar, developed the "Flying Geese Paradigm" to explain technological development in Southeast Asia. Embraced also by Kojima (2000), the paradigm views Japan as a leading power—the lead "goose" with the other countries in the region aligned in a "wild geese" pattern, based on their differing stages of growth. As the lead nation moves out of labor-intensive production to capital-intensive production, its low-productivity production moves down the hierarchy and the pattern repeats itself. This model of comparative advantage described

Figure 6.1 Regional Growth Poles

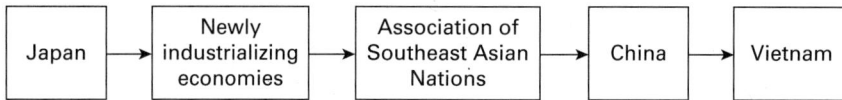

```
┌──────────┐     ┌──────────────┐     ┌──────────────┐     ┌──────────┐     ┌──────────┐
│          │     │   Newly      │     │ Association of│     │          │     │          │
│  Japan   │ ──> │industrializing│ ──>│Southeast Asian│ ──> │  China   │ ──> │ Vietnam  │
│          │     │  economies   │     │   Nations    │     │          │     │          │
└──────────┘     └──────────────┘     └──────────────┘     └──────────┘     └──────────┘
```

Source: Author's illustration.

the economic development of Japan, the second-tier of nations consisting of the new industrializing economies of the Republic of Korea; China; Taiwan, China; Singapore; and Hong Kong SAR, China, followed by the main countries of the Association of Southeast Asian Nations (the Philippines, Indonesia, Thailand, and Malaysia, with China and Vietnam at the rear) (figure 6.1). The paradigm depended on the catalytic role of Japan as the lead nation. It is difficult to identify lead nations in other developing regions of the world.

High-Income Inequality Constrains Economic and Political Development

There is now enough evidence that in a country with relatively higher income and wealth inequality, the incumbent government (1) resorts to redistributive policies to maintain political and social stability; and (2) is faced with credit market imperfections as powerful groups corner the credit flows, thus impeding the formation of both physical and human capital among the have-nots. For example, Sachs (1989) finds that Latin American and Caribbean countries have higher income equality than other regions, and this is deterring their economic development. Persson and Tabellini (1994) find that, indeed, a relatively equal distribution does have a positive impact on economic growth in democratic countries.

Poor Institutions

To trace the variety of institutions prevailing in postcolonial nations, Acemoglu, Johnson, and Robinson (2002) estimate the effect of institutions on economic performance, based on differences in European mortality rates. Where Europeans faced high mortality rates, due to an adverse climate or disease environment, institutions tend to be extractive. Colonizers were unable to settle in these areas and thus concentrated on extracting as much and as many of the resources as possible, without developing institutions to protect property or to limit government expropriation. In areas where climate was favorable and the disease environment was manageable, colonizers facing lower mortality rates had incentives to develop institutions that protected property rights and enforced checks and balances on government.

Europeans settled in large numbers in the United States, Canada, and Australia, where climate was favorable. Institutions conducive to growth evolved. The fate of much of Africa was very different, however. Even after the demise of colonialism, extractive institutions prevailed. In a separate article, Acemoglu, Johnson, and Robinson (2002) note the exceptional case of Botswana, where due its unfavorable geographic location, the colonial masters did not tamper with the local tradition of checks and balances. This fostered democracy and sustained economic growth.

According to North and Weingast (1989), British institutions were better in fostering growth because of superior commercial law. Consequently, British settler-colonies fared better eventually. Latin America was a Spanish and Portuguese colony. Similar to their colonial masters, these nations had regulatory monopolies, which prevailed well into current times and impeded growth. Despite the same initial advantage during 19th century, each continent was led to a different predicament during the next 100 years or so.

Formal Rules Are Required for Development

During the 11th century, the West was far behind in almost all dimensions, compared with Islamic and Chinese civilizations; but industrialization took place in Great Britain and not elsewhere. Greif (1989, 1994) makes a compelling argument that juxtaposes the individualistic nature of the West with the collaborative nature of the East. Contracts in the West were mostly bilateral, compared with multilateral contracts in the Muslim world. Even though initially efficient, multilateral contracts prevented the formation of formal legal institutions. The absence of formal legal institutions forced trade to take place within a certain community. This curtailed the growth of exchanges farther afield. Bilateral transactions did not enforce communal ties; therefore, the society had greater need to build formal laws and regulations that eventually fostered economic growth.

Perennial Crisis in Governance Destabilizes Development

What do we learn from the troubles of modern-day corporations? These are the most sophisticated corporations ever formed, yet they are victims of their own governance failures. Public sector governance problems are known from time immemorial. The first description of state governance problems in the form of bribery, corruption, and other misgovernance is attributed to Patañjali, who lived in India around 53 CE. Conversely, corporate governance problems are relatively recent. With the industrial revolution came the need for a corporation to organize and manage capital and labor. The board of directors, by law, is given full authority in a corporation. In the initial days of industrialization, the family-owned corporation had family members on its board. However, as the corporations became more complex over time, the board has occupied more a role of overseeing the management team (comprising chief executive and financial officers). This is the problem of principal-agent, where the agent (management team) usurps power from the principal (board of directors and shareholders). The oversight function has been diluted further, owing to the complexity of business transactions and the managers often providing obfuscation. In addition, more and more boards are stacked with insiders and friends. As a result, we have reached a stage in several big and small corporations where there is a crisis in corporate governance. The recent financial crisis is but one manifestation of this corporate crisis, where complexity is deliberately created in the name of financial innovation that, in turn, obfuscates information given to the board of directors, stakeholders, and the public.

The crisis in corporate governance is compounded by public sector governance where politicians and bureaucrats are influenced by the large corporations. State capture is defined by Hellman et al. (2000) as the "propensity of firms to shape the underlying rules of the game by 'purchasing' decrees, legislation, and influence at the central bank, which is found to be prevalent in a number of transition economies" (p. i). This "shaping" may be done not only by the private firms or richer elites (top 20 percent on the income distribution scale), but also by ethnic groups or powerful economic groups in some countries. As such, to fully understand the dynamics of state capture, the analysis must be based on winners and losers—not only in terms of income groups, but also in terms of powerful groups and vested interests (including bureaucracy). In almost all the countries, this argument of state capture by a small group of corporations or elites appears to hold because these elites have been colluding with politicians and, with the help of bureaucracy, extracting rents rather than investing in productive activities (which Eifert and Gelb 2005 call "low-level political equilibrium"). Private investment and growth are higher in stronger states than in weaker states, and garnering of subsidies by the elites is relatively lower.

Countries that are "highly captured" may exhibit capture of all or most institutions—such as parliament, political parties, the executives (including ministries and public enterprises), judicial courts, and bureaucrats. Firms and groups that cannot compete with favored firms or accommodated groups will go under or have no choice but to resort to "informality" or "unofficialdom" and a "shadow financial system." By choosing to be in the shadows, these informal enterprises are able to circumvent government regulations relating to property rights, labor laws (such as minimum wages and workers' safety restrictions), environmental regulations, price controls, and licensing and to avoid taxes and fees. To avoid the costs arising from detection and punishment for operating informally (usually illegally), the big corporations and informal enterprises operate through "trust" in the form of transactions, based on reputation, among closed networks of customers and suppliers.

Political development is blocked by the elites and powerful groups. Acemoglu and Johnson (2007) studies a number of countries and finds that the movement from dictatorship or authoritarianism to democracy is blocked by groups that benefit from the status quo. In such societies, the reward structure favors the elites. Only when there is outside pressure (for example, from donors) or when the vast majority of citizens take to the streets will there be some concessions made to ease restrictions, reduce rent-seeking, and change the reward structure to promote incentives for the many—not just the few. There has to be a continuous pressure exerted on closed regimes to provide more equitable services and develop institutions that provide incentives. Enlightened leadership and coalition building in civil society (that emphasizes social accountability) can bring forth change agents and place a country on a path of gradual reforms and opening up.

In Conclusion

Growth and development have been uneven over time and across countries. Some of the issues considered here—high income inequality, state capture by elites and powerful groups, weak state and private institutions, and the "lack of a regional growth pole"—highlight this disparity in growth and development.

References

Acemoglu, D., and S. Johnson. 2007. "Disease and Development: The Effect of Life Expectancy on Economic Growth." *Journal of Political Economy* 115 (6): 925–85.

Acemodlu, D., S. Johnson, and J. A. Robinson. 2002. "Reversal of Fortune: Geography and Institutions in the Making of the Modern World Income Distribution." *Quarterly Journal of Economics* 117 (4): 1231–94.

Akamatsu, K. 1962. "A Historical Pattern of Economic Growth in Developing Countries." *Developing Economies* 1 (Suppl 1): 3–25.

Eifert, B., and A. Gelb. 2005. "Coping with Aid Volatility." *Finance and Development* 42 (3): 24–27.

Greif, A. 1989. "Reputation and Coalitions in Medieval Trade: Evidence on the Maghribi Traders." *Journal of Economic History* 49 (4): 857–82.

——. 1994. "Cultural Beliefs and the Organization of Society: An Historical and Theoretical Reflection on Collectivist and Individualist Societies." *Journal of Political Economy* 102 (5): 912–50.

Hellman, J., G. Jones, D. Kaufmann, and M. Schankerman. 2000. "Measuring Governance, Corruption, and State Capture: How Firms and Bureaucrats Shape the Business Environment in Transition Economies." Policy Research Working Paper 2312, World Bank, Washington, DC.

Kojima, K. 2000. "The 'Flying Geese' model of Asian Economic Development: Origin, Theoretical Extensions, and Regional Policy Implications." *Journal of Asian Economics* 11: 375–401.

North, D. C., and B. R. Weingast. 1989. "Constitutions and Credible Commitment: The Evolution of the Institutions of Public Choice in 17th Century England." *Journal of Economic History* 49 (4): 803–32.

Persson, T., and G. Tabellini. 1994. "Is Inequality Harmful for Growth?" *American Economic Review* 84: 600–21.

Sachs, J. 1989. "Social Conflict and Populist Policies in Latin America." Working Paper 2897, National Bureau for Economic Research, Cambridge, MA.

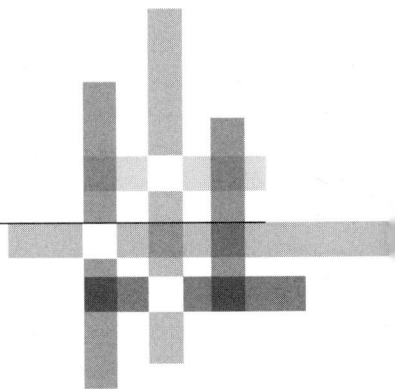

Development Challenges

Raj Nallari

The global financial and economic crisis of 2008 brought an urgency to focusing on shorter-term policy issues related to managing bubbles, a transformed economic landscape, and a new normal that sees a key role for the emerging markets.

From Home Mortgages to the U.S. Credit Freeze

The bursting of the housing bubble in the United States (as reflected in a surge in defaults and foreclosures since mid-2006) resulted in a plunge in the prices of mortgage-backed securities, assets whose value ultimately comes from mortgage payments. These financial losses have left many financial institutions with too little capital—that is, too few assets compared with their debt. (U.S. financial firms lost over $1 trillion by December 2008.) This problem is especially severe because households, corporations, and the government took on so much debt during the bubble years—debt that accumulated to over 400 percent of gross domestic product (GDP) in the United States and about 450 percent of GDP in the United Kingdom.

Because financial institutions have too little capital relative to their debt, they have not been able or willing to provide the credit the economy needs. U.S. and European banks have been raising capital of about $400 billion from oil-producing countries and China, but the gap remains large as banks continue to write down bad loans. Financial institutions have been trying to pay down their debt by selling assets (including those mortgage-backed securities), but this action drives asset prices down and makes the institutions' financial positions even worse. This vicious circle is what some call the "paradox of deleveraging." The U.S. financial system is being crippled by inadequate capital, which will continue unless the federal government hugely overpays for the assets it buys, giving financial firms—and their stockholders and executives—a giant windfall at taxpayers' expense.

Regulators in some cases facilitated and in other cases failed to respond to the buildup in imbalances. The current economic crisis had many other culprits. A long period of abundant liquidity, rising asset prices, and low interest rates—in the context of international financial integration and innovation—led to the buildup of global macroeconomic imbalances as well as to a global "search-for-yield" and general underpricing of risk by investors. Complex, nontransparent instruments were mispriced and misunderstood.

By early 2007, sovereign wealth funds managed over $3 trillion, in addition to foreign exchange reserves in emerging markets of $7 trillion. The uncertainty surrounding the losses to financial firms led to a flight to quality, as reflected by widening spreads between the London interbank offered rate and U.S. Treasury bill yields as well as among other financial instruments. At about the same time as the financial crisis was engulfing the United States, the excess asset demand that produced the crisis did not collapse. The financial instruments were deemed not as sound by capital investors (who were primarily from emerging markets) and by oil producers (who were in search of investment opportunities).

Managing booms and busts is still the main economic policy challenge for developed and developing countries. The global oil price, which doubled between February 2007 and July 2008, is one such bubble that coincided with an endogenous response of a world economy that was trying to increase the global supply of financial assets (see figure 7.1). It is not the increased demand for oil from fast-growing China and India but the search for higher yields that is driving the commodity and financial bubbles.

Figure 7.1 Monthly Price Indexes, 2005–09

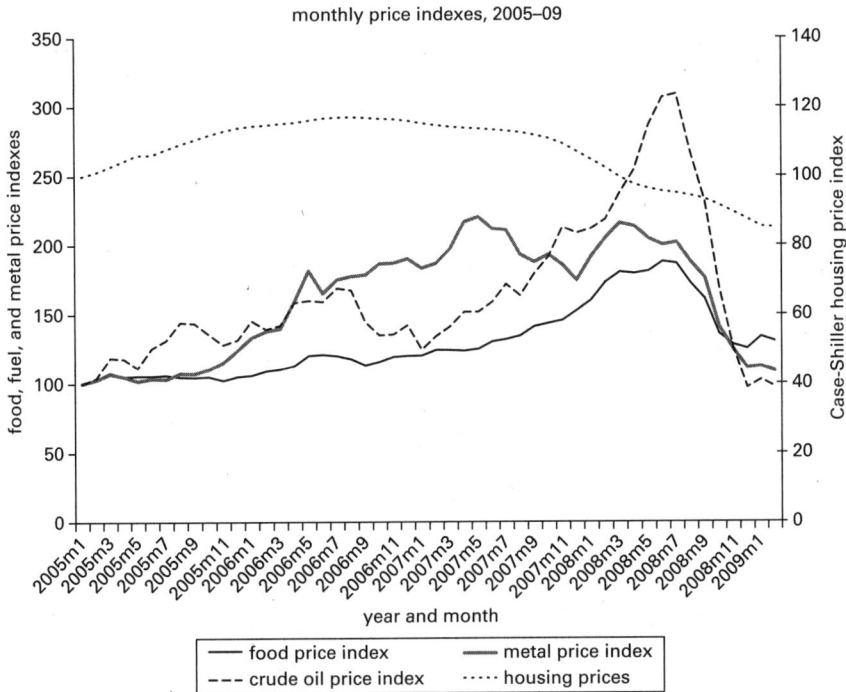

monthly price indexes, 2005–09

Source: IMF 2011a. Compiled from International Monetary Fund data at http://www.imf.org/external/data.htm.

The Global Economic Crisis Has Transformed the Economic Landscape

Patterns of trade flows, financial flows, innovation, and growth are all rapidly changing (see figure 7.2). It is no longer the dominance of the neoclassical model (Washington Consensus), but one of many models—the Republic of Korea; China; Brazil; India; Taiwan, China. Neither is the model G-3 or G-7, but G-20 and expanding. There is a degree of inertia in currencies—moving away from the dominance of the U.S. dollar could be expected to be a gradual process. Creation of the euro and the growing economic clout of Brazil, the Russian Federation, India, and China (the so-called BRIC countries) over the past decade, however, have led to a new environment in which a multipolar international monetary system is beginning to emerge.

Development is no longer just North-South. It is South-South, even South-North, with lessons for all with open minds. It is conditional cash

Figure 7.2 Development Is No Longer Just North-South

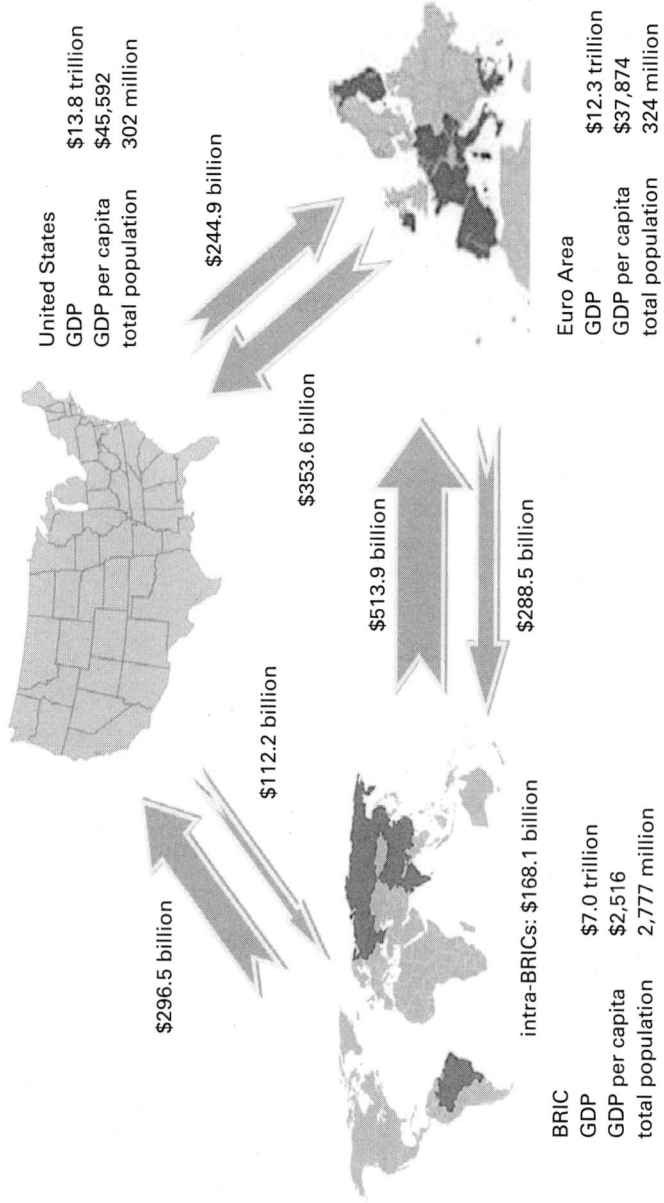

United States
GDP $13.8 trillion
GDP per capita $45,592
total population   302 million

Euro Area
GDP $12.3 trillion
GDP per capita $37,874
total population   324 million

BRIC
GDP $7.0 trillion
GDP per capita $2,516
total population   2,777 million

intra-BRICs: $168.1 billion

$244.9 billion

$353.6 billion

$513.9 billion

$288.5 billion

$112.2 billion

$296.5 billion

Source: Author illustration.

Note: BRIC = Brazil, the Russian Federation, India, and China.

transfer programs in Mexico being studied around the world. It is Indians in Africa explaining the so-called white revolution that boosted milk production. It is a new world where developing countries are not only recipients but also providers of aid and expertise. And it is not about ideological panaceas, blueprints, or one-size-fits-all solutions.

This also means that it is harder to reach a consensus on "global commons." The Doha Round of the World Trade Organization and the climate change talks in Copenhagen revealed how hard it will be to share mutual benefits and responsibilities between developed and developing countries. Those debates also exposed the diversity of challenges faced by different developing countries. Brazil, Russia, India, and China cannot represent all. As President Ernesto Zedillo of Mexico pointed out, the problem for poor people is not too many markets, but too few. We need markets for microfinance or small and medium-size enterprises, especially if run by women; markets to move, store, and sell goods; and markets to save, insure, and invest.

The New Normal

The Western world is likely to have a low output performance in the next two to three years because the financial systems in the United States and in European countries have broken down and the fiscal burden and public debt arising from the economic and financial crisis is quickly mounting. These circumstances would contribute to credit restraint and a crowding-out of the private sector. Very little has changed in terms of regulating the U.S. and European financial systems. If anything, the U.S. financial system has become even more concentrated around Goldman Sachs, J.P. Morgan, AIG, Citibank, and a few others; transparency in transactions has not improved much; and financial firms are continuing their merry ways of the past. Many of these larger financial firms have received large bailouts and could still go under. Unemployment rates are likely to be higher for the next few years. The result is that governments of major countries will be expanding their roles further in protecting too-big-to-fail financial firms—including reregulating the financial sector, protecting the politically connected industrial companies in the name of protecting jobs, and spending more money on social protection. All this means that higher taxes may be warranted. More government and less financial leverage will be the new norm, characterized by deleveraging, deficits and debt, and reregulation.

In Conclusion

Emerging and developing economies whose financial systems are intact are expected to grow at about 6.5 percent during 2010–12, on average (IMF 2011b, 4); and China, India, and other Asian countries are pulling the world wagon with continued adoption of technology and institutions. China and other East Asian countries need to cooperate in increasing their domestic spending, particularly on consumption, so as to maintain the world output and export growth of the early 2000s.

Under these economic conditions, will the U.S. dollar and the euro be strong enough to continue to be major currencies in the world? More recently, China, Russia, and a few others have been pushing for an international reserve currency such as the already existing special drawing rights. Geopolitics will play a major role in determining whether the world will have a new reserve currency.

References

IMF (International Monetary Fund). 2011a. "Data and Statistics." Washington, DC. http://www.imf.org/external/data.htm.

———. 2011b. "Global Recovery Advances but Remains Uneven." *World Economic Outlook Update* January. http://www.imf.org/external/pubs/ft/weo/2011/update/01/pdf/0111.pdf.

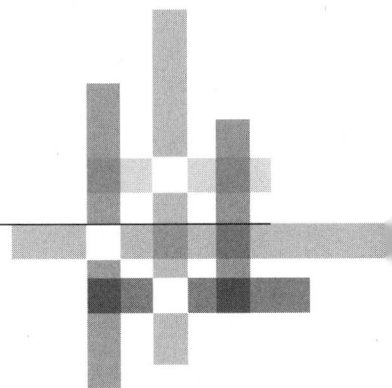

Political Economy

Raj Nallari and Rwitwika Bhattacharya

A social contract requires that citizens give up some of their rights in return for protection provided by the government. The government, in turn, promises to protect citizens from conditions like unemployment, physical insecurity, and hunger. Unfortunately, governance realities in developed and developing countries mean that political leadership does not always deliver the implicit promises made through the social contract.

In "dominant states," the failure to deliver services might be because the government has a short-term view of policy and development. In other "competitive clientelism" states, this might be because the state does not have the infrastructural organization to support development policies. These are two of the many causes that make it hard for governments to implement effective policies. Therefore, even if the most effective policies are developed, it is ultimately the government's role to implement them efficiently. Political economy deals with the ground realities of hindrances faced because of politics in implementing the policies.

In extreme cases, the failure to deliver basic services might result in a reaction from constituents. However, changes in the political system can come in various forms. Levy argues that there are four approaches through which political reform can come about (Levy 2011). The first approach is to choose policy options that do not directly confront stakeholders—in other words, what is feasible (given the country trajectory); second is for small governance reforms—"small-g" or an incremental approach; third is to garner support for reform from the grassroots—a multistakeholder approach; and forth is big governance—"big-g" approach. Each of these can usher in reforms in the governance systems. However, to bring in sustained changes there is a need for political will.

State Capture

The lack of political will to bring substantive changes is often attributed to unequal distribution of power. State capture—defined as the efforts of affluent individuals, groups, private firms, or oligarchs to shape law, public policies, and rules and regulations to their own advantage—is one of the primary issues in public governance. How else can one explain former U.S. Treasury Secretary Henry Paulson calling his former colleagues from Goldman Sachs three times more often in the days before the run-up to the collapse of Lehman Brothers in September 2008 that triggered a financial meltdown first in the United States and later in Europe?[1]

States are often captured by influential elites (particularly those in the top 20 percent of the income distribution scale), consisting of richer elites or ethnic groups, or both. Consequently, the elites are able to exert themselves on the bureaucracy; and this oftentimes translates into preferential treatment for the "privileged" while the poor continue to suffer because of weak policies. In other words, state capture and redistributive conflicts are part of the same spectrum of good-to-bad governance. Countries that fall victim to state capture often end up having elites and corporations working in tandem with political leaders to extract rents rather than build and develop the state (which Eifert and Gelb [2005] call "low-level political equilibrium"). The only difference in "weak states" of several low-income countries is that the private sector is uncertain.

In contrast, stronger states—despite rhetoric about "limited government" and a "constrained executive" (such as in Organisation for Economic Co-operation and Development countries)—tend to have higher revenue-to-GDP ratios and to invest in public goods because elites in these countries are confident that rents can accrue to them now and in the future.

For firms working in "highly captured" states, the limited accessibility to political elites makes it particularly hard for them to compete. Inevitably, many firms choose to work informally because this is the only way for them to surpass governmental regulation. The presence of an informal economy leads to further labor-related issues. For elites who have captured the state, this might include all wings of governance (including executive, judicial, and legislative) or those related to the interest of the vested party.

For example, in Mauritius, 12 families of French origin had controlled all the sugar plantations. Since Mauritius was economically reliant on sugar production, control over the plantations meant control over resources. The monopolistic control over the financial resources inevitably led to the elites capturing the state. Because the majority of the population was deprived of government support (and was of a different ethnic background—that is, of Indian descent), it was inevitable that political tensions eventually arose. The World Bank and the United Nations Development Programme came in as external mediators during this process to alleviate the tension. Eventually, the elites controlling the plantations had to concede some power to balance the overall power structure. Most sustainable movements for change tend to come from the bottom up (Gulhati and Nallari 1990).

Movement from the Bottom Up

Recent tensions in the Arab Republic of Egypt are an example of an organized movement that started in the grassroots and ultimately created a change in the political system. Even though the causes of the tension are yet to be deciphered, the movement did engage "average" citizens and led them to take some strong actions. Inevitably, the impact of these actions was tremendous. Similarly in India, the Right to Information Act, passed in 2005, was started by farmers in rural India who wanted to seek more information about their backgrounds. As the movement gained ground and started coming to national attention, there was even more grassroots support. Finally, with the support of some senior political leaders, the bill was passed.[2]

Even though the Right to Information movement was not as drastic as the actions in Egypt, both of these movements illustrate that civic engagement and unrest at the grassroots can push the government to reconsider its position and bow to the demands. Although movements started in the grassroots ended peacefully in Egypt and India, that is not always the case. Often, grassroots movements can turn violent and cause further setbacks for the country. In these conditions, intervention is often needed. The two major types of interventions applied have used external support or unbiased internal support.

Additionally, there is a stark difference between legislating programs in support and implementing effective programs. An organized movement can often give enough ammunition to bring about change, and governments can often concede to bringing change (especially if it is from the bottom up); however, civil society organizations need to ensure that the change brought about through the legislation is sustained and implemented effectively. Thus, although political will is important to ensure the foundations for good governance, there are various other stakeholders involved in ensuring successful governance. For example, if the government is failing to deliver basic services, then citizens are likely to express their grievances.

Notes

1. "Henry Paulson's links to Goldman Sachs raises questions." France 24 News Source. http://www.france24.com/en/20090810-henry-paulsons-links-goldman -sachs-raise-questions-.
2. Right to Information Act (India), http://www.righttoinformation.gov.in/.

References

Eifert, B., and A. Gelb. 2005. "Coping with Aid Volatility." *Finance and Development* 42 (3): 24–27.

Gulhati, R., and R. Nallari. 1990. *Successful Stabilization and Recovery in Mauritius.* EDI Development Policy Case Series, Analytical Case Studies. Washington, DC: World Bank.

Levy, B. 2011. "The Politics of Development." *Development Outreach Magazine,* April. http://wbi.worldbank.org/wbi/devoutreach/article/1072/politics -development.

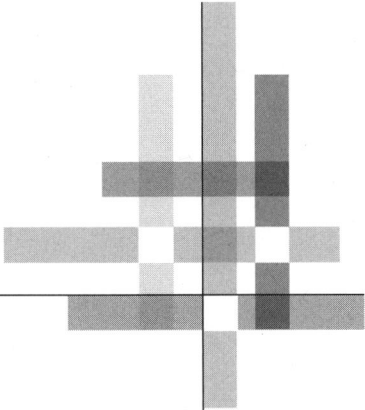

Part II

PRIVATE ENTERPRISE AND DEVELOPMENT

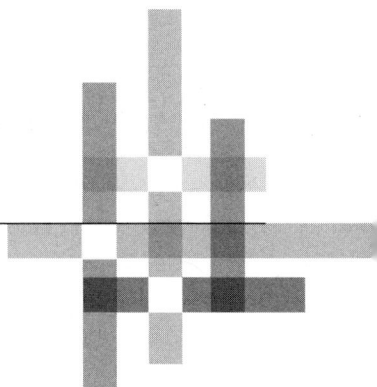

SECTION 9

Overview

Shahid Yusuf, Breda Griffith, and Raj Nallari

Innovation is a favorite catchword among policy makers in most industrializing countries[1]; but as it has gained in currency, the meaning of innovation has tended to blur. Innovation should refer to a product, a process, a design, or an organizational form that is a significant improvement over or a departure from existing products. Even incremental innovation—and most innovation belongs in this category—entails a nontrivial change in a process or an attribute of a product. An innovation that passes the market test by increasing the productivity of an activity or the demand for a product or by giving rise to an entirely new market contributes to the competitiveness and profitability of an organization. After innovation ceases to be episodic, but instead becomes a routine activity systematically and successfully pursued by many business entities in an economy, then positive macroeconomic consequences generally follow. That is, widespread innovation—much of it of an incremental nature by enhancing productivity,[2] widening markets for products and services, raising the quality of what is produced, and creating markets where none existed—swells the ranks of successful (that is, profitable) firms and, most important, leads to higher growth. When policy makers talk longingly of innovation, it is growth they are after. Innovation is a means—and a powerful one—for firms to strengthen their performance. On an economywide scale, innovation can lead to rising exports, higher real wages, and larger gross domestic product (GDP) numbers. How GDP responds is the real acid test: from the policy maker's perspective, the value of innovation and the reason for pursuing it rest on its contribution to the economic bottom line.

An emerging consensus among development specialists is that growth in low- and middle-income countries will hinge increasingly on continuous gains in productivity because a significant portion of the difference in incomes between poor and rich countries can be traced to the inefficiency of factor use in developing economies (Jones and Romer 2009). This is not to minimize the contribution of investment, which is likely to remain dominant—especially in countries where the ratio of capital to labor is low[3] and where industrialization is in its early stages. But, efforts at raising or sustaining investment (which also affects productivity) need to be complemented by measures to raise factor productivity.

There is no one recipe for enhancing productivity. What countries need are steady gains in the efficiency with which resources are used; progress toward the technological frontier; and the capacity to innovate, which can increase efficiency, enlarge the set of technological possibilities, and improve competitiveness. For the majority of lower- and middle-income countries, the first orders of business (which can take two to three decades) are to acquire production capabilities and to narrow technological and intraindustry efficiency gaps in key subsectors. Once these are close to being achieved, further gains in productivity are likely to be paced by innovation in a variety of areas. Innovation to enhance competitiveness is a valuable asset at any stage of development, but its importance increases as technological catch-up shrinks the pool of unexploited possibilities. That is when new combinations of existing ideas and the pushing of the knowledge frontier acquire greater salience.

Learning Comes First

Innovation is only one of several means of achieving desired macroeconomic results. Before an economy can begin to derive a significant growth impetus from innovation, it must go through a lengthy preparatory apprenticeship. The less industrial a country is, the longer is the apprenticeship. But many low- and middle-income countries seduced by the possibility of "stage skipping" and of "leapfrogging" are impatient.[4] They are looking for a short route to an innovative economy that will deliver the growth they are unable to generate from other sources. Because innovation has come to be viewed as a panacea for firms and economies in a hurry, its meaning is being

Frontiers in Development Policy

confused with learning and technology absorption in the preparatory stage of development. Mastering an existing body of technology and the associated scientific knowledge and translating this mastery into production capabilities, whether in manufacturing or services, is a necessary prelude to the kind of activity that seeks to push the technology frontier through ideas and innovations.[5] It is next to impossible to be innovative[6] until a substantial fund of knowledge, expertise, tacit understanding, and production skills has been accumulated. (See figure 9.1, which underscores the concentration of innovation in high-income countries.) A large percentage of the gains in productivity attained by developing economies is from an internalization of what is already commonplace in more-advanced countries.

How quickly an economy—or, rather, firms and other entities in an economy—catches up is the true test of good policy, effective institutions,[7] entrepreneurship, and an enabling culture of industrial learning. In this process, a small subset of firms invariably takes the lead in borrowing and mastering technologies from abroad; and, within subsectors, a wide gap can separate the pacesetters in an economy from the rest (Bloom et al. 2010). This defines the opportunities for productivity growth through internal reallocation of resources (Syverson 2010). Thus, for low- and middle-income countries, there is vast scope for ratcheting-up productivity in all segments of the economy by more fully leveraging existing

Figure 9.1   Scientific Innovation: Penetration of New Technologies

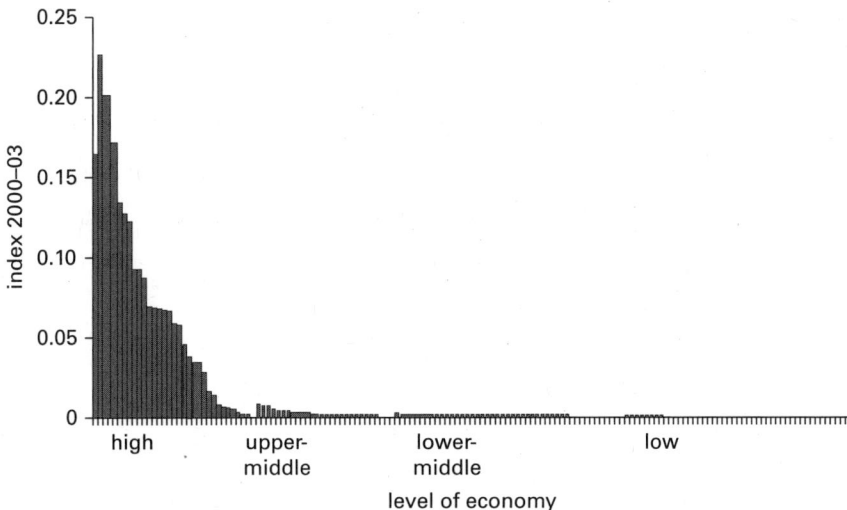

Source: Chandra and others 2009.

technologies. The learning, mastering, and applying of technological knowledge as it evolves underpins innovation by leading firms, once they pull abreast of the global leaders.

Innovation capacity indexes constructed by various groups of researchers (see tables 9.1 and 9.2) provide a window onto the relative competitiveness of countries using a variety of quantitative indicators combined with subjective assessments. In Asia, the frontrunners (not surprisingly) are Japan; the Republic of Korea; Singapore; and Taiwan, China. For example, according to these indexes, firms in Malaysia, China, and India are now demonstrating the ability to innovate. But the signs of

Table 9.1 Innovation Capacity Index

Economy	Rank	Score	Economy	Rank	Index
2009–10			*2001–02*		
Singapore	6	76.5	Japan	12	26.4
Taiwan, China	13	72.9	Singapore	13	26.0
Japan	15	72.1	Taiwan, China	14	26.0
Korea, Rep.	19	70.0	Korea, Rep.	23	22.9
Malaysia	34	57.3	China	43	18.1
Thailand	43	54.6	Thailand	46	17.4
China	65	49.5	Malaysia	52	16.8
Philippines	75	47.0	Indonesia	54	16.4
Vietnam	78	46.4	Philippines	56	15.8
Indonesia	88	44.9	Vietnam	61	13.8
Cambodia	112	37.5	Cambodia	—	—

Sources: Lopez-Claros and Mata 2009; Porter and Stern 2001.

Note: — = not available.

Table 9.2 Boston Consulting Group/National Association of Manufacturers' Global Innovation Index, 2009

Country	Rank	Overall score	Innovation input score	Innovation performance score
Singapore	1	2.45	2.74	1.92
Korea, Rep.	2	2.26	1.75	2.55
Japan	9	1.79	1.16	2.25
Malaysia	21	1.12	1.01	1.12
China	27	0.73	0.07	1.32
Thailand	44	0.12	−0.12	0.35
Philippines	54	−0.15	−0.76	0.48
Indonesia	71	−0.57	−0.63	−0.46
Vietnam	73	−0.65	−1.09	−0.16

Source: Andrew, DeRocco, and Taylor 2009.

nascent innovative capacity in these middle-income countries draw attention to the broad-ranging effort required to fully assimilate the technology that is already in circulation before trying to extend it in fresh directions.

Regulation and Economic Growth

Developing countries have been actively involved in deregulating various industries—infrastructure, production, labor, and finance and banking—since the 1980s. Efforts to liberalize the public service have not always delivered the anticipated increased competition or diminished market failures. In fact, regulations imposed by developing countries often limit productivity, growth, and service delivery; and they cost three times more than regulations in advanced countries.

Despite the increase in regulations, some areas such as property rights are not that developed, and labor market regulations tend to protect jobs rather than people. Land and property regulations hinder investment rather than promote it.

Private enterprise and development rely on regulations that encourage competition and break up monopolies where possible. Simple, transparent, flexible guidelines that are evenly enforced across sectors and industries are necessary for growth and development.

Notes

1. It is integral to the growth mantra in developed economies as well.
2. Hulten and Isaksson (2007) estimate that the major differences in levels of income among countries are explained by total factor productivity, although more than half the growth rate in incomes is traceable to differences in capital investment.
3. Jorgenson and Vu's (2009) recent estimation of the global sources of growth during 1989 and 2006 shows that capital dominated over the entire period; however, its share has declined from 54 percent during 1989–95 to 46 percent during 1995–2000, and then to 41 percent during 2000–06. The contribution of total factor productivity climbed from 16 percent to 36 percent between 1989–95 and 2000–06 (table 2A, 12).
4. Gottinger (2006) examines how firms engage in technological races and what leads to leapfrogging, the size of a jump, frontier sticking, and other criteria of performance in races.
5. Viotti (2002) sees the national learning system as the foundation of what can, in time, become an innovation economy.

6. One cannot exclude the possibility of chance innovations that are like manna from heaven.

7. Jones and Romer (2009) assign special significance to institutions.

References

Andrew, J. P., E. S. DeRocco, and A. Taylor. 2009. "The Innovation Imperative in Manufacturing: How the United States Can Restore Its Edge." Report prepared for the Boston Consulting Group, Boston, MA.

Bloom, N., B. Eifert, A. Mahajan, D. McKenzie, and J. Roberts. 2010. "Does Management Matter? Evidence from India." Working Paper 16658, National Bureau of Economic Research, Cambridge, MA.

Chandra, V., D. Erocal, P. C. Padoan, and C. A. Primo Braga, eds. 2009. *Innovation and Growth: Chasing a Moving Frontier*. Paris: OECD Publishing.

Gottinger, H. W. 2006. "Global Technological Races." *Japan and the World Economy* 18 (2): 181–93.

Hulten, C. R., and A. Isaksson. 2007. "Why Development Levels Differ: The Sources of Differential Economic Growth in a Panel of High-and Low-Income Countries." Working Paper 13469, National Bureau of Economic Research, Cambridge, MA.

Jones, C. I., and P. Romer. 2009. "The New Kaldor Facts: Ideas, Institutions, Population, and Human Capital." Working Paper 15094, National Bureau of Economic Research, Cambridge, MA.

Jorgenson, D. W., and K. M. Vu. 2009. "Growth Accounting within the International Comparison Program." *ICP Bulletin* 6 (1): 3–28.

Lopez-Claros, A., and Y. N. Mata. 2009. "The Innovation Capacity Index: Factors, Policies, and Institutions Driving Country Innovation." In *The Innovation for Development Report 2009–2010: Strengthening Innovation for the Prosperity of Nations*, ed. A. Lopez-Claros, 3–68. New York: Palgrave Macmillan.

Porter, M., and S. Stern. 2001. "National Innovative Capacity." In *The Global Competitiveness Report 2001–2002*, ed. M. E. Porter, J. D. Sachs, P. K. Cornelius, J. W. McArthur, and K. Schwab, 102–19. New York: Oxford University Press.

Syvreson, C. 2010. "What Determines Productivity?" Working Paper 15712, National Bureau of Economic Research, Cambridge, MA.

Viotti, E. B. 2002. "National Learning Systems: A New Approach on Technological Change in Late-Industrializing Economies and Evidences from the Cases of Brazil and South Korea." *Technological Forecasting and Social Change* 69 (7): 653–80.

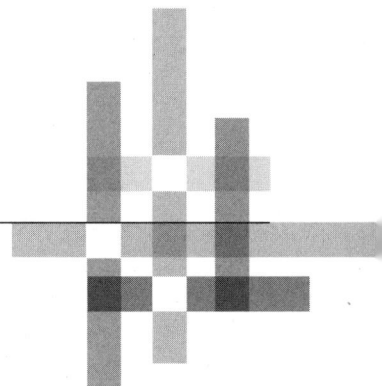

Firms Are the Prime Movers

Shahid Yusuf

The epicenter of technology learning and application in the low- and lower-middle-income countries (and not just these, but all countries) is the business sector, and firms are the ultimate "deciders." Their entry, survival, competitiveness, profitability, and growth depend in large part on how effectively they organize themselves and deploy their resources to learn and apply available technologies. This is the first order of business. For the majority, innovation comes much later—if it figures at all in their decision-making calculus. For industrializing countries, the cycle of learning technologies starts at the level of the firm; and, depending on policies and circumstances, it is complemented and reinforced by a strengthening of market institutions, the accumulation of human capital, better infrastructure, lower transaction costs, and so on. Where firms are slow to take the initiative, efforts to educate workers and build knowledge and physical infrastructure will make limited headway in inducing the assimilation of technology and preparing the ground for an innovative economy.

If firms are key, then it stands to reason that entrepreneurship and management skills have a vital role to play in the technology cycle. Entrepreneurs not only bring firms into existence but, together with professional managers, they also are important conduits for technology and drivers of technological change in their companies (Audretsch 2008, Glaeser 2007).

In innovative economies, high-tech firms are frequently the brainchild of entrepreneurs who are ready to test the commercial potential of fresh ideas and technologies.

Firing up the animal spirits of entrepreneurs with the help of policies and institutions that mobilize the energies latent in culture and social capital needs to be the primary objective of a growth strategy that sees technology as a significant lever. In the Republic of Korea during the 1960s and 1970s, in Taiwan, China, from the 1950s onward, and in China after the mid-1980s, it was the nurturing of entrepreneurship[1] and of policies promoting new starts, as well as the rapid expansion of existing firms and the ambition to enter foreign markets, that was responsible for a virtuous spiral of industrial development fueled by investment and technology acquisition.

Recent research by Bernard and Jensen (2001); Bernard, Redding, and Schott (2006); Melitz (2003); and others has revealed how the activities of a minority of firms prompted by opportunities inherent in exporting can initiate a cycle of technology enhancement and rising productivity. Firms active in international markets are more likely to extract the maximum productivity advantage from the available technologies. Moreover, competing for export markets creates a feedback loop stimulating effort at technological learning, at upgrading, and at raising productivity. The actions and the example of this minority of pioneering exporters set the pace for other domestic firms that have not ventured abroad. They can trigger the exit of less-productive firms and the entry of competitors; and, in so doing, they infuse dynamism into the industry—a process that has contributed to the unusual performance of the leading East Asian countries. Capital of all kinds and technology were the ultimate sources of growth; but firms raised the capital, acquired the technology, and put it to use by organizing skilled workers. Firms such as Samsung and Hyundai in Korea and their counterparts in China and other Southeast Asian economies were and are the standard-bearers of Asia's signature export-led growth model; and they are now helping build the innovation capabilities of their respective economies, having first drawn abreast of the global technological frontier.

Large companies do most of the applied research and innovation.[2] Such companies are responsible for most of the incremental process and product innovation; and through their own efforts and the marketing of innovations by others, they achieve commercial success for radical advances.[3] Large firms are generally less receptive and often do not give rise to breakthrough innovations, for reasons delineated by Christensen and Raynor (2003); nevertheless, their development and marketing inputs frequently determine the success of disruptive innovations.[4] Some research by Zucker and Darby (2007) also shows that, notwithstanding the drawbacks of industrial concentration and oligopolistic producers, consumers derive larger welfare gains from the innovativeness of large oligopolistic firms. In fact, no substitute exists for the initiative and leadership that large firms with transnational strategies can provide. Government incentives and purchasing policies can encourage innovation, universities and research institutions can assist, incubators can nurture new ideas, and science parks can provide space; but large firms that seek to compete and earn profits on the basis of innovation must provide a good part of the impetus—the demand for innovation—and some of them need to become the innovation hothouses.

One striking finding from the research on leading international firms is that only a weak relationship seems to exist between the level of research and development (R&D) spending and the metrics used to measure the success of firms. Increasing R&D can raise the number of patents; but patents do not readily translate into desired business outcomes, such as profitability and market share. In fact, excessive spending can be dysfunctional if it throws up barriers to innovation by making scientists into constituents who become wedded to the status quo (Jaruzelski, Dehoff, and Bordia 2005). The most successful innovative companies are ones that can extract the maximum innovation from a moderate R&D budget. These companies share a number of characteristics:

- They have an innovation culture deliberately cultivated and constantly reinforced by top management and an innovation strategy fully aligned with corporate strategy.

- The innovation strategy is comprehensive and keyed to long-run competitiveness and the avoidance of frequent restructuring and changes of direction.[5] It embraces not only product but also process innovation, innovations in marketing, associated services, and the business model of the firm itself. A study of innovative firms by Hargadon and Sutton (2000) found that serial innovators had perfected a "knowledge brokering cycle made up of four intertwined work practices: capturing good ideas, keeping ideas alive, imagining new uses for old ideas, and putting promising concepts to the test" (p. 158). Some research suggests that the firms with the most innovative business models—and not the ones with the innovative products—achieved the highest stock market returns and growth of revenues (Hagel, Brown, and Davison 2008).

- Successful innovators adopt an open and collaborative approach to innovation, recognizing that they cannot excel in more than a few areas of research and need to canvass ideas from a variety of sources.[6]

- The focus of the research efforts and the quality of leadership is critical to success, as is the closeness of interaction between the research wing of the firm and the production and marketing departments.

- Successful innovators tend to have a flatter and nimbler managerial structure and effective procedures for vetting research proposals, tracking progress, and screening out failures (Lynch 2007). These companies also have well-articulated procedures for developing and commercializing products.

- In industrializing countries, the successful innovators leverage their knowledge of the local market to innovate by customizing products. They also innovate in the distribution of products.

The Role of Small and Young Firms

Although large corporations are the serial innovators, young innovative companies are significant contributors and the source of most radical innovations. From the standpoint of innovation, the entry of many new firms and their presence in an urban economy are advantageous because they accelerate the technology refresh rate and raise growth rates (Rosenthal and Strange 2008). One reason the United States is the innovation front-runner is that it provides a hospitable environment for large numbers of young, innovative firms that contribute to both R&D and sales (see Veugelers 2009 and table 10.1).

Table 10.1 Major Innovations by Small U.S. Firms in the 20th Century

Air conditioning	Hydraulic brake	Pacemaker
Biomagnetic imaging	Kidney stone laser	Polaroid camera
Electronic spreadsheet	Microprocessor	Quick-frozen food
Heat sensor	Magnetic resonance scanner	Soft contact lenses
High-resolution CAT scanner	Optical scanner	Two-armed mobile robot

Source: Veugelers 2009.

Note: CAT = computed axial tomography.

In Conclusion

Bolstered by policy support, entrepreneurship allied with management skills and technological expertise can, through the medium of firms, generate productivity gains during the catch-up stage of development and enable an economy to transition to a stage when productivity accrues more from innovation than from learning. But the formation and growth of firms, their responsiveness to incentives, and their capacity to push technological change are not independent of other factors. Firms may be the prime movers, but how fast they move, how effectively they mobilize technology, and how much innovation they are capable of, along with the quality of this innovation, are functions of other factors examined in subsequent sections of this publication.

Notes

1. The rise of an entrepreneurial tradition in these economies dates back to the (proto)industrialization stage in the 1920s and 1930s, which survived a long spell of dormancy in the 1940s and 1950s in Korea and Taiwan, China, and an even longer spell in China.
2. Huawei Technologies, Datang Telecom Technology, and Zhongxing Telecom lead the way, each devoting about 10 percent of sales revenue to research and development (Cao 2008, 7).
3. Baumol (2004) notes that "technical progress requires both breakthrough ideas and a protracted follow-up process of cumulative incremental improvement of those breakthroughs with the combined incremental contribution of this second phase often exceeding that of the first" (p. 4). Baumol continues, "In today's economy, many rival firms use innovation as their main battle weapon with which they protect themselves from competitors....The result is precisely analogous to an arms race" (p. 10).
4. The spread of electricity and the internal combustion engine was expedited by takeovers that consolidated production in a few large firms that could reap scale advantages and sustain technological advance.
5. The Hay Group (2009) finds that companies that have consistent and stable strategies and can avoid paroxysms of restructuring have a better chance of forging and sustaining a reputation for performance. The experience of General Motors highlights the limited utility of frequent restructuring that leaves the firm culture and the fundamental strategic orientation untouched.
6. Open innovation systems that emphasize tools such as alliances, licensing, consortia and innovation exchanges, and joint ventures assume that innovation is a cumulative process that requires melding a number of different and intersecting technologies. Tetra Pak concluded that it had to draw on the

expertise of a number of other companies before it could develop a paperboard container that could be sterilized and was lightweight, rectangular, and easy to hold and pour. Similarly, Cargill managed to perfect a new family of corn-based plastics only when it teamed up with Dow Chemical (Rigby and Zook 2002). During World War II, the large-scale production of penicillin became a reality after U.S. agricultural scientists and technicians who knew a lot about culturing molds became involved.

References

Audretsch, D. B. 2008. *The Entrepreneurial Society*. New York: Oxford University Press.

Baumol, W. J. 2004. "Education for Innovation: Entrepreneurial Breakthroughs vs. Corporate Incremental Improvements." Working Paper 10578, National Bureau of Economic Research, Cambridge, MA.

Bernard, A. B., and J. B. Jensen. 2001. "Who Dies? International Trade, Market Structure, and Industrial Restructuring." Working Paper 01-04, Center for Economic Studies, Bureau of the Census, University of Maryland, College Park, MD.

Bernard, A. B., S. J. Redding, and P. K. Schott. 2006. "Multi-Product Firms and Trade Liberalization." Working Paper 12782, National Bureau of Economic Research, Cambridge, MA.

Cao, C. 2008. "Technological Development Challenges in Chinese Industry." In *China's Science and Technology Sector and the Forces of Globalization*, ed. E. Thomson and J. Sigurdson, 1–30. Singapore: World Scientific Publishing.

Christensen, C. M., and M. E. Raynor. 2003. *The Innovators' Solution: Creating and Sustaining Successful Growth*. Boston, MA: Harvard Business School Press.

Glaeser, E. L. 2007. "Entrepreneurship and the City." Working Paper 13551, National Bureau of Economic Research, Cambridge, MA.

Hagel, J. III, J. S. Brown, and L. Davison. 2008. "Shaping Strategy in a World of Constant Disruption." *Harvard Business Review* (October): 81–89. http://www.johnseelybrown.com/shapingstrategy.pdf.

Hargadon, A., and R. I. Sutton. 2000. "Building an Innovation Factory." *Harvard Business Review* (May-June): 157–66. http://www.stanford.edu/group/WTO/cgi-bin/docs/2000HargadonSutton.pdf.

Hay Group. 2009. "Managing Growth, Innovation, Talent, Engagement, and Performance When the Pressure Is to Do More with Less." Paper presented at the Hay Group International Conference, Valencia, Spain, May 18–20.

Jaruzelski, B., K. Dehoff, and R. Bordia. 2005. "The Booz Allen Hamilton Global Innovation 1000: Money Isn't Everything." *Strategy+Business* 41: 1–14.

Lynch, L. M. 2007. "Organizational Innovation and US Productivity." *VOX*, http://www.voxeu.org/index.php?q=node/775.

Melitz, M. J. 2003. "The Impact of Trade on Intra-Industry Reallocations and Aggregate Industry Productivity." *Econometrica* 71 (6): 1695–1725.

Rigby, D., and C. Zook. 2002. "Open-Market Innovation." *Harvard Business Review* 80 (10): 80–89.

Rosenthal, S. S., and W. C. Strange. 2008. "Small Establishments/Big Effects: Agglomeration, Industrial Organization and Entrepreneurship." In *Agglomeration Economics,* ed. E. L. Glaeser, 277–302. Chicago: University of Chicago Press.

Veugelers, R. 2009. "A Lifeline for Europe's Young Radical Innovators." Policy Brief 301, Bruegel, Brussels.

Zucker, L. G., and M. R. Darby. 2007. "Star Scientists, Innovation, and Regional and National Immigration." Working Paper 13547, National Bureau of Economic Research, Cambridge, MA.

Industrial Mix, Research Intensity, and Innovation by Firms

Shahid Yusuf

A competitive environment stimulates, but technological change and innovation are strongly influenced by the composition of industry. Historically, the pattern of scientific inventions has tended to be concentrated in certain fields, and this is reflected in the intensity of innovation. Certain industries are far more innovative than others, and countries specializing in these industries have greater opportunities for catch-up and for developing new products and processes.

The composition of economic activities has a strong bearing on technological change. Producers of garments, food products, footwear, furniture, light consumer electronics, and a variety of services have been innovation laggards in every country. Where these industries have registered gains in productivity, it is because they have moved closer to an international production frontier and rarely because of innovations that have shifted the frontier outward. Industries producing electronics, telecommunications and office equipment, machinery, and engineering products have been in the vanguard of productivity advances in the manufacturing sector; while finance, retailing, and wholesaling have also registered significant gains in the United States over the past two decades.

Among U.S. manufacturing industries, equipment, components, and materials-producing firms were in the 20 that registered the greatest gains in total factor productivity between 1960 and 2005; office equipment and electronic components were the first and the fourth on the list (Jorgenson et al. 2007). A number of factors contributed to these gains, and it is not surprising that innovation is prominent among them. The most productive manufacturing industries are also the most research intensive, and this research has produced numerous patents that tangibly delimit the extent of technological advance and the expanding scope for innovation.

Figure 11.1, which uses data from 10 leading Organisation for Economic Co-operation and Development (OECD) countries, presents the variation in research intensity across different subsectors. Clearly, the manufacturing industries (led by office and computing machinery) are in the forefront, followed by pharmaceuticals and by machinery and transport equipment. The productivity contributions of the science-based industries (such as electronics and pharmaceuticals) and the specialized suppliers producing complex capital goods in the OECD countries are reinforced by Castaldi (2009): "They remain fundamental contributors to technologies' knowledge and aggregate productivity growth" (p. 721).

Patent data from the U.S. Patent and Trademark Office reaffirm the relative importance of innovation in manufacturing. Invention patents are more numerous in manufacturing industries, notwithstanding a considerable jump in patents for services (inventions) over the past decade. Within manufacturing industries, only a dozen or so industrial subsectors account for 60–70 percent of the invention patents (figure 11.2).

Innovative manufacturing industries can be grouped into three categories. Producers of customized, complex capital goods (for example, plant equipment, power-generating equipment, and transport equipment) depend on a slow accumulation of learning, tacit knowledge, and specialized skills. They have significant backward links and involve a host of specialized suppliers that frequently cluster near the main assemblers and collaborate in conducting research and development (R&D) programs to meet specific needs of end users and in producing new generations of equipment.[1] Global suppliers of complex goods can sustain a flotilla of affiliated firms that provide well-paid jobs in an urban environment. (Complex capital goods, components, and electrical equipment are among the industrial products most suited for capital-abundant economies with a skilled and high-wage workforce.)[2]

Figure 11.1 R&D Intensity, by Industry, in 10 OECD Countries

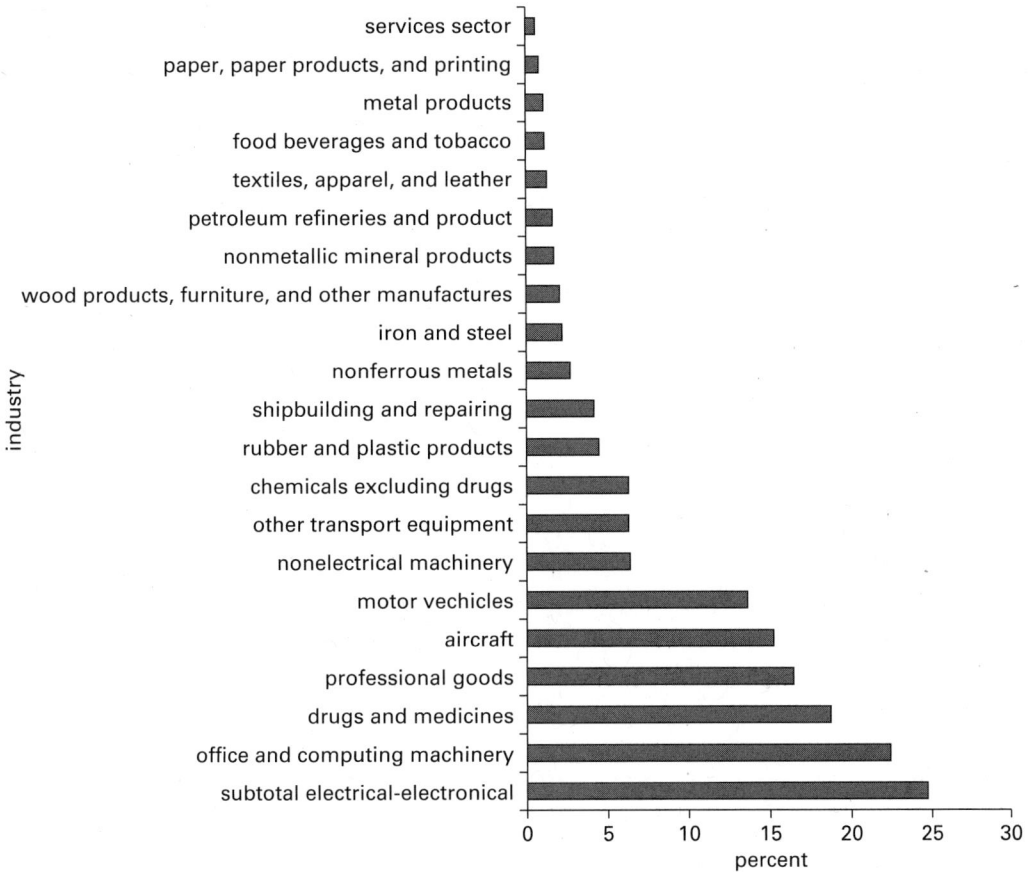

Source: Mathieu and van Pottelsberghe de la Potterie 2008.

A second category of manufacturing activities innovate incrementally and, every so often, introduce a revolutionary (disruptive) new product that redraws market boundaries and brings new firms to the forefront.[3] This category of manufacturing industries ranges from cosmetics to medical imaging and from nanotechnology to new materials. These industries are R&D intensive, often rely on research covering several fields, and frequently draw on the basic or applied research conducted in universities or specialized institutes (Boozer et al. 2003; Jaruzelski and Dehoff 2007; Jaruzelski, Dehoff, and Bordia 2005, 2006). Small and medium-size firms are the lifeblood of these industries because they are responsible for a significant share

Figure 11.2 Share of U.S. Patents, by Industry, 2006

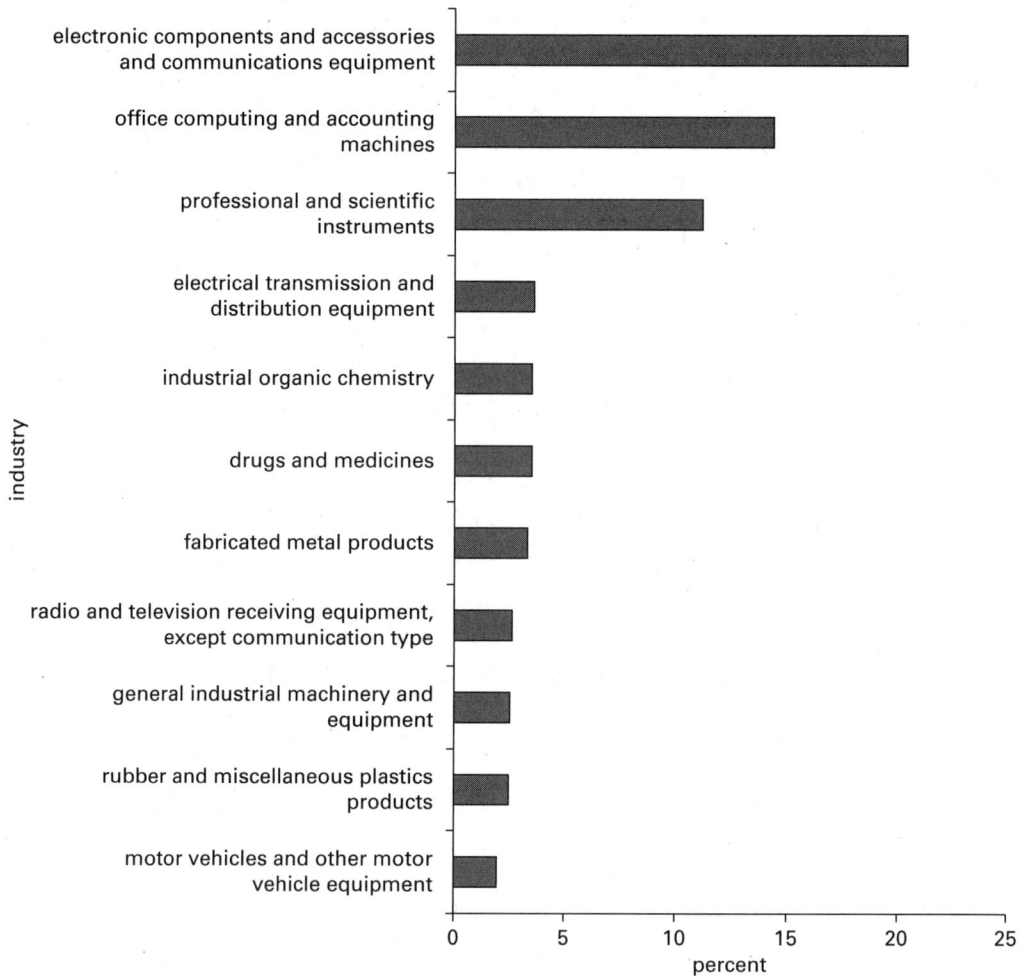

Source: Author's calculation based on U.S. Patent and Trademark Office data.

of innovation. Firms in industries associated with the life sciences and with advanced materials not infrequently are started by university faculty from nearby schools; draw on the research conducted in universities; and are heavy users of legal,[4] consulting, managerial, and financial services. Consequently, they integrate closely with the service providers in urban centers (see Bresnahan et al. 2001). Both types of industries depend for their growth, profitability, and longer-term survival on knowledge deepening and on product differentiation through customization, innovation of all kinds (including business models), and packaging of products with services ("The World's Most" 2006).[5]

The automobile industry and its suppliers are in yet another category with a widening scope for innovation for a number of reasons. First, the development of commercially viable "clean" automobiles and the supporting infrastructure will absorb a large volume of R&D in hybrid, electric, and fuel cell technologies, plus other alternatives; and in the physical facilities for delivering fuel or power.[6] Second, the increasing use of electronics in improving the performance of automobile engines, entertainment systems, dashboard displays, and safety and handling features opens fruitful opportunities for innovation (including in embedded software). Premium cars already require 100 million lines of code to operate their electronic control units, and electronics accounts for almost 40 percent of the value of such vehicles. Third, the auto industry is also investing in advanced materials that can reduce weight without compromising safety and can facilitate the repair and recycling of the vehicle (Charette 2009; Zhao 2006).[7]

Innovation is also responsible for rising productivity in several service industries, such as wholesale and retail trade, real estate, and banks. Much of this increase occurred after the mid-1990s as a result of major advances in information technology, the parallel reorganization of work practices, and logistics coupled with innovations in business models (Brynjolfsson and Hitt 2003; Oliner and Sichel 2000; Brynjolfsson and Saunders 2009; and Gordon 2003). The introduction of new equipment (computers, other office equipment, and telecommunications equipment and software)[8] has enabled providers of services to increase the quality and variety of their services—for example, in finance, to raise the efficiency of their supply chains and warehousing, to consolidate their activities, and to outsource and massively reduce the labor intensity of their operations. This surge of productivity in services has yet to filter through into the industrializing countries.

Notes

1. This collaborative activity between assemblers and their suppliers—most notably in the transport sector—is well known and associated with the embracing of just-in-time delivery practices. Subcontractors have taken on the responsibility for major modules (see Smitka 1991). Collaboration and proximity might be taken a step farther if Toyota, for example, realizes its ambition to further minimize the movement of parts (Stewart and Raman 2007).

2. The most dynamic Japanese firms in the country's shrinking manufacturing sector are ones that specialize in components, engineering, plant equipment,

and materials technologies. These companies contribute to the success of some of the latest Apple products and the newest generation of jet airliners—most notably, the Boeing 787 Dreamliner (Schaede 2008).

3. Leading firms are reorganizing the way in which they conduct their R&D by embracing an open approach to innovation to enrich and extend their own efforts in fruitful ways to promote radical innovation (*Business Week* 2006). Two Indian firms (Tata and Reliance) were included in the 2008 edition of *Business Week*'s "World's 50 Most Innovative Companies" (http://bwnt.businessweek.com/interactive_reports/innovative_companies/). See also Christensen and Raynor (2003).

4. Intellectual property protection is frequently a concern for high-tech firms in areas such as biotechnology and electronics.

5. The success of innovations in advanced materials has been closely associated with complementary innovations that can delay adoption or widespread use for many years. Realizing the full potential of glass fiber was paced by the evolution of laser technology, which brought the fiber-optic infrastructure into existence; Kevlar came into widespread use following advances in the design of body armor. Currently, proton exchange membrane fuel cells for automobiles are in a holding pattern, waiting for other innovations that will reduce production costs and lead to superior catalysts and fuel cell stacks that together will result in an economically viable substitute for the internal combustion engine (Maine and Garnsey 2005).

6. To stimulate the demand for hybrid and electric cars, the Chinese government is requiring the power companies to install charging stations for electric cars in Beijing, Shanghai, and Tianjin (Bradsher 2009).

7. Automobiles have evolved into highly complex systems, and the trend with hybrids, electric, and fuel cell–based automobiles is toward greater technical complexity entailing a vast amount of groundbreaking research. A premium car now has 70–100 microprocessor-based electronic control units, which can execute up to 100 million lines of code. This quantity is comparable to the number of electronic control units in the Airbus 380 (not including the aircraft's entertainment system). A car's electronics and software amount to between 15 percent and 40 percent of the vehicle's total cost, and as cars become smarter, this share could soon approach 50 percent (Charette 2009).

8. Digital technology has been reinforced by organizational changes, changes in work practices, and training.

Bibliography

Boozer, M., G. Ranis, F. Stewart, and T. Suri. 2003. "Paths to Success: The Relationship between Human Development and Economic Growth." Discussion Paper 874, Economic Growth Center, Yale University, New Haven, CT.

Bradsher, K. 2009. "China Vies to Be World's Leader in Electric Cars." *New York Times*, April 1.

Branscomb, L. 2008. "Research Alone Is Not Enough." *Science* 321: 915–16.

Bresnahan, T., A. Gambardella, A. L. Saxenian, and S. Wallsten. 2001. "'Old Economy' Inputs for 'New Economy' Outcomes: Cluster Formation in the New Silicon Valley." Discussion Paper 00–43, Stanford Institute for Economic Policy Research, Stanford, CA.

Brynjolfsson, E., and L. M. Hitt. 2003. "Computing Productivity: Firm-Level Evidence." *Review of Economics and Statistics* 85 (4): 793–808.

Brynjolfsson, E., and A. Saunders. 2009. *Wired for Innovation: How Information Technology Is Reshaping the Economy*. Cambridge, MA: MIT Press.

Business Week. 2006. "The World's Most Innovative Companies." April 24. http:// www.businessweek.com/magazine/content/06_17/b3981401.htm.

Castaldi, C. 2009. "The Relative Weight of Manufacturing and Services in Europe: An Innovation Perspective." *Technological Forecasting and Social Change* 76: 709–22.

Charette, R. N. 2009. "This Car Runs on Code." *IEEE Spectrum,* February. http:// www.spectrum.ieee.org/feb09/7649.

Christensen, C. M. and Mi. E. Raynor. 2003. *The Innovators' Solution: Creating and Sustaining Successful Growth*. Boston, MA: Harvard Business School Press.

Gordon, R. J. 2003. "Hi-Tech Innovation and Productivity Growth: Does Supply Create Its Own Demand?" Working Paper 9437, National Bureau of Economic Research, Cambridge, MA.

Jaruzelski, B., and K. Dehoff. 2007. "The Booz Allen Hamilton Global Innovation 1000: The Customer Connection." *Strategy+Business* 49: 1–16.

Jaruzelski, B., K. Dehoff, and R. Bordia. 2005. "The Booz Allen Hamilton Global Innovation 1000: Money Isn't Everything." *Strategy+Business* 41: 1–14.

——. 2006. "The Booz Allen Hamilton Global Innovation 1000: Smart Spenders." *Strategy+Business* 45: 46–61.

Jorgenson, D. W., S. H. Mun, J. D. Samuels, and K. J. Stiroh. 2007. "Industry Origins of the American Productivity Resurgence." *Economic Systems Research* 19 (3): 229–52.

Maine, E., and E. Garnsey. 2005. "Commercializing Generic Technology: The Case of Advanced Materials Ventures." Working Paper 2004/4, Centre for Technology Management, University of Cambridge, Cambridge, UK.

Mathieu, A., and B. van Pottelsberghe de la Potterie. 2008. "A Note on the Drivers of R&D Intensity." Discussion Paper 6684, Centre for Economic Policy Research, London.

Melitz, M. J. 2003. "The Impact of Trade on Intra-Industry Reallocations and Aggregate Industry Productivity." *Econometrica* 71 (6): 1695–725.

Oliner, S. D., and D. E. Sichel. 2000. "The Resurgence of Growth in the Late 1990s: Is Information Technology the Story?" *Journal of Economic Perspectives* 14 (4): 3–22.

Schaede, U. 2008. *Choose and Focus: Japanese Business Strategies for the 21st Century*. Ithaca, NY: Cornell University Press.

Smitka, M. J. 1991. *Subcontracting in the Japanese Automobile Industry*. New York: Columbia University Press.

Stewart, T. A., and A. P. Raman. 2007. "Lessons from Toyota's Long Drive." *Harvard Business Review* 85 (7/8): 74–83.

Syverson, C. 2010. "What Determines Productivity?" Working Paper 15712, National Bureau of Economic Research, Cambridge, MA.

Zhao, J. 2006. "Whither the Car? China's Automobile Industry and Cleaner Vehicle Technologies." *Development and Change* 37 (1): 121–44.

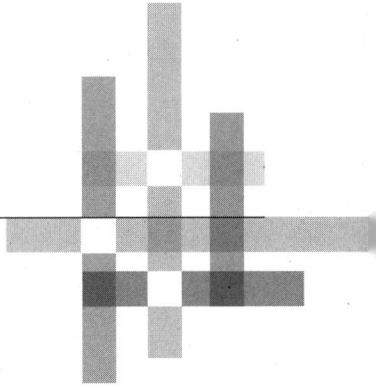

Investing in Technology and Human Capital: An Example from Asia

Shahid Yusuf

Investing in Technological Capacity

Expenditure on research and development (R&D) is the most frequently used metric of technological capacity. The level of research activity can reinforce the technological capacity inherent in the industrial structure. Japan is, by far, the largest spender on R&D as a share of gross domestic product (GDP), with 3.4 percent of GDP devoted to R&D in 2006 (see table 12.1), followed closely by the Republic of Korea (3.2 percent) and Singapore (2.4 percent). All three economies rely on manufacturing as the driver of growth and exports. The fastest increase in spending occurred in China—a manufacturing economy par excellence—with outlay on R&D rising from 0.6 percent of GDP in 1999 to 1.4 percent in 2008. By comparison, the spending on R&D by the sample of Southeast Asian economies (the Philippines, Singapore, Thailand, Vietnam) in table 12.1 that are oriented toward processing and assembly manufacturing activity is quite low, with less than 1.0 percent of GDP devoted to R&D.

Table 12.1   R&D Spending, by Country, Selected Years, 1996–2006
percentage of GDP

Country	1996	2000	2002	2004	2005	2006
China	0.6	0.9	1.1	1.2	1.3	1.4
Japan	2.8	3.0	3.2	3.2	3.3	3.4
Korea, Rep.	2.4	2.4	2.5	2.9	3.0	3.2
Indonesia	—	0.1	—	—	—	—
Malaysia	0.2	0.5	0.7	0.6	—	—
Philippines	—	—	0.2	—	—	—
Singapore	1.4	1.9	2.2	2.2	2.4	2.4
Thailand	0.1	0.3	0.2	0.3	—	—
Vietnam	—	—	0.2	—	—	—

Source: World Bank World Development Indicators Database.

Note: — = not available.

Mirroring the overall pattern in countries of the Organisation for Economic Co-operation and Development, firms account for two thirds or more of R&D spending in East Asia—except in Hong Kong SAR, China; Indonesia; Thailand; and Vietnam (see table 12.2).

Government is the major source of R&D spending in Indonesia and Vietnam. In Hong Kong SAR, China, and in Thailand, universities are the largest spenders on R&D. While the public sector usually finances the bulk of basic and early-stage applied research, the tasks of developing technology and commercializing innovation fall on firms. R&D spending during the early stage of development can be thought of as a part of the effort by manufacturing industries to assimilate and internalize foreign technology as well as to build the foundations of a national innovation system. Firms are in a much better position to identify the technologies with the greatest commercial payoff, and they need to expend some effort in understanding these technologies.

Absorbing and Generating Technology

Royalty and license fee payments are a proxy for technology absorption. In this regard, Singapore and China stand out because of the presence of multinational companies. Korea also actively purchases technologies from abroad, although the pace of increase has slowed in the last five years (figure 12.1). Other economies in East Asia are not active in the market for technology (despite the scale of manufacturing activities and

Table 12.2 Composition of R&D Spending, by Type of Organization
percentage of total

Economy	Business enterprise	Government	Higher education	Private nonprofit
China	71.1	19.7	9.2	—
Hong Kong SAR, China	48.3	2.2	49.5	—
Indonesia	14.3	81.1	4.6	—
Japan	77.2	8.3	12.7	1.9
Korea, Rep.	77.3	11.6	10.0	1.2
Malaysia	71.5	10.4	18.1	—
Philippines	68.0	19.1	11.1	1.8
Singapore	65.7	10.4	23.9	—
Thailand	43.9	22.5	31.0	2.6
Vietnam	14.5	66.4	17.9	1.1

Source: United Nations Educational, Scientific, and Cultural Organization's Institute for Statistics Data Centre.

Note: — = not available. Hong Kong SAR, China; India; and Malaysia 2004; Philippines and Thailand 2003; Vietnam 2002; Indonesia 2001.

Figure 12.1 Royalty and License Fee Payments, 1995–2006

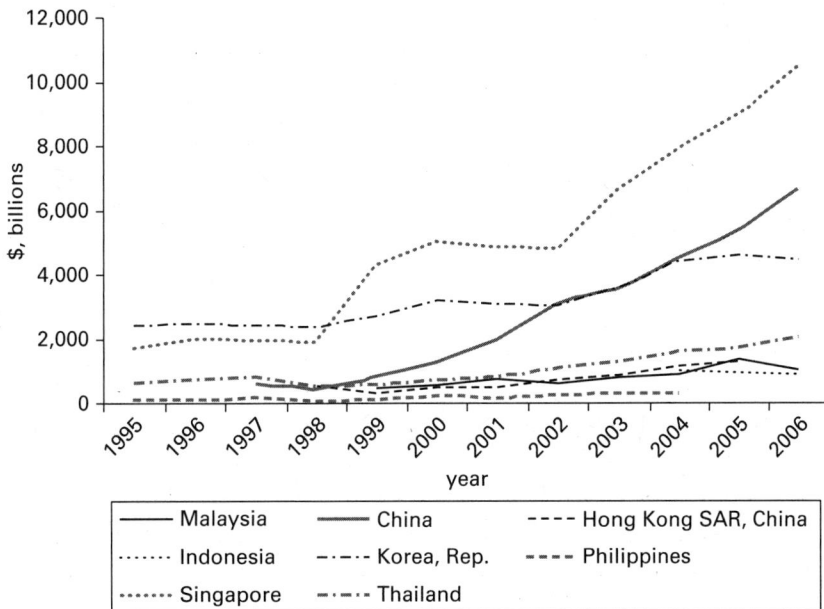

Source: World Bank World Development Indicators Database.

the role of multinational corporations), probably because their focus is mainly on assembly and processing rather than R&D.

Figure 12.2 shows the royalty and license fee receipts for selected East Asian economies. The increase in royalty and license fee receipts in Korea and Singapore suggests an emergence of technological capabilities in the last 10 years. The sale of technology by other countries is insignificant, reflecting their modest technological capacities. China is currently the leading importer of technologies.

Patenting and Innovation Potential

Patents, while far from ideal as an indicator of the productivity of R&D, are generally the metric of choice (see Scotchmer 2004). The United States is the major market for East Asian economies, so we examine the data from the U.S. Patent and Trademark Office (USPTO). Using data from a specific

Figure 12.2 Royalty and License Fee Receipts, 1995–2006

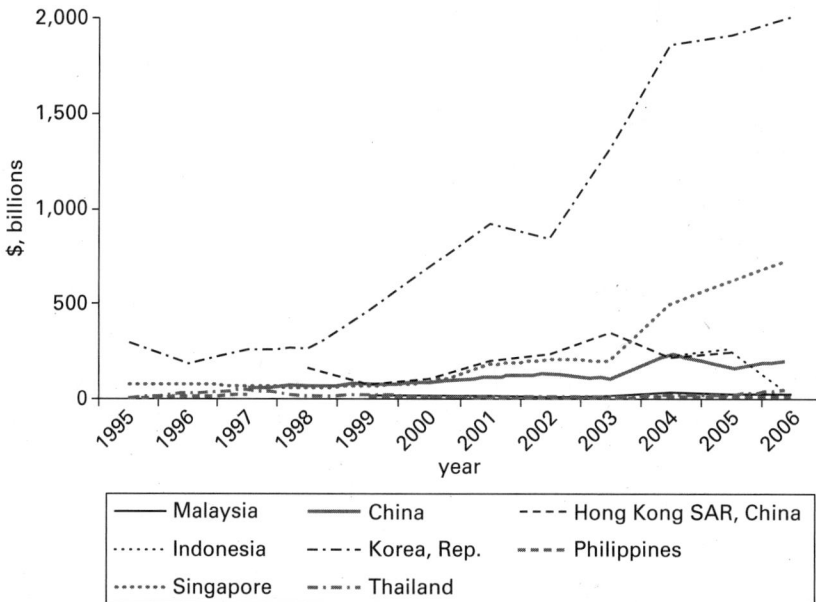

Source: World Bank World Development Indicators Database.

patent office (such as the USPTO) eliminates the incompatibility arising from cross-country differences in the criteria for submission, examination, and award of patents.

Table 12.3 lists the number of patents granted by the USPTO to East Asian economies in 1992, 2000, and 2008. Japan is the leader by a wide margin, with more than 36,000 patents awarded in 2008.[1] Korea is a distant second, followed by Taiwan, China. The number of patents granted to these economies grew quite rapidly between 1992 and 2008. China now ranks fourth among East Asian economies. In 2000, China received 163 patents— less than Singapore with 242 patents. However, by 2008, Chinese residents received four times those granted to residents of Singapore. Malaysia also saw the number of patents granted to its residents increase steeply during this period, albeit starting from a base of just 11. Thailand, the Philippines, and Indonesia have not received many patents from the USPTO during this period, and the numbers of patents granted to their residents is growing at a slow pace. Vietnam, a latecomer, did not receive any patents during this period.

Spending on R&D and the volume of patenting help move economies closer to the technological frontier and prepare the ground for innovation. But the productivity of R&D spending, the assimilation of technology, and the effective commercialization of innovative ideas require the mobilization of specific skills. Entrepreneurship[2] transfers ideas into the commercial domain; and it is vital not only to the absorption of existing technologies by industrializing countries, but also to the process of innovation.

Table 12.3 Number of Patents Granted to East Asian Economies by the USPTO, 1992, 2000, and 2008

Economy	1992	2000	2008
Japan	23,151	32,922	36,679
Korea, Rep.	586	3,472	8,731
Taiwan, China	1,252	5,806	7,779
China	41	163	1,874
Singapore	35	242	450
Malaysia	11	47	168
Thailand	2	30	40
Philippines	7	12	22
Indonesia	9	14	19
Vietnam	0	0	0

Source: USPTO.

Becoming Innovative:
The Human Capital Dimension

Creating a manufacturing base that can lead to technological development and innovation and can flexibly accommodate new research-intensive industries as existing ones migrate requires a solid human source of knowledge and technical expertise. The starting point is the quality of the education imparted by schools, how effectively it instills science and math skills, and whether it nurtures a spirit of inquiry and an aptitude for solving problems (Yusuf 2009). A sound university system with several world-class universities produces the advanced science, technology, engineering, and mathematics skills and the talent for management, design, and marketing required by dynamic industries—whether manufacturing or services.[3]

East Asian economies have relatively high levels of primary and secondary gross enrollment, but quality is a different matter; in fact, there is wide dispersion. Higher-income economies such as Hong Kong SAR, China; Japan; Korea; Singapore; and Taiwan, China, are among the top-ranked economies in terms of international test scores in science and mathematics (see table 12.4). This group is followed by mainly Southeast Asian economies, all of which fall below the international average. Among the Southeast Asian economies, Malaysia is closest to the international average and leads

Table 12.4   Eighth-Grade TIMSS Scores for Science and Mathematics, Selected East Asian Economies, 1999, 2003, and 2007

	Science			Mathematics		
Economy	1999	2003	2007	1999	2003	2007
Hong Kong SAR, China	530	556	530	582	586	572
Indonesia	435	420	427	403	411	397
Japan	550	552	554	579	570	570
Korea, Rep.	549	558	553	587	589	597
Malaysia	492	510	471	519	508	474
Philippines	345	377	—	345	378	—
Singapore	568	578	567	604	605	593
Taiwan, China	569	571	561	585	585	598
Thailand	482	—	471	467	—	441
United States	515	527	520	502	504	508
International average	488	473	500	487	466	500

Sources: Gonzales et al. 2004; Gonzales et al. 2008; Mullis et al. 2000.

Note: — = not available; TIMSS = Trends in International Mathematics and Science Study. Economies are ranked by their scores in 2007.

other economies. The quality of secondary education in Indonesia and the Philippines is low, especially in mathematics.

Because the potential capacity to absorb and develop technology depends upon science, technology, engineering, and mathematics skills, enrollment in science and engineering fields is a better indicator than the overall enrollment rates in tertiary education.[4] The experience of leading East Asian economies suggests that indigenous technological capabilities require an abundance of scientists and engineers, necessitating the enrollment or graduation percentage in these fields of between one third and one half of the total in the earlier stages of industrialization. More than one half of students earn science and engineering degrees in China, Japan, Singapore, and Thailand (see table 12.5). A significant percentage of students in Korea; Hong Kong SAR, China; and Taiwan, China, also earn their degrees in science and engineering fields, while relatively few students are graduating with science and engineering degrees in the Philippines.

Beyond Educating: Links with Firms

Universities and other tertiary entities can assist firms in assimilating and upgrading technology. Many countries have introduced various reforms, often packaged together with governance reforms (for example, university autonomy) to increase university-industry links.[5] But firms have been slow to cultivate links with universities. The problem (which is universal) stems from the difference in capabilities between universities and firms. The advantage of universities lies in their knowledge of a given subject

Table 12.5 Percentage of First University Degrees in Science and Engineering

Economy	Year	Percentage
China	2004	56.2
Hong Kong SAR, China	2004	37.7
Japan	2005	63.3
Philippines	2004	25.5
Singapore	2004	58.5
Korea, Rep.	2004	45.6
Philippines	2006	27.4
Taiwan, China	2005	40.8
Thailand	2001	68.9

Sources: NSF 2008. Data for the Philippines are from the World Bank Knowledge Assessment Methodology data set (http://www.worldbank.org/kam).

area and multidisciplinary reach. At the same time, their knowledge tends to be more theoretical. While this is an asset for industries that are more science oriented (such as chemicals, metallurgical, electronics, and tele-communications), practical knowledge is more relevant for the other industrial subsectors. In addition, firms may lack the capability to iden-tify and use the knowledge that is available at universities (Kodama and Suzuki 2007). Hence, the demand from firms to collaborate with univer-sities is relatively weak throughout East Asia, although members of cer-tain faculties may engage in consulting assignments. Even where there is a demand from firms, domestic universities and research institutes may not have the capacity to collaborate with firms or the interest in doing so.

This is not to deny episodic examples throughout the region of advanta-geous collaboration; but these are not numerous and, as yet, there is no trend pointing to an intensification of university-industry links (see Yusuf and Nabeshima 2007 and World Bank and NESDB 2008).

Notes

1. In fact, among the foreign countries, Japan receives the most patents (60 percent), followed by Germany. In any given year, about half of patents granted by the USPTO are to residents of countries other than the United States.

2. Antoinette Schoar (2009) draws an interesting distinction between "subsistence entrepreneurs" and "transformational entrepreneurs." Subsis-tence entrepreneurs set up small businesses with their own capital or the small amounts available from relatives, friends, and microfinance providers. These firms rarely grow. Transformational entrepreneurs have access to larger amounts of capital and are able to initiate ventures with the potential for growth. Such financing cannot be supplied by microfinance providers or venture capitalists; it must come from banks. Transformational entrepre-neurship is also influenced by the regulatory environment, and innovation by smaller firms is promoted by competition with foreign firms (Hall, Lotti, and Mairesse 2008).

3. In the United States, math-related occupations are the most well paid (Needleman 2009).

4. Gross enrollment rates for 2006 show Korea at 93 percent, Japan at 57 percent, Thailand at 46 percent, the Philippines at 29 percent, and Indonesia at 17 percent (World Bank World Development Indicators 2006).

5. Firms conducting R&D are more likely to establish research links with universi-ties. Firms' support can be invaluable for government initiatives to improve the quality of tertiary education, to strengthen the research capabilities of universi-ties, and to develop a local research culture.

References

Gonzales, P., J. C. Guzman, L. Partelow, E. Pahlke, L. Jocelyn, D. Kastberg, and T. Williams. 2004. "Highlights from the Trends in International Mathematics and Science Study (TIMSS) 2003." National Center for Education Statistics, Washington, DC.

Gonzales, P., T. Williams, L. Jocelyn, S. Roey, D. Kastberg, and S. Brenwald. 2008. "Highlights from TIMSS 2007: Mathematics and Science Achievement of U.S. Fourth- and Eighth-Grade Students in an International Context." National Center for Education Statistics, Washington, DC.

Hall, B., F. Lotti, and J. Mairesse. 2008. "Innovation and Productivity in SMEs: Empirical Evidence for Italy." Working Paper 14594, National Bureau of Economic Research, Cambridge, MA.

Kodama, F., and J. Suzuki. 2007. "How Japanese Companies Have Used Scientific Advances to Restructure Their Business: The Receiver-Active National System of Innovation." *World Development* 35 (6): 976–90.

Mullis, I.V.S., M. O. Martin, E. J. Gonzalez, K. D. Gregory, A. R. Garden, K. M. O'Connor, S. J. Chrostowski, and A.T. Smith. 2000. "TIMSS 1999 International Mathematics Report: Findings from IEA's Repeat of the Third International Mathematics and Science Study at the Eighth Grade." International Association for the Evaluation of Educational Achievement, Amsterdam.

Needleman, S. E. 2009. "Doing the Math to Find the Good Jobs." *Wall Street Journal*, January 6.

NSF (National Science Foundation). 2008. "Science and Engineering Indicators." Arlington, VA. http://www.nsf.gov/statistics/seind08/.

Schoar, A. 2009. "The Divide between Subsistence and Transformational Entrepreneurship." Working Paper 14861, National Bureau of Economic Research, Cambridge, MA.

Scotchmer, S. 2004. *Innovation and Incentives*. Cambridge, MA: MIT Press.

World Bank. 2006. *2006 World Development Indicators*. Washington, DC: World Bank.

World Bank/NESDB (National Economic and Social Development Board). 2008. "Towards a Knowledge Economy in Thailand." NESDB, Bangkok.

Yusuf, S. 2009. "From Creativity to Innovation." *Technology in Society* 31 (1): 1–8.

Yusuf, S., and K. Nabeshima. 2007. *How Universities Promote Economic Growth*. Directions in Development Series. Washington, DC: World Bank.

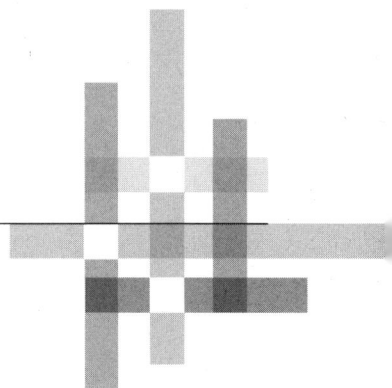

Impact of Regulation on Growth and Informality

Breda Griffith and Raj Nallari

Regulation and Economic Growth

Developing countries have regulated and deregulated firms in industry and services since the 1980s as a way of liberalizing their public services. The expectation is that regulation encourages competition leading to greater productivity and growth. "Yet the regulations of most developing countries in fact limit productivity, growth, and service delivery—and cost three times more than those of advanced economies" (Nallari and Griffith 2011, 388). Loayza, Oviedo. and Servén (2005) find that a high level of regulation hinders economic growth in product and labor markets. They highlight the distortionary effect of (too much) regulation on firms that may lead some firms to move their operations to the informal sector.[1] On the other hand, increased governance would lessen the risk of moving to the informal sector, as would greater fiscal regulation, better public services, and tax compliance.

Regressing growth of the gross domestic product (GDP) per capita on overall indexes of regulation[2] suggests that heavily regulated economies fare worse (figure 13.1), with product and labor market regulations slowing

Figure 13.1   Regulation and GDP Per Capita

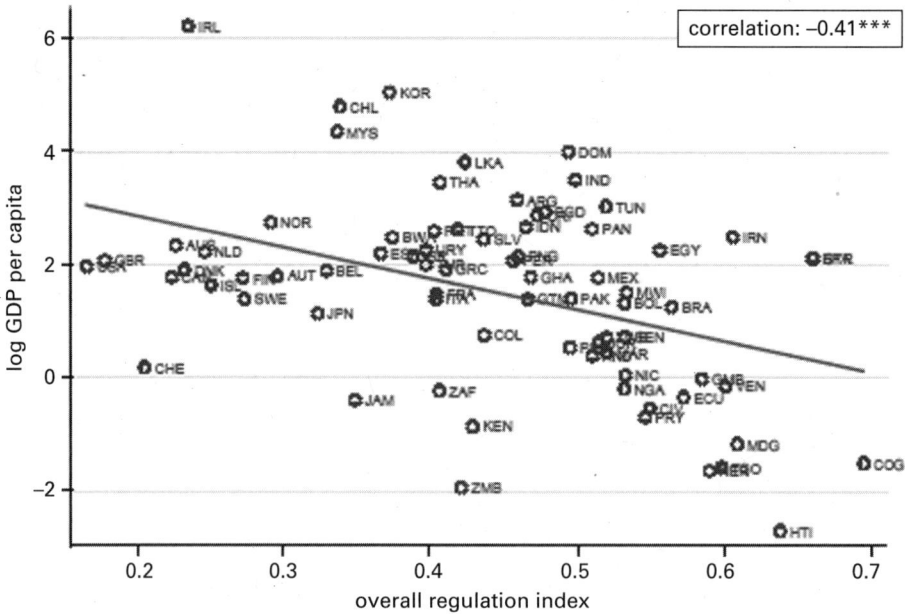

correlation: −0.41***

(y-axis: log GDP per capita; x-axis: overall regulation index, 0.2 to 0.7)

Data point labels include: IRL, KOR, CHL, MYS, LKA, DOM, THA, IND, ARG, BGD, TUN, NOR, IDN, PAN, BWA, TTO, SLV, IRN, ESP, URY, GBR, AUS, NLD, GRC, PNG, EGY, BER, USA, DNK, FIN, AUT, BEL, GHA, MEX, ISL, SWE, JPN, FRA, PAK, MWI, BOL, BRA, COL, YEN, CHE, PRY, NIC, GMB, BEN, JAM, ZAF, NGA, ECU, CIV, KEN, MDG, LSO, COG, ZMB, HTI

Source: Loayza, Oviedo, and Servén 2005, 18.

*** p < .001.

growth the most (Loayza, Oviedo, and Servén 2005). Reducing product market regulations to the level of those pertaining in an advanced economy and maintaining its level of governance, the typical developing country would see growth rise by 1.7 percentage points (Loayza, Oviedo, and Servén 2005, 8). Increasing labor regulations by one standard deviation for the group of developing economies considered by Loayza, Oviedo, and Servén and maintaining the world median level of governance would see growth in the developing economy fall by 0.3 percentage point (p. 8). Thus, reforming regulation and improving governance in highly regulated economies may help economic growth.

Regulation and Informality

Heavily regulated economies tend to have a larger informal sector than do less-heavily regulated countries. Low growth and high regulation are more typical of developing economies. Firms that operate in the informal economy tend to avoid fiscal and regulatory obligations. These might include value-added taxes, income taxes, and other labor market obligations (such as social security taxes and minimum wage requirements). Product market regulations (such as quality standards, copyrights, and intellectual property laws) are also compromised in the informal economy. The scope of avoidance depends on the sector. For example, retailers operating in the informal economy may avoid paying value-added tax and companies in the food-processing industry may not adopt all of the product quality and health regulations. Construction firms in the informal economy may underreport their number of employees. According to Farrell (2006), governments are not fully aware of the significant economic and social benefits that would arise from reducing the informal economy (figure 13.2). For example, the amount of resources allocated to enforcing tax laws and other regulations is insufficient.

Three readily identifiable factors contribute to informality: (1) government does not devote the necessary resources to enforcing legal obligations, (2) the cost of operating formally is prohibitive, and (3) the informal economy is tolerated by society and there is little social pressure to comply with the law. As noted in this section, informality suppresses economic growth and development by keeping economic activity in the gray area. Furthermore, firms that continue to operate informally are at a competitive advantage and steal market share from those operating in the formal economy—thus also stifling their contribution to economic growth and welfare.

In Conclusion

Developing economies have embraced regulation since the 1980s. For some, the situation appears to have been too much regulation and without the benefit one would expect. In many cases, too much regulation has pushed economic activities into the informal sector.

Figure 13.2 Informal Economy across Several Countries and Sectors

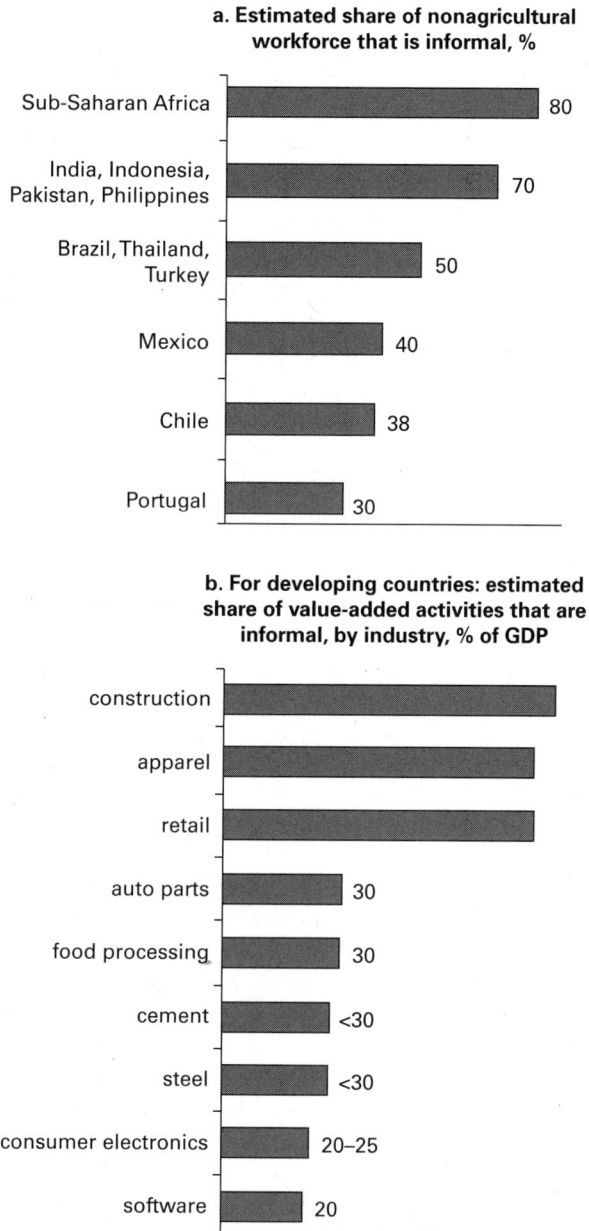

a. Estimated share of nonagricultural workforce that is informal, %

Sub-Saharan Africa	80
India, Indonesia, Pakistan, Philippines	70
Brazil, Thailand, Turkey	50
Mexico	40
Chile	38
Portugal	30

b. For developing countries: estimated share of value-added activities that are informal, by industry, % of GDP

construction	
apparel	
retail	
auto parts	30
food processing	30
cement	<30
steel	<30
consumer electronics	20–25
software	20

Source: Farrell 2006, 144.

Frontiers in Development Policy

Notes

1. The "informal" sector comprises (noncriminal) economic activities that go undeclared specifically to avoid compliance with costly regulations (such as employment protection laws), tax payments, and social security contributions.
2. The overall regulation index comprises seven regulation categories—fiscal, labor, and an average of the five components that make up product regulations (that is, entry, trade, financial markets, bankruptcy, and contract enforcement indexes).

References

Farrell, D. 2006. *Driving Growth—Breaking Down Barriers to Global Prosperity.* Boston, MA: Harvard Business School.

Loayza, N. V., A. M. Oviedo, and L. Servén. 2005. "The Impact of Regulation on Growth and Informality: Cross-Country Evidence." Policy Research Working Paper 3623, World Bank, Washington, DC.

Nallari, R., and B. Griffith. 2011. *Understanding Growth and Poverty: Theory, Policy, and Empirics.* Washington, DC: World Bank.

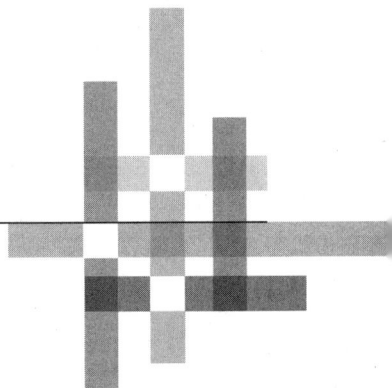

Private Sector Regulation and Financial Regulation

Breda Griffith and Raj Nallari

Regulation and the Private Sector

Regulations play a key role in private sector development. Market failures can adversely impact consumers through, for example, information asymmetries, negative externalities, and monopoly power. The existence of regulations ameliorates the negative impact. However, getting the amount of regulation right is not easy. Too little regulation fails to address the underlying issues, whereas too much regulation can hamper growth and runs the risk of firms moving to the informal economy. Simple, transparent, and enforceable regulations are the goal.

Firms in advanced economies find it easier to comply with regulations as they are more streamlined. Complying with regulation is not seen as a major or severe constraint to their business growth. The opposite is true for low-income countries that have the most regulatory procedures and time delays associated with compliance. As income increases, the burden of procedures and delays lessens.

Along with access to finance and infrastructure services, the regulatory and institutional environment correlates strongly with firm performance.

Aterido, Hallward-Driemeier, and Pages (2007) suggest that weaknesses in the business environment have contributed to a downward shift in the size distribution of firms. Countries with better financial regulations can attract foreign direct investment (FDI). On the other hand, excessive regulation that prevents the reallocation of human and capital resources is likely to restrict the potential economic growth stemming from FDI (Nallari and Griffith 2011).

Using the World Bank's 2004 Ease of Doing Business Database, Busse and Groizard (2006) confirm that economies with limiting regulations are unable to make efficient use of FDI inflows. Moreover, FDI is unable to stimulate growth in countries with excessive business and labor regulations. Reaping full benefits from FDI and foreign capital requires simple, transparent, and enforceable regulations. Regulatory quality determines overall income levels and is negatively correlated with income per capita levels, with gross domestic product (GDP) per capita growth rates, and with FDI. Figure 14.1 shows the correlation between ease of doing business and average per capita growth of GDP. The figure shows the negative relationship between per capita GDP growth and ease of doing business as the latter becomes progressively more difficult.

Figure 14.1 Average Per Capita GDP Growth and Ease of Doing Business, 2000–05

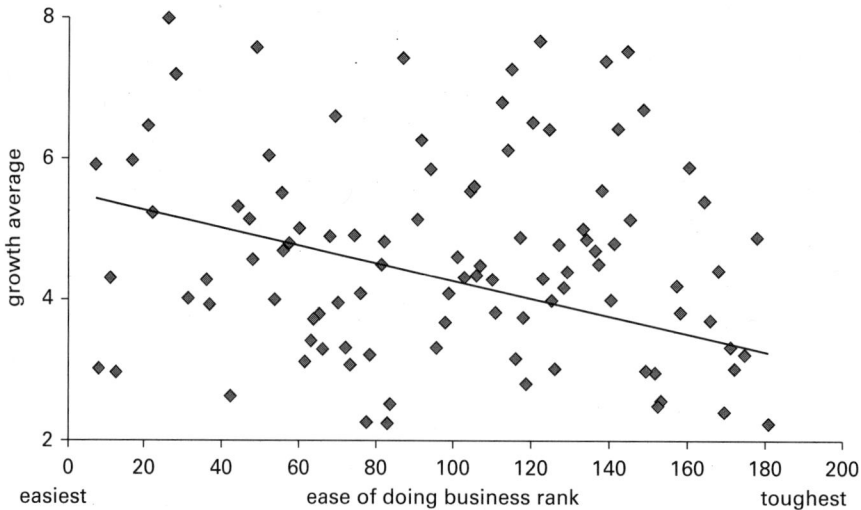

Sources: Authors' computation from World Bank data on growth and the World Bank's 2009 Doing Business Database.

Frontiers in Development Policy

Financial Regulation

In regard to bank regulation, governments can intervene to correct market failures or regulate to support political constituencies. Barth, Caprio, and Levine (2001) categorize these two competing approaches as (1) the helping-hand approach and (2) the grabbing-hand approach. In the former, government appoints regulators and supervisors to oversee a well-functioning banking system. The industry is plagued with information asymmetries, and sometimes the regulation may lead to a moral hazard problem. For example, the deposit insurance schemes adopted by many countries create incentives for banks to take on excessive risks and for depositors to be less mindful of their deposits. Strong supervision can improve this moral hazard.

Conversely, too much regulation stymies the development of a competitive banking and financial sector. At the limit, too much regulation increases government power and may create a role for corruption through granting exceptions to the rules.

In summary, specific regulations affect country performance in different ways:

- Excessively generous official deposit insurance regimes inhibit bank development and increase bank fragility.

- Fewer restrictions allow banks to perform better, subject to a lower probability of crisis.

- Fewer limits on foreign bank entry enhance banking sector stability.

- Policies that promote the private monitoring of banks improve bank performance and reduce corruption. This supports the view that legal and regulatory reforms that promote and facilitate private monitoring of financial institutions constitute a useful financial reform strategy (Nallari and Griffith 2011).

In Conclusion

The recent financial crisis was largely an advanced-economy experience. Yet the lessons for regulation and supervision are relevant for developing and developed countries alike. The recent financial crisis exposed the weaknesses in regulation and supervision and the misalignment of incentives with this regulation and supervision. Financial stability requires financial regulation. Components of this might include capital requirements that can be adjusted over the business cycle, thus facilitating the holding of more liquid assets in good times.[1] Other instruments that can also be countercyclical are provisions, leverage ratios, and additional capital buffers.

Note

1. "By switching the basis of capital adequacy requirements from levels of risk-weighted assets to their rates of growth, these measures require additional capital and liquidity when bank lending and asset prices are rising fast—and the relaxing of such requirements during downturns" (Nallari and Griffith 2011, 384).

Bibliography

Aterido, R., M. Hallward-Driemeier, and C. Pages. 2007. "Investment Climate and Employment Growth: The Impact of Access to Finance, Corruption, and Regulations Across Firms." Working Paper 626, Inter-American Development Bank, Washington, DC.

Barth, J. R., R. D. Brumbaugh, and J. A. Wilcox. 2000. "The Repeal of Glass-Steagall and the Advent of Broad Banking." *Journal of Economic Perspectives* 14 (2): 191–204.

Barth, J. R., G. Caprio Jr., and R. Levine. 2001. "Bank Regulation and Supervision: What Works Best." Policy Research Working Paper 2725, World Bank, Washington, DC.

Busse, M., and J. L. Groizard. 2006. "FDI, Regulations and Growth." Discussion Paper 3882, World Bank, Washington, DC.

Nallari, R., and B. Griffith. 2011. *Understanding Growth and Poverty: Theory, Policy, and Empirics.* Washington, DC: World Bank.

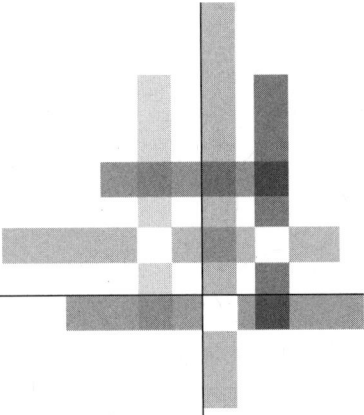

Part III

GROWTH AND DEVELOPMENT STRATEGIES AND RETHINKING DEVELOPMENT

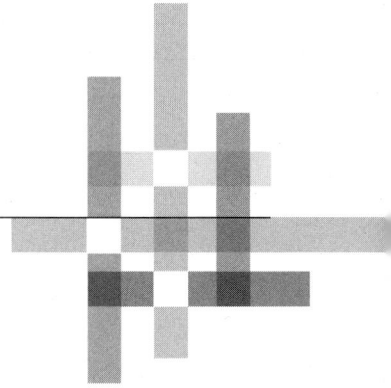

Overview

Breda Griffith, Raj Nallari, and Shahid Yusuf

World output declined by an unprecedented 2.25 percent (annualized) in the last quarter of 2008 (Nallari 2009, 5). Global trade and industrial activity have fallen abruptly between October 2008 and January 2009. All the major industrial economies entered a period of deep recession, and several emerging markets were sputtering in late 2008. Emerging and developing economies' growth has decelerated abruptly to 3.25 percent, mostly because of *external* pressures—lower foreign demand, reversal of capital inflows (including foreign direct investment, portfolio flows, and remittances), and plunging commodity prices (Nallari 2009, 6). But the reforms of past decades and accumulation of large foreign exchange reserves made emerging markets more resilient than in previous crises, and they were faring relatively better. Anemic global growth has reversed the commodity price boom and lowered inflation. These price declines (except for gold) have dampened growth prospects for a number of commodity-exporting economies. About 50 million people may have been pushed below the poverty line during the first few months of crisis (Ravallion 2009, 17). If the Asian crisis is any indication, poverty is likely to be much higher in several affected countries long after the global economy recovers.

Is there a need to rethink development? This is a big question. First, we need to take stock of where we are, especially in light of the recent financial crisis and what we have learned from past crises. As was the case with previous crises, the most recent one calls for short-term policy responses. The experience with this in the 1970s and 1980s was a focus on stabilization policies. Against this background, the longer-term objectives of development economies were cast to the side. It is important this time around not to renege on development. What are the questions we should be asking at this point?

Ensuring Growth and Competitiveness

Growth remains paramount in the quest to reduce poverty. But growth remains elusive for a number of countries. For example, with the exception of East Asian countries and (more recently) India, why are African, Eastern European, Central Asian, and other South Asian countries unable to sustain high growth rates for more than five to seven years? Perhaps a better way to ask this question is to examine the reasons why a number of countries—13—were able to sustain growth beyond seven years (Commission on Growth and Development, 2008).

Sustainable high growth is catch-up growth that relies on the global economy, an abundant and flexible labor market, and domestic savings, among other things. At home, growth depends on a credible government committed to the pursuit of policies that promote investment (in education, health, infrastructure), job creation, mobile resources, social protection, equity and inclusiveness, and competitiveness (in innovation and technology transfer). Also crucial to the mix are macroeconomic stability and policies that mitigate uncertainty about interest rates, the price level, and tax burden.

The results from the countries that were able to maintain growth rates beyond seven years suggest a role for government and the market. Economists have been divided into two groups: those believing in primacy of free markets and those advocating a greater role for government in regulating the markets and protecting the consumers from the excesses of the private sector.

The Changing Development Paradigm

What of the financial crisis and the developing world? Western economies are revisiting their macro-fiscal-monetary policies and pursuing stimulus policies. The developing world faces its own issues in a changed world order with depressed growth, reduced capital flows, and dwindling aid budgets. Some developing countries are better placed than others in facing these issues. Developing countries with low deficits and significant reserve holdings are in a good position. Countries having a good governance record and open to international trade have opportunities to pursue South-South trade. On the other hand, low-income and fragile state economies continue to exist and did not benefit from the expected trickle-down effects of macroeconomic stabilization policies and efforts to promote economic growth and reduce poverty. For these countries, the Millennium Development Goals Initiative and the Poverty Reduction Strategy Program are at the forefront of the development effort.

We know a lot about development and growth. The recent crisis exposed the weakness of the financial system and global interdependence; it has caused us to reexamine macro-fiscal-monetary policies. The human development needs of developing countries are still there and are just as relevant today.

Enhancing Competitiveness

Achieving macroeconomic stability is important for economic growth. At the microeconomic level, the issue of competiveness is paramount, and policies to enhance competitiveness are critical to the development effort.

In theory, a firm (or country) has a comparative advantage in labor-intensive traditional sectors, but the firm (or country) with government support embarks on a somewhat risky, skill-intensive activity. In general, as the skill level crosses a certain line, the marginal cost declines steeply; but as the skill level continues to grow, productivity ceases to grow at the same pace, and the wages in the primary sector outpace it. This trend happens because skill level does enhance productivity, but it does so to different degrees during the product's life. Thus, productivity takes the form of a U-shaped curve. In the beginning, the wage rate (as well as the skill level) is low, and the country is forced to import. Gradual familiarity leads to more productivity. Despite a concomitant rise in wages, such productivity gains lead to increased exports. A further increase in the wage depletes the comparative advantage in a particular product. Thus, the nation is forced to produce another good that uses labor less intensively, and higher-skilled workers can be used more effectively. This story explains a country's gradual upgrading of exports, from textiles to chemicals to iron and steel to automobiles and, finally, to electronics. The Republic of Korea and Finland are two examples of countries that have used this approach.

As one nation grows in skill and its products are upgraded from labor-intensive to capital-intensive goods, another nation grows and takes over the market in labor-intensive products. This phenomenon happened in East Asia. A skill ladder began with Japan as the most skilled country, followed by other Asian Tigers. Kojima (2000) extended the Flying Geese model to incorporate the transport of one industry to another country where the wage is lower, even though the productivity of the workers in the second country is not as high as in the parent country. This gradual shift of comparative advantage causes a high growth rate in a particular economy at a particular time. For example, Taiwan, China, supplanted Japan in the production of certain goods when Japan lost its comparative advantage in that industry.

The further the government moves away from comparative advantage, the more the costs of subsidization and support increase and, over time, become fiscally burdensome. Moreover, once government support is withdrawn, the industry may become uncompetitive, may generate fewer surpluses and resources to reinvest, and may have to close down. When such support is stopped, the industry's profits evaporate—whereas they do not evaporate in the private sector. Opponents still believe that East Asian countries would have grown even faster had they not used industrial policies.

The new industrial policy group argues that state intervention is needed in research and development and innovation policy to encourage low-carbon, high-growth industries. The group argues that the private sector does not internalize the carbon emissions and that state intervention will deal with this negative externality.

Effective Use of Natural Resources and Land Policy

Enhanced stewardship of natural resources is an important key to sustainable growth and development. In particular, land is a key resource: those who own land can exchange it in the marketplace, they can use it as collateral to raise investment funds, and they can make it productive and contribute positively to their livelihood and to national income. Land is of paramount importance to the poor.

The capacity to escape from poverty for many of the world's poor depends on their economic relationship to land. Many do not have access to or ownership of the land they work, and such groups as the rural poor and women suffer disproportionately. Governmental efforts in land titling and registration have not always yielded the desired outcomes, and many of the poor have lost access without gaining ownership.

Poverty is higher in countries with a predominantly agricultural base and where two thirds of the population live in rural areas. Thus, agriculture remains a viable instrument in the fight against poverty. Developing and growing the agricultural sector in a sustainable manner represents the key to poverty reduction. Government has a large role to play in this regard. Furthermore, government may play a role in achieving a more equitable distribution of land, particularly in areas where unequal land allocation and utilization have contributed to poverty.

Cities as Engines of Growth

Over the past 60 years, two economic trends have proved surprisingly durable. One is urbanization; the other is the declining share of agriculture in gross domestic product (GDP). The advanced countries are highly urbanized; and urban populations are expanding ceaselessly in virtually all of the middle- and low-income countries, irrespective of economic performance. According to UN-Habitat (2009) projections, a global urbanization rate of 50 percent in 2009 is expected to reach 70 percent by 2050. The salience of agriculture in national economies has changed even faster. Data from the World Development Indicators Database show that, in 1970, 8.8 percent of global GDP was derived from agriculture; even advanced economies, such as the United States, sourced 3.5 percent of their GDPs from agriculture. In 2008, agriculture generated just 1.2 percent of the United States' national product; and, globally, the share of agriculture decreased to 4.0 percent. It has fallen to 20.0 percent in Pakistan and to less than 10.0 percent in China. Economic activity in rich nations and poor is concentrated in urban services and urban industries, with services comfortably in the lead in all but a handful of countries.

The massive and continuing intersectoral transfer of the population and, in parallel, the redistribution of productive activities have had far-reaching consequences for development. Urban industry and services are, by a wide margin, the drivers of growth in the vast majority of economies; and new jobs are mostly generated in urban areas, including those in the informal sector. Modern industry and services have proved to be significantly more productive per input unit of labor than has agriculture; and where urban centers have created plentiful jobs to absorb migrants from rural areas, countries have benefitted from a productivity dividend that has buoyed growth rates.[1] The activities proliferating in urban areas—whether services or manufacturing—have also induced far more innovation than has agriculture, thereby reinforcing the economic gains from urbanization.[2] Moreover, by offering diverse opportunities and widening the sources of financing, cities (especially the ones attracting dynamic young migrants) have stimulated entrepreneurship, which introduces innovations into the blood stream of the economy.[3]

Urbanization does not necessarily result in rapid development of urban industry and services, however. For low- and middle-income countries to fully realize the potential of urban development and to achieve sustainable growth that mitigates some of the problems and costs associated with urbanization is no less urgent than is grasping the opportunities. The problems and costs that rank uppermost are

1. congestion, pollution, crime, urban sprawl,[4] and the proliferation of slums—each of which has a cost that erodes the advantages of urban living and of cities as centers of production;

2. the energy and resource intensity of urban activities that is related to poor planning and design of cities, inefficient land use, weak regulatory and pricing mechanisms, inadequate public services (especially transport), and slowness in harnessing technological advances; and

3. urban poverty and inequality arising from a mismatch between the growth of the urban population and the availability of well-paid jobs, the composition of economic activity, affordable housing, and adequate urban infrastructure.

In Conclusion

Since 2008–09, the deceleration of the financial markets has led to the rethinking of the development paradigm. To be competitive, markets need to strengthen financial regulation, legislation, and infrastructure, among other factors.

Notes

1. Fogel (2010) estimates that the transfer of workers from agriculture to jobs in the urban sector added 3 percentage points to China's growth rate.
2. Not only does most innovation take place in cities, but patent statistics suggest that a few cities account for the lion's share, and often these tend to be large metro areas well endowed with education and research entities

(see Bettencourt, Lobo, and Strumsky 2007; Carlino, Chatterjee, and Hunt 2007; and Chapple et al. 2004).

3. See Audretsch (2008) and Glaeser (2009) on the role of entrepreneurship and entrepreneurial activity in cities.

4. For a discussion of some of the causes of urban sprawl—in particular, demand for space and the reliance on private autos—see Gonzalez (2009) and Glaeser and Kahn (2003).

References

Audretsch, D. B. 2008. *The Entrepreneurial Society*. New York: Oxford University Press.

Bettencourt, L.M.A., J. Lobo, and D. Strumsky. 2007. "Invention in the City: Increasing Returns to Patenting as a Scaling Function of Metropolitan Size." *Research Policy* 36 (1): 107–20.

Carlino, G. A., S. Chatterjee, and R. M. Hunt. 2007. "Urban Density and the Rate of Invention." *Journal of Urban Economics* 61 (3): 389–419.

Chapple, K., A. Markusen, D. Yamamoto, G. Schorock, and P. Yu. 2004. "Gauging Metropolitan 'High-Tech' and 'I-Tech' Activity." *Economic Development Quarterly* 18 (1): 10–24.

Commission on Growth and Development. 2008. *The Growth Report. Strategies for Sustained Growth and Inclusive Development*. Washington, DC: World Bank.

Fogel, R. W. 2010. "$123,000,000,000,000: China's Estimated Economy by the Year 2040. Be Warned." *Foreign Policy* January/February.

Glaeser, E. 2009. "Entrepreneurship and the City." Working Paper 13551, National Bureau of Economic Research, Cambridge, MA.

Glaeser, E., and M. E. Kahn. 2003. "Sprawl and Urban Growth." Working Paper 9733, National Bureau of Economic Research, Cambridge, MA.

Gonzalez, G. A. 2009. *Urban Sprawl, Global Warming, and the Empire of Capital*. Albany, NY: State University of New York Press.

Kojima, K. 2000. "The 'Flying Geese' Model of Asian Economic Development: Origin, Theoretical Extensions, and Regional Policy Implications." *Journal of Asian Economics* 11 (4): 375–401.

Nallari, R. 2009. "Growing Out of Crisis." Guest editorial. *Development Outreach* 11 (3): 5–7.

Ravallion, M. 2009. "The Crisis and the World's Poorest." *Development Outreach* 11 (3): 16–18.

UN-Habitat (United Nations Human Settlements Programme). 2009. *Global Report on Human Settlements 2009. Planning Sustainable Cities*. New York: UN-Habitat.

Why Is Growth Higher in Some Countries?

Breda Griffith

The Commission on Growth and Development examined the reasons for high and sustained growth in 13 economies from 1950 to 2005. These economies—Botswana; Brazil; China; Hong Kong SAR, China; Indonesia; Japan; Republic of Korea; Malaysia; Malta; Oman; Singapore; Taiwan, China; and Thailand—achieved an average annual growth rate of 7 percent for at least 25 years, (table 16.1). Their findings are presented here in answer to the posed question, Why is growth higher in some countries (than others)?

Globalization is critical for economic growth and for facilitating catch-up among countries. The global economy facilitates technology transfer, ideas, and know-how—for example, through foreign direct investment that will be imported by the fast-growing economy. The fast-growing economy may look to its domestic market for growth, but the global economy provides for a much larger market for the fast-growing economy's goods.

Fast-growing economies rely on an abundant supply of labor that is mobile in helping bring about the structural transformation from an agricultural to an industrial base that is also characteristic of these high and sustained growth economies. Growth is limited in the short term to the pace of

Table 16.1 Success Stories of Sustained High Growth

Economy	Period of high growth[b]	Per capita income beginning	2005[c]
Botswana	1960–2005	210	3,800
Brazil	1950–80	960	4,000
China	1961–2005	105	1,400
Hong Kong SAR, China[a]	1960–97	3,100	29,900
Indonesia	1966–97	200	900
Japan[a]	1950–83	3,500	39,600
Korea, Rep.[a]	1960–2001	1,100	13,200
Malaysia	1967–97	790	4,400
Malta[a]	1963–94	1,100	9,600
Oman	1960–99	950	9,000
Singapore[a]	1967–2002	2,200	25,400
Taiwan, China[a]	1965–2002	1,500	16,400
Thailand	1960–97	330	2,400

Source: Commission on Growth and Development 2008, 20.

a. Economies that have reached industrialized countries' per capita income levels.

b. Period in which annual GDP growth was 7 percent or more.

c. In constant 2000 U.S. dollars.

investment by the private and public sectors; and that is linked, in turn, to the rate of savings. The Commission on Growth and Development report (2008) notes that "a national saving rate of 20–25 percent or higher, is not unusual" (p. 3) (figure 16.1). Foreign savings via capital inflows are not as reliable as domestic savings.

The third factor noted by the commission was "an increasingly capable, credible, and committed government" (p. 3). The form of government—single or multi-party—did not matter as much as did a commitment to pursuing policies that ensured "high levels of investment, job creation, competition, mobility of resources, social protection, equity, and inclusiveness" (p. 5). Policies that promoted accumulation, innovation, allocation, stabilization, and inclusion were characteristic of the high-growth economies.

"Accumulation" refers to public investment and spending on infrastructure, education, and health. Data on spending on infrastructure are relatively scarce, and the available data indicate low levels of spending. The economies that are not high growth economies suggest spending on the order of 2 percent of gross domestic product (GDP), whereas the high-growth economies of South Asia, for example, show spending between 5 percent and 7 percent of GDP. All of the high-growth economies had put

Figure 16.1 GDP Percentage and Investment Rates, by Growth in 13 Economies, 1971–2004

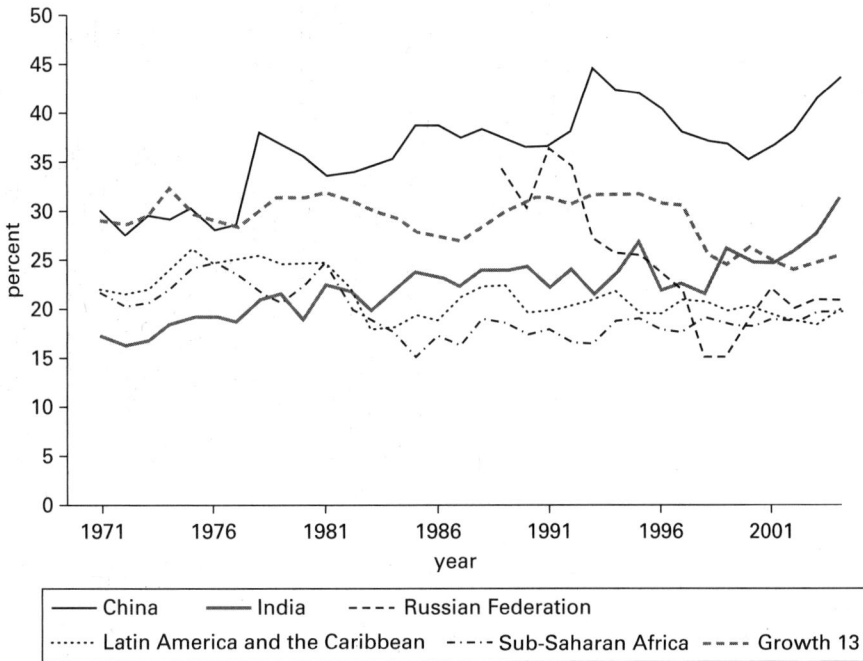

Source: Commission on Growth and Development 2008, 35.

significant resources into education and human capital. However, the quantitative measures—years of schooling, rates of enrollment—did not always translate into a qualitative education as measured by numeracy and literacy, for example. Health affects economic performance in many ways. In particular, ensuring healthy children—both prenatally and beyond—is positive for economic growth. Children who are malnourished or undernourished fail to develop sufficient cognitive skills, impairing their ability to benefit from education and damaging their productivity in the workplace. The rapid rise in world food prices may lead to undernourished children and a strain on long-term growth.

Policies of innovation and imitation help an economy do new things. Technology transfer has been enormously important in helping fast-growth economies catch up. One of the main conduits has been foreign direct investment. Whereas its contribution to total investment in the developing economy is minimal, its knowledge transfer is extremely important to the local economy. Foreign education has proved to be an important means of knowledge transfer. In some countries—for example, Japan and China—active policies to bring personnel from the United States and Europe and to send students to Western universities have been pursued for many years.[1]

Allocation and stabilization policies work hand in hand to bring about an environment conducive for growth. Labor and capital are allocated on the basis of their relative prices. Ensuring a stable environment where prices do not fluctuate wildly—causing uncertainty—requires a strong macroeconomy and stabilization policies.

Labor mobility is key to sustaining growth and employment. There is a surplus of labor in poor, populous countries; and employment opportunities are scarce. Creating gainful employment in the export sectors is one avenue to move labor from the land to industry. As the economy develops and grows, better educated and more skilled workers are required. Government can help labor mobility by providing opportunities for training and education. As workers move to the cities, the government has a role to play in easing urbanization.

The export sector was a crucial growth engine for all 13 economies. Some countries pursued export promotion policies as part of an industrial policy, whereas others did not. The significance of these policies was difficult to prove. The Commission on Growth and Development (2008) concludes that "export promotion is not a good substitute for other key supportive ingredients: education, infrastructure, responsive regulation, and the like" (p. 49).

Governments in high-growth economies also pursued exchange rate policies to sustain competitiveness. Policies included managed exchange rates, selected capital controls, and reserves of foreign currency. The commission notes the benefits and risks associated with these policies. Its bottom line is that any industry or enterprise that needs "permanent subsidies or price distortions to survive does not deserve to do so" (p. 7).

Macroeconomic stability is a key underpinning for growth. Private investment is adversely affected when economies suffer from uncertainty in price level, interest rates, and tax burden. Consensus on these issues is difficult to reach; but Western opinion on the inflation rate, for example, suggests keeping the inflation rate stable and in single digits. The central banks in most developed countries occupy independent positions. This may not yet be advisable for developing economies where a coherent economic strategy must be maintained. Such a strategy that embraces the global economy for growth relies on the central bank's choices on exchange rate, interest rate, and inflation policy. Maintaining economic coherence of the growth strategy and central bank autonomy is a difficult balancing act. "In some countries this balance is achieved by having the Minister of Finance set the objectives and broad parameters of macroeconomic policies, and then leaving the Central Bank free to operate within these parameters" (Commission on Growth and Development 2008, 54). Similarly, enforcing fiscal balance may at times run counterproductively to growth. For example, running a fiscal deficit may not be so bad in an economy where GDP is increasing rapidly enough so that the debt-to-GDP ratio remains unaffected.

Going forward, the commission describes the importance of a number of policies necessary to sustain further growth and development. These policies include financial sector development policies, urbanization policies, policies to promote equity and equality, and policies to protect the environment.

In Conclusion

The Commission on Growth and Development identified a number of characteristics that the 13 sustained-growth economies had in common. First, the importance of globalization in promoting sustainable growth was noted. This growth, in turn, relied on an abundant supply of flexible labor rich in human capital. Government played a crucial role in implementing growth-promoting policies. Future policies should embrace the financial sector, urbanization, development, and the environment. Finally, macroeconomic stability policies were key.

Note

1. During the Meiji Reformation (1868), Japan brought experts from the United States and sent Japanese students to Western universities.

Reference

Commission on Growth and Development. 2008. *The Growth Report. Strategies for Sustained Growth and Inclusive Development.* Washington, DC: World Bank.

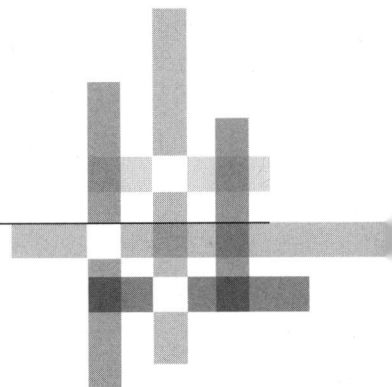

The Role for State Intervention

Raj Nallari

Do successful development and economic transformation require state intervention in industry and technology? Proponents of state intervention argue that market failures in information, coordination, credit, and other aspects of economies necessitate "infant-industry protection" and, therefore, an activist role for government. For example, information about success or failure of new industries or adopted technologies may be available only to investors and innovators and may not be shared with other entrepreneurs. Also, new industries and technologies require complementary human capital and basic infrastructure, among other things. In addition, credit market imperfections in developing countries and inequality in access to finance impede the formation of highly skilled workforces and the large entrepreneurial class needed for industrialization.

Positive stimulus from governments might include subsidies, tax breaks, and directed credit favoring certain industries and bestowing them with a comparative advantage. Other measures include establishing public enterprises in these targeted industries, investing in research and development related to the industry, and erecting barriers to foreign direct investment unless it was needed for new technology.

External to government policy, the conditions in competing markets also often affect how the labor market grows. As discussed earlier in this publication, for example, when Japan shifted from a labor-intensive market to a capital-intensive market, the impact was felt by other countries, and other Asian Tigers came in to fill the space in the labor-intensive market. Economies such as China and Taiwan, China, benefited from Japan's losing its competitive advantage. Taiwan, China, was followed by the member-countries of the Association of Southeast Asian Nations and, finally, China took over.

Japan; the Republic of Korea; Taiwan, China; and a few other Southeast Asian economies have been successful with state intervention in promoting industrial and technological development. Whether this is a policy prescription that other economies should emulate does not necessarily follow. Most governments are better off staying away from picking winners and losers; development experience during the past 60 years is replete with government failures—not only in industry but also in agriculture, tourism, financial services, and other sectors. Even when the cause is shown to be market failure, opponents argue that industries never become adults following their starts as infant industries because they depend on government support for decades on end. Such opponents argue that the comparative advantage defying state intervention takes the form of the government favoring industries that are capital and skilled-labor intensive through subsidies and trade protection. The government aims to put the economy on a higher growth path by a strategy of leapfrogging development. The further the government moves away from comparative advantage, the more the costs of subsidization and support increase; and, over time, they become fiscally burdensome. Moreover, once government support is withdrawn, the industry may become uncompetitive, may generate fewer surpluses and resources to reinvest, and may have to close down. Opponents still believe that East Asian countries would have grown even faster had they not used industrial policies.

In Conclusion

Combining the market mechanisms with an important role for government, depending on a country's stage of economic development, is called "new structural economics." A lower-income country may require the government to provide a lot of public goods (such as education, subsidization of technology development and adaption, and so on), whereas an advanced economy may require a regulatory and clearly less prominent role for the government. This is the new structural economics framework that requires government to reinforce an economy's comparative advantage. The new structural economics recognizes the importance of state intervention in areas such as research and development and innovation policy because the private sector will not necessarily internalize the production of public goods and the government will have to step in.

Reference

Kojima, K. 2000. "The 'Flying Geese' Model of Asian Economic Development: Origin, Theoretical Extensions, and Regional Policy Implications." *Journal of Asian Economics* 11 (4): 375–401.

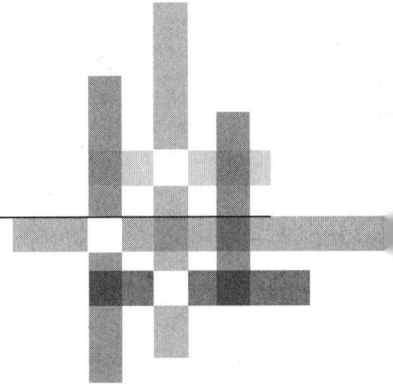

Private Participation in Infrastructure

Breda Griffith

The shift to private provision of infrastructure in developing countries took off in the 1990s. By 2009, low- and middle-income developing countries had seen investment flows of $1.56 million from 4,570 infrastructure projects (table 18.1). However, the unexpected takeoff in private participation was not maintained, and today's figures underestimate the potential for private participation in infrastructure (PPI).

PPI[1] declined between the latter half of the 1990s and 2003 and increased between then and 2008 and the recent financial crisis (figure 18.1). Macroeconomic stability in developing economies and developments in overall risk mitigation helped attract greater private flows to infrastructure. These private flows were curtailed in the wake of the financial crisis, and infrastructure projects faced higher costs of financing. Furthermore, demand for infrastructure services in some sectors decreased. The impact of the crisis was felt primarily in delayed projects and in some project cancellations.

Private activity continued in the wake of the crisis (figure 18.1). In the first quarter of 2010, 53 infrastructure projects amounting to $22.6 billion across 21 developing economies reached closure and represented the second-highest investment of any quarter since 1995. The rate of

Table 18.1 Totals of Infrastructure Projects and Investments, Low- and Middle-Income Developing Economies, 1990–2010

Item	Energy	Telecom	Transport	Water and sewerage	Total
Total number of projects	1,852	807	1,196	715	4,570
Total investments ($, millions)	481,695	719,645	253,197	60,280	1,554,817

Source: PPI Database, http://ppi.worldbank.org/.

Figure 18.1 Investment Commitments to PPI Projects Reaching Closure in Developing Countries, by Quarter, 1995–2010

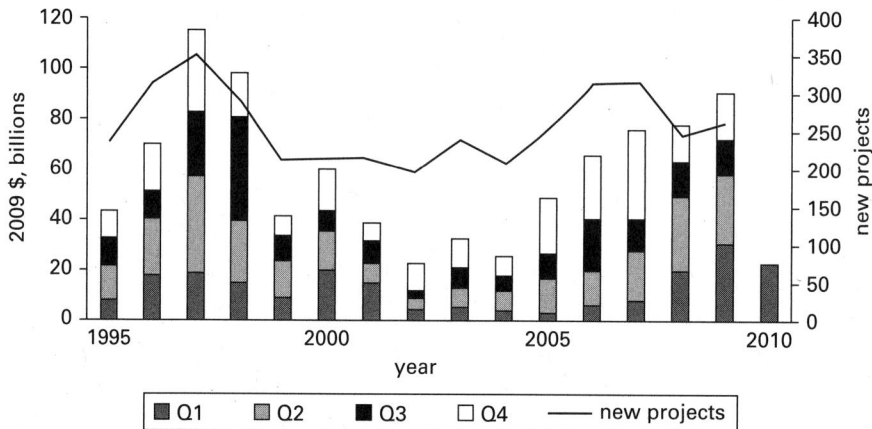

Source: PPIAF 2010, 2, http://ppi.worldbank.org/features/September2010/assessment.

project closure continues to suffer. The most recent data indicate a decrease of 25 percentage points between the first quarter in 2009 and the first quarter in 2010 (figure 18.1). The data, however, are influenced by the dollar amount of a project, so some big projects in one quarter influence the percentage growth when comparing with investment projects in another quarter. For example, if investments of $4 billion were excluded from the first quarter of January 2009, investment would have increased by 17 percent in the first quarter of 2010. Including the projects of $4 billion-plus meant that investment fell by 25 percent. Most of the investment in the first quarter was in projects of $1 billion or more, maintaining recent trends.[2]

Cancellations and delays were also less evident in this first quarter since the crisis began. Other issues, such as delay in government approvals or land

Frontiers in Development Policy

acquisitions, were more evident (PPIAF 2010, 1). The financial crisis continues to be felt in more stringent conditions on debt and equity financing, and
projects face less liquid markets than they faced heretofore. Risk mitigation
is an attempt to mobilize greater (private) debt and equity for infrastructure
projects. There has been increasing interest in and discussion of the role of
risk mitigation instruments among multilateral and bilateral agencies and
the private sector. Private infrastructure financiers highlight regulatory
risks, devaluation risk of local currency, and subsovereign risk that impact
their willingness to invest[3] (table 18.2).

Although most creditworthy subsovereigns have access to the market on
their own credit, the smaller subsovereigns face insufficiently developed
capital markets and weak capacity; and, thus, they rely on multilaterals,
bilaterals, and local state-owned banks as their main financiers. In the first
quarter of 2010, 14 of the 53 projects (33 percent of investment) reaching
closure had funding from local state-owned banks, while multilateral and
bilateral agencies provided funding to 8 projects (17 percent of investment).

Telecommunications dominated investments over the period and
accounted for 40 percent of investment in 2009. Investments, however, have
declined since 2006. At the same time, investments in energy have improved
and they accounted for 45 percent of the total in 2009. Investment in transport has declined over the period, apart from some pickup in the early

Table 18.2 Risk Mitigation Instruments

Risk	Proposed risk mitigation instrument
Regulatory risk	Provide partial risk guarantee.
	Provide political risk insurance.
Devaluation risk	Extend loans in local currency, or intermediate cross-currency swaps.
	Allow for tariff indexation of foreign currency cost components to foreign exchange rates.
	Partial risk guarantees and political risk insurance have been used to cover a government's or a public counterparty's contractual performance, indirectly covering the devaluation risk.
Subsovereign risk	In investment-grade developing countries, private monoline insurers provide wrap guarantees for municipal bonds.
	The European Bank for Reconstruction and Development and the International Finance Corporation have municipal finance units and provide loan and partial credit guarantee support to selected subsovereign governments and entities, based on their own credit.
	The Inter-American Development and the Multilateral Investment Guarantee Agency provide Partial Risk Guarantees and political risk insurance for municipal concession projects.

Source: Matsukawa and Habeck 2009.

2000s. It accounted for 14 percent of total investment in 2009. Investment in water and sewerage continued its decline in 2009, hovering around the $2 billion mark and well below the levels in the late 1990s (figure 18.2).

The number of projects in energy declined in the first quarter of 2010 (by 14 percent), with investment falling by 33 percent when compared with the first quarter of 2009. The decline in investment took place primarily in $1 billion-plus projects. The majority of energy projects took place in power plants. The pipeline of energy projects is strong (table 18.3), but activity is concentrated in a few countries—Brazil and India.[4] The impact of the crisis on new energy projects has declined.[5]

There were no new projects in telecommunications in the first quarter of 2010. Investment in telecoms is concentrated in existing operators. Activity in the pipeline is for new licenses for mobile phones. Five new projects in water and sewerage reached closure in the first quarter of 2010, representing a 70 percent gain on the first quarter in 2009. The pipeline is limited to a few projects to take place in China and Brazil (table 18.3). In transport, 16 new projects[6] reached closure, with an investment of $5.3 billion—equivalent to the level in the first quarter of 2009. Brazil, India, and Mexico account for over half of the transport projects in the pipeline and "half of the associated investment" (PPIAF 2010, 6). Transport has the largest share of projects cancelled or delayed, but the impact of the financial crisis has waned and other issues as

Figure 18.2   Investment Commitments to Infrastructure Projects with Private Participation in Developing Countries, by Sector, 1990–2009

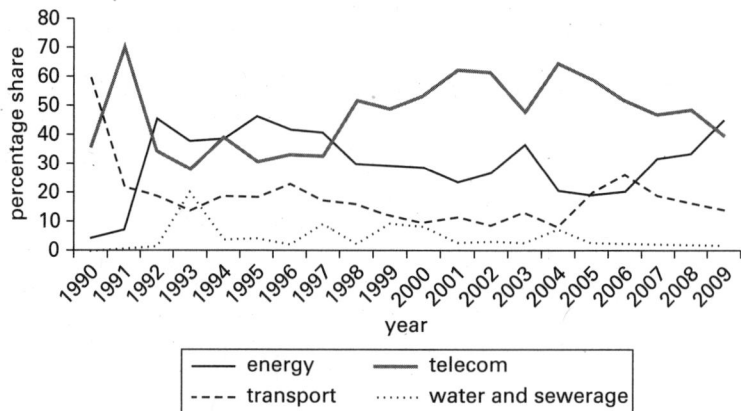

Source: PPI Database, http://ppi.worldbank.org/.

Table 18.3   PPI Project Pipeline in Developing Countries, by Sector and Project Status, January 2008–March 2010

Sector and status	Number of projects	Investment commitments	Countries
Energy			
Looking for financing	66	40.4	22
Awarded	131	22.9	33
Final tender stage	46	20.1	13
Telecom			
Looking for financing	0	0	0
Awarded	11	0.3	10
Final tender stage	13	0.9	8
Transport			
Looking for financing	40	24.5	15
Awarded	57	24.3	21
Final tender stage	51	39.9	15
Water			
Looking for financing	4	1.0	2
Awarded	21	1.3	6
Final tender stage	2	0	1

Source: PPIAF 2010, 5.

mentioned above have taken over (concerns over land acquisitions and government permits). Private activity has become more evenly spread among regions and country income groups since 2002. This is due to declining investment in Latin America and East Asia and previous leaders and growth in Europe and Central Asia since 1999 and South Asia since 2004. Approximately one third of investment in 2009 took place in Latin America and the Caribbean, an increase in the share compared with the mid-2000s. Roughly 26 percent of all investment in 2009 took place in South Asia. Europe and Central Asia accounted for 18 percent of overall investment in 2009. Sub-Saharan Africa experienced a peak in investment in 2006[7] and accounted for just over 6 percent of total investment in 2009 (figure 18.3).

Within the regions, Turkey stands out as the largest investee in Europe and Central Asia; Brazil in Latin America and the Caribbean; and India in South Asia. India accounted for 54 percent of total investment in the first quarter of 2010.

South Asia had 17 projects reach closure in the first quarter of 2010—a 63 percent increase on the number in the first quarter of 2009—accounting for $12.2 billion in investment. As noted above, all of this activity was due to investment taking place in India. In East Asia and Pacific, 11 new

Figure 18.3 Investment Commitments to Infrastructure Projects with Private Participation in Developing Countries, by Region, 1990–2009

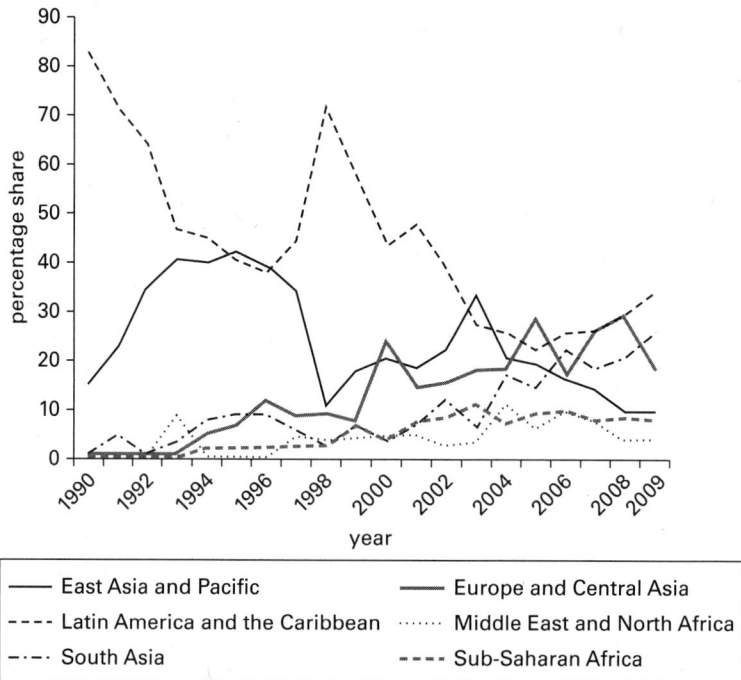

Source: PPI Database, http://ppi.worldbank.org.

projects reached closure in the first half of 2010, a 50 percent decline from the number in the first quarter in 2009; but investment levels were broadly similar at $4.9 billion. Project activity was more evenly spread across the region.[8] Eleven projects also reached closure in Latin America and the Caribbean, with investment down by 88 percent when comparing the first quarter in 2010 with that in 2009. The decline was due to a lack of activity in Brazil. Ten new projects reached closure in the first quarter of 2010 in Europe and Central Asia—a decline of six projects when compared with 2009 and an investment decline of 48 percent. Activity in the Middle East and North Africa was broadly similar to that pertaining in the first quarters of 2008 and 2009, with three new projects reaching closure. No new projects reached closure in Sub-Saharan Africa.

In Conclusion

The pipeline of projects suggests that developing countries are committed to PPI. Most of this investment is large scale—projects in excess of $1 billion—and is concentrated in the larger developing economies. Energy is the largest sector of investment, and its growth stems from new power plants. The impact of the recent financial crisis is abating, with implementation issues stemming from government commitments and licensing issues the more likely reason for a project's cancellation or delay. Projects rely on financing from local public funds and the multilateral and bilateral agencies. More stringent conditions are attached to funding from the financial markets, and the selectivity in investment growth suggests a "flight to quality" (PPIAF 2010, 10).

Notes

1. The data are drawn from the Private Participation in Infrastructure Database at the World Bank. See http://ppi.worldbank.org.
2. "This activity maintains the concentration of PPI investment in projects of US$1 billion or more experienced in the last few years. The share of these projects in total investment rose from low 20%s in 2004 to 30%s in 2005–06 to 40%s in 2007–08 to 50% in 2009 and the first quarter of 2010" (PPIAF 2010, 3).
3. Regulatory risk is the risk of losses as a result of adverse regulatory actions by the host government. Devaluation risk is risk of losses arising from unfavorable movements in foreign exchange rates. Subsovereign risk is the risk of losses as a result of breach or repudiation of contracts or nonperformance by the subnational host government, subnational contractual counterparties, or both (Matsukawa and Habeck 2009).
4. Brazil and India account for 25 percent of projects in the pipeline and 47 percent of the associated investment. Projects of $1 billion or more represent 62 percent of investment in projects in the pipeline. The two largest projects in the pipeline are the $5 billion, 4-gigawatt Krishnapatnam Ultra Mega power plant in India, which was looking for financing by March 2010; and the $13 billion, 11.3-gigawatt Brazilian Belo Monte hydro power plant in Brazil, which was in the final tender stage (PPIAF 2010, 5).
5. The database is available at http://ppi.worldbank/org/.
6. Of the transport projects, nine were road projects that involve investment of $4.3 billion and four were port projects that involve investment of $560 million. The remaining investment was directed to one railroad and two airport projects.
7. The peak in 2006 was driven by a large project (the $3.4 billion Gautrain light rail project in South Africa) with government cash support of approximately $3 billion.

8. Just one project (the concession of the Philippines' transmission company) accounted for 60 percent of investment in the first quarter of 2009.

References

Matsukawa, T., and O. Habeck. 2009. *Review of Risk Mitigation Instruments for Infrastructure Financing and Recent Trends and Developments.* Trends and Policy Options No. 4. Washington, DC: World Bank.

PPIAF (Public-Private Infrastructure Advisory Facility). 2010. "Investment in New Private Infrastructure Projects in Developing Countries Slowed Down in the First Quarter of 2010." Data Update Note 38, September, World Bank, Washington, DC. http://ppp.worldbank.org/reatures/September2010/assessment.

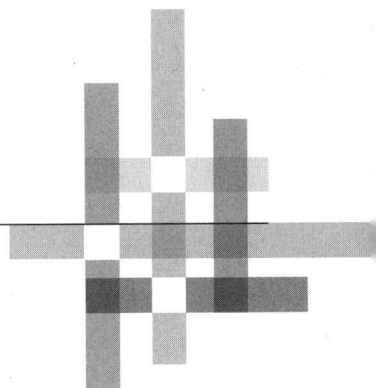

Changing Development Paradigms

Breda Griffith

Rethinking development had begun even before the financial crisis took place. The ensuing recession has given further impetus to development and poverty reduction strategies. The changing development paradigm is one that advocates a strong role for government in the economy and a move away from the so-called Washington Consensus that held sway in the 1980s and 1990s and that espoused macroeconomic stability, deregulated markets, globalization, and market-based growth. At the turn of the 21st century, the adoption of the Millennium Development Goals (MDGs) and the introduction of the Poverty Reduction Strategy Papers placed human development and poverty reduction at the forefront of the development agenda.

The targets set by the MDGs show us the progress that countries have made[1] and the reality is that many countries are off target.[2] The United Nations Department of Economic and Social Affairs (UNDESA 2010) blames the macroeconomic liberalization policies of the 1990s that were too narrowly focused on inflation, government budgets, and current account deficits. Furthermore, trade and financial policies were focused on further integration with the global economy. The hoped-for trickle-down effects that would address poverty reduction and employment growth did not occur in many low-income countries.[3] UNDESA (2010) calls for a broad-based development approach to macroeconomic policy that encompasses countercyclical monetary and fiscal policy supportive of employment creation and that protects household income; an emphasis on agricultural development policy in countries that continue to have low agricultural productivity; a sustainable development agenda that includes climate change adaptation and mitigation in all policies; and social policies that foster a more broadly based approach to social protection, encompassing more people and aiming for human development and household-level social reproduction (UNDESA 2010, xii).

Foreign Aid Landscape

The unrealized commitment to 0.7 percent of gross national income from the Organisation for Economic Co-operation and Development/Development Assistance Committee countries that was first brought up for discussion in the 1960s remains unfulfilled. Lack of aid predictability,[4] lack of coordination, and aid fragmentation constrain aid effectiveness.[5] Improving aid effectiveness is difficult, given the myriad of actors involved—more than 280 bilateral donor agencies, 242 multilateral programs, 24 development banks, and about 40 United Nations agencies together with an increasing number of private foundations, nongovernmental organizations, and "an estimated 340,000 development projects around the world" (Deutscher and Fyson 2008, 16). An emerging trend in the 1990s saw private sources of external financing become more important than official sources[6] (figure 19.1).

However, the destination of private flows tends toward the emerging markets or those fragile states that are either resource-rich or small economies benefitting from workers' remittances. Official financing has not been very important in the emerging market economies in recent years, even becoming negative, on average, as many countries prepaid their debts to the official creditors.[7] The improved macroeconomic environment and high growth rates spurred the demand for bonds and private equity. Debt-generating financing (both official and private) became less important in emerging markets as foreign direct investment (FDI) and workers' remittances increased considerably.[8] Conversely, official financing remains important in the other developing countries and fragile states, although net private flows have also increased in both country

Figure 19.1   Flows of FDI, Remittances, and Official Development Assistance to Developing Countries, 1980–2007

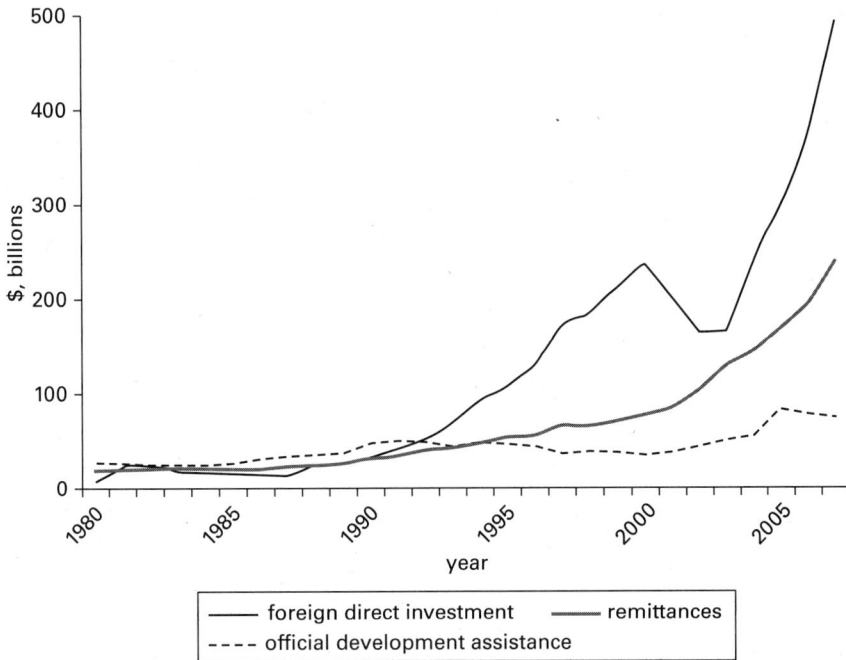

Source: UNDESA 2010, xiv.

groups. Private capital flows positively affect economic growth, increasing productive capacity, technology transfer, and quality standards and contributing to financial deepening in the recipient country.

The recent financial crisis has, of course, tested the resilience of the relationship between international banks and developing countries, reopening the role that the multilaterals and bilaterals can play in the coming years. UNDESA opts for a more involved role for developing countries as a way of overcoming aid fragmentation and improving aid effectiveness. It suggests a "needs-based allocations and alignment of aid flows behind national development strategies, which is consistent with the principles of the Paris Declaration" (2010, xv). New forms of partnerships between donors and developing-country governments aligned with national sustainable development policies and funded by innovative sources of development finance (such as internationally coordinated levies) would make up the new aid architecture.

Trade and the Financial Crisis

Arvind Subramanian discusses the effects of the recent financial crisis on the trade policies of developing economies. He differentiates the countries on the basis of foreign capital and trade. In the first category, the "foreign finance fetish model," are countries in Eastern Europe—Latvia, Hungary, Romania, and Poland—with lots of foreign capital and trade. In the other group—the "export fetish or mercantilism model"—is China with lots of exports and FDI. In the middle are India and Brazil. The recent crisis has adversely affected those countries in the foreign finance fetish model—in particular, those countries that over borrowed. Those countries that were not overborrowed were able to respond to reduced flows of foreign capital by pursuing countercyclical monetary policy. They had the economic space to do so. The real sector suffered in the export fetish mercantilism model. Subramanian notes that China's excellent fiscal position served it well during the crisis, but declining exports may hurt the economy in the long run. Thus, a move to a domestic demand–led model may be in the offing. Subramanian concludes that a middle ground—neither foreign finance nor mercantilist trade model—is preferable and "less prone to giving rise to systemic tensions and troubles."[9] UNDESA calls for a more focused agenda for trade liberalization that would allow developing economies more space to pursue active trade policies for "production sector and export promotion" (2010, xv). The report calls also for "multilateral rules for trade in financial services as part of a reformed international financial regulatory framework" (p. xvi).

Is There a New Development Paradigm?

What are the implications for developing economies and development policy from the recent crisis? The first point is that the financial crisis was external to the developing economies. It began in the West and, although Western economies are pursuing stimulus measures and revisiting the role of macro-fiscal-monetary policies, developing economies continue to face their own issues in a changed world order with depressed growth, reduced capital flows, and dwindling aid budgets. Second, many developing countries, with low deficits and significant reserve holdings, are in a good position to weather the storm. Third, many developing countries now have better governance; "more robust democracies; more frequent elections;

initiatives to reduce corruption and end conflicts; and to empower women that are all largely homegrown" (Naudé 2009, 5). The route to growth for most developing economies—that is, those without large domestic markets—depends on global growth that includes both developing and advanced economies. Apart from the necessary reforms to the financial architecture to restore trust in banks and create strong financial systems that underlie growth, a window of opportunity for greater South-South trade, progress in regional integration, and coordination is now open (Naudé 2009). Is there a new development paradigm needed? It would seem that the financial crisis has exposed many weaknesses of the financial system; has caused us to examine macro-fiscal-monetary policies; and has highlighted global interdependence, revealing those economies that have been able to weather the storm and the continued existence of low-income and fragile economies.

In Conclusion

We will conclude with the words of Anne Krueger: "I don't think there's anything wrong with the old development paradigm. I think, if anything, very few people paid enough attention to it. I don't think that there is only one way to do things, but I do think you cannot borrow in good times and in bad times."[10]

Notes

1. The Center for Global Development recently developed an MDG Progress Index that provides a more nuanced view of the progress made by countries on the MDGs. The lack of baseline data for many countries stymies the MDG effort in many cases.
2. The multidimensional poverty index developed at the Oxford Poverty and Human Development Initiative takes into account an individual's health (nutrition status and child mortality of their offspring), education (years of schooling, number of his or her children enrolled in school), and living standard (access to cooking fuel, sanitation, water, electricity, and assets; and whether his or her home has a floor). An individual is classified as poor if he or she is deprived in 30 percent or more of these areas. Using the Multidimensional Poverty Index, the initiative has found that 51 percent of the world's poor live in South Asia, 28 percent in Sub-Saharan Africa, and 15 percent in East Asia and Pacific. The eight poorest Indian states have more poor people than all of Sub-Saharan Africa (World Bank 2010).

3. At the same time, many developing economies—in particular, the emerging markets—benefitted from macroeconomic liberalization policies that were successful in generating economic growth.
4. Celasun and Walliser (2008), using data in International Monetary Fund staff reports from 1992 to 2007 for a set of 13 countries, found that, on average, disbursed budget aid differed from the amount expected by about 30 percent.
5. For any average country, just 45 percent of aid arrives on time. In 2005–06, 38 developing countries received official development assistance from 25 or more Development Assistance Committee and multilateral donors; in 24 of these countries, 15 (or more) donors collectively provided less than 10 percent of the country's total aid budget. Furthermore, some countries are ignored by donors. Fragmentation of aid means that some countries receive a small amount of aid from a plethora of donors, all requiring adherence to different procedures and standards (OECD 2008).
6. During the 1990s, about half (as a proportion of GDP) of total external financing came from private sources, increasing to two thirds in 2007.
7. Net liabilities to official creditors have decreased due to shifts in the composition of external financing and debt reduction operations.
8. Most of the FDI was for investment in infrastructure projects, but the success of the macroeconomic stabilization policies also prompted investment in other sectors (World Bank 2008).
9. Arvind Subramanian's comments were made during Panel 1: Causes of the Global Financial Crisis and the Implications for National Development Strategies at the Center for Global Development conference, "New Ideas in Development After the Financial Crisis, Washington, DC, April 22, 2009.
10. Krueger made this statement during Panel 1: Causes of the Global Financial Crisis and the Implications for National Development Strategies at the Center for Global Development conference, "New Ideas in Development After the Financial Crisis, Washington, DC, April 22, 2009.

References

Celasun, O., and J. Walliser. 2008. "Managing Aid Surprises." *Finance and Development* 42 (3): 34–37.

Deutscher, E., and S. Fyson. 2008. "Improving the Effectiveness of Aid." *Finance and Development* 45 (3): 15–19.

Naudé, W. 2009. "The Global Economic Crisis after One Year: Is a New Paradigm for Recovery in Developing Countries Emerging?" Policy Brief No. 2, United Nations University, Tokyo.

OECD (Organisation for Economic Co-operation and Development). 2008. "Scaling Up: Aid Fragmentation, Aid Allocation, and Aid Predictability: Report of 2008 Survey of Aid Allocation Policies and Indicative Forward Spending Plans." OECD, Paris.

UNDESA (United Nations Department of Economic and Social Affairs). 2010. *World Economic and Social Survey 2010: Retooling Global Development*. New York: United Nations.

World Bank. 2008. *Global Monitoring Report 2008: MDGs and the Environment— Agenda for Inclusive and Sustainable Development*. Washington, DC: World Bank.

———. 2010. "Towards a New Development Paradigm: Rethinking the Concepts and Measures of Development and Social Progress." Presentation to the Civil Society Policy Forum, International Monetary Fund/World Bank Annual Meetings, Washington, DC, October 6–10. http://www.pnowb.org/admindb/docs/RTR _New%20Development%20Paradigm.pdf.

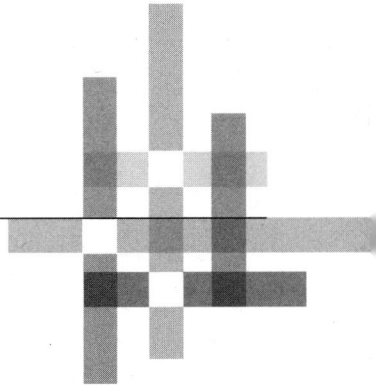

Aid Effectiveness

Breda Griffith and Raj Nallari

Ensuring aid effectiveness means managing aid so that it makes a positive impact on development. Aid effectiveness is about delivering on the commitments that donors and recipient governments have made to one another. These commitments are underpinned by the agreements reached in the 2005 Paris Declaration on Aid Effectiveness and the 2005 Accra Agenda for Action. The forthcoming Fourth High Level Forum on Aid Effectiveness to be held in the Republic of Korea (November 2011) will further set the stage for aid effectiveness for the remaining years of the Millennium Development Goals Initiative. Developing countries have already identified their priorities for the Fourth High Level Forum. These are

- predictability of aid,

- use of country systems,

- removal of policy conditionality,

- country-driven capacity development,

- mutual accountability, and

- reduction of transaction costs.

The record of development aid has been poor. At the beginning of the 21st century, increases in the quantity of aid, in dollar terms, were not having the desired growth and development impact. Some studies—most notably, those by Easterly (2001, 2006)—at the time found that aid had no effect on growth. Radelet, Clemens, and Bhavnani (2005) found a conditional relationship where increased aid under certain conditions accelerated growth. And Rajan and Subramanian (2005) found no relationship whatsoever, regardless of time period, recipient country characteristics, type of donor, or type of aid. Against this backdrop, international opinion turned to a consideration of the quality of aid and methods to improve it.

The development agenda that evolved during this period rose to meet these challenges. Various initiatives at the international level incorporated in a comprehensive manner the national, international, and systemic issues relating to financing for development in the context of globalization and interdependence. The launch of the Millennium Project and the commitment to the Millennium Development Goals are endorsed at high-level meetings (table 20.1) that provide a road map to achieving effective aid by 2015.

The International Conference on Financing for Development, held at Monterrey, Mexico, in March 2002, suggested recommendations in six key areas[1] that were adopted by the participants—both donors and recipients. In addition, a commitment to a larger volume of aid was expressed. The high-level meeting at Rome resulted in the Rome Declaration on the Harmonization of Aid that was adopted by multilateral and bilateral donors and representatives from recipient countries. This declaration emphasized the involvement of the recipient countries with the donors in

Table 20.1 Measures to Achieve Aid Effectiveness

Year	Initiative	Venue	Output
2002	International Conference on Financing for Development	Monterrey, Mexico	Monterrey Consensus
2003	High Level Forum on Harmonization	Rome, Italy	Rome Declaration on Harmonization of Aid
2005	Second High Level Forum	Paris, France	Paris Declaration on Aid Effectiveness
2008	Third High Level Forum on Aid Effectiveness	Accra, Ghana	Accra Agenda for Action
2011	Fourth High Level Forum on Aid Effectiveness	Busan, Republic of Korea	An assessment of whether targets have been met

Source: Author's compilation.

harmonizing aid to meet their needs and priorities. Promoting aid effectiveness was the mainstay of the Paris meeting in 2005. Five principles of aid effectiveness were adopted by the same development community (multilateral and bilateral donors and recipient-country representatives) that had met in Rome. These five mutually reinforcing principles were developed in line with 12 indicators by which progress was to be assessed. The five principles are the following:

- *Ownership*—Partner countries exercise effective leadership over their development policies and strategies and coordinate development actions (indicator 1).

- *Alignment*—Donors base their overall support on partner countries' national development strategies, institutions, and procedures (indicators 2–8).

- *Harmonization*—Donors' actions are more harmonized, transparent, and collectively effective (indicators 9 and 10).

- *Managing for results*—Resources are managed and decision making is improved for development results (indicator 11).

- *Mutual accountability*—Donors and partners are accountable for development results (indicator 12).

An Organisation for Economic Co-operation and Development study in 2008 examined the 12 indicators to assess the progress achieved (figure 20.1). The performance was less than stellar. The Accra Agenda called for greater efforts.

Targets were on track for three indicators—aligning and coordinating technical cooperation (indicator 4), public financial management systems (indicator 2), and untying aid (indicator 8). The report suggested that, with greater country efforts and international efforts, three further indicators may be on track. For example, the number of parallel implementation units had declined and, with no further increase, the target would be reached (indicator 6); similarly, with greater international effort and recipient country commitment, aid flows could be more accurately recorded in national budgets (indicator 3) and disbursed with greater predictability (indicator 7).

The report makes three major policy recommendations aimed at accelerating progress and transforming the aid relationship into a full partnership between donors and recipient countries: (1) step up the use and capability of national institutions as a way of reinforcing country ownership, (2) strengthen accountability for development resources, and (3) make aid management more cost effective[2] (Nallari and Griffith 2011).

Figure 20.1 Progress Toward the 2010 Paris Declaration Targets

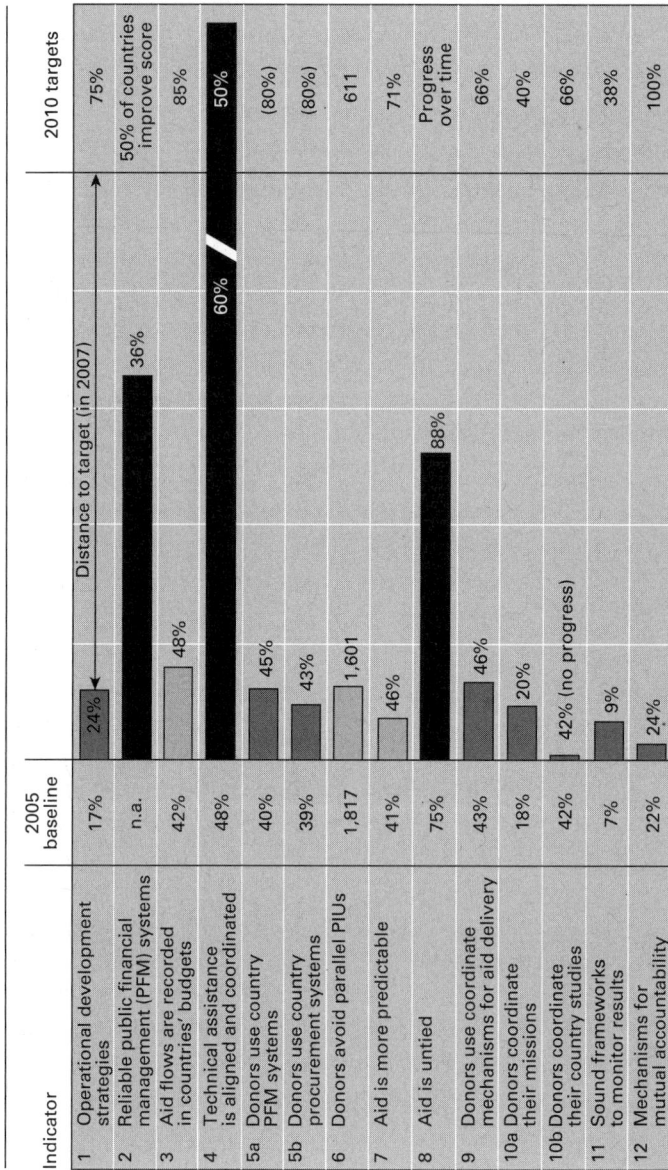

Indicator	2005 baseline	Distance to target (in 2007)	2010 targets
1 Operational development strategies	17%	24%	75%
2 Reliable public financial management (PFM) systems	n.a.	36%	50% of countries improve score
3 Aid flows are recorded in countries' budgets	42%	48%	85%
4 Technical assistance is aligned and coordinated	48%	60%	50%
5a Donors use country PFM systems	40%	45%	(80%)
5b Donors use country procurement systems	39%	43%	(80%)
6 Donors avoid parallel PIUs	1,817	1,601	611
7 Aid is more predictable	41%	46%	71%
8 Aid is untied	75%	88%	Progress over time
9 Donors use coordinate mechanisms for aid delivery	43%	46%	66%
10a Donors coordinate their missions	18%	20%	40%
10b Donors coordinate their country studies	42%	42% (no progress)	66%
11 Sound frameworks to monitor results	7%	9%	38%
12 Mechanisms for mutual accountability	22%	24%	100%

Source: OECD/DAC 2008.

Note: n.a. = not applicable; PIU = project implementation unit.

Financing for Development

The 189 countries that signed the Millennium Declaration in September 2000 endorsed the Millennium Development Goals. These goals set targets for poverty reduction, improvement of well-being (health and education), and promotion of sustainable development. The declaration called for increased public funding of aid, which did transpire—although not at the promised levels.[3]

Increased public funding of aid, referred to as the scaling up of aid, has implications for the government budget, a country's competitiveness, and the macroeconomic managing of aid flows. Ensuring aid effectiveness—that is, maximizing the development impact of this—is not an easy task.

It is difficult for governments to produce accurate, sustainable budgets when questions surround the volume, duration, and disbursement of aid. Celasun and Walliser (2008) note that almost one third of development assistance to 13 countries between 1992 and 2007 failed to arrive on time, leading to budgetary shortfalls. An Organisation for Economic Co-operation and Development survey in 2008 indicated that just 45 percent of aid arrives on time for an average country. Oftentimes, aid is tied to a particular sector or project, and this also presents budgetary challenges. The absorptive capacity of a sector may be exceeded. Public financial management systems in many developing countries are ill equipped to meet the challenges of substantial increases in aid (Nallari and Griffith 2011).

Increased development aid flows may damage a country's competitiveness through a Dutch disease effect. An increased inflow of foreign currency may push up prices in both the traded and nontraded sectors, leading to an appreciation of the domestic currency and compromising the competitiveness of exports.

Managing the macroeconomic effect of aid flows depends on how fiscal and monetary policies interact with increased development aid. Typically, fiscal policy will be concerned with directing aid to priority projects while monetary and exchange rate policies try to ameliorate inflation and competitiveness issues. Fiscal and monetary policies should be undertaken together to maximize the positive impact of development aid. Assuming the most usual scenario in which aid dollars are sold by the government to the central bank for local currency, the government's macroeconomic response is to decide on a combination of absorption and spending.

- *Absorption* is defined as the widening of the current account deficit (excluding aid) because of the presence of incremental aid. It measures the extent to which aid engenders a real transfer of resources through higher imports or through a reduction in the domestic resources devoted to producing exports. Absorption depends on both exchange rate policy and policies that influence the demand for imports. The central bank controls the exchange rate through its sales of foreign exchange, while monetary policy can be used to control aggregate demand—and the demand for imports.

- *Spending* is defined as the widening of the fiscal deficit, excluding incremental aid (Nallari and Griffith 2011).

In Conclusion

Aid effectiveness is difficult to prove. The lack of evidence for a direct effect of aid on growth should not mean that aid should be cut back. Rather, a broader view of aid should emerge whereby the effect of aid is evaluated for its role in improving governance and economic management and its role in meeting human development objectives such as education, health, and infant mortality.

Notes

1. The areas were domestic financial resources for development, mobilizing international resources for development (including foreign direct investment and other private flows), international trade as an engine of development, international financial and technical cooperation for development, external debt, and several systemic issues (enhancing the coherence and consistency of the international monetary, financial, and trading systems in support of development) (Nallari and Griffith 2011).
2. Achieving these recommendations might prove challenging in a developing-country context where capacity is lacking, the national vision is not linked to a specific budget process, and transparency in the expenditure of public funds is basic at best (Deutscher and Fyson 2008).
3. Deutscher and Fyson (2008) caution that the commitment gap between the spending plans of 23 members of the Development Assistance Committee (the World Bank; the African, Asian, and Inter-American development banks; the main United Nations organizations; and the global funds for health and the environment) fall short (by $30 billion) of the overall aid targets set by the committee members individually for 2010.

References

Celasun, O., and J. Walliser. 2008. "Managing Aid Surprises." *Finance and Development* 42 (3): 34–37.

Deutscher, E., and S. Fyson. 2008. "Improving the Effectiveness of Aid." *Finance and Development* 45 (3): 15–19.

Easterly, W. 2001. *The Elusive Quest for Growth—Economists' Adventures and Misadventures in the Tropics.* Cambridge, MA: MIT Press.

———. 2006. *The White Man's Burden: Why the West's Efforts to Aid the Rest Have Done So Much Ill and So Little Good.* New York: Penguin Press.

Nallari, R., and B. Griffith. 2011. *Understanding Growth and Poverty: Theory, Policy, and Empirics.* Washington, DC: World Bank.

OECD/DAC (Organisation for Economic Co-operation and Development/Development Assistance Committee). 2008. *2008 Survey on Monitoring the Paris Declaration.* Paris: OECD.

Radelet, S., M. Clemens, and R. Bhavnani. 2005. "Aid and Growth." *Finance and Development* 42 (3): 16–20.

Rajan, R., and A. Subramanian. 2005. "Aid and Growth: What Does the Cross Country Evidence Really Show?" Working Paper WP/05/127, International Monetary Fund, Washington, DC.

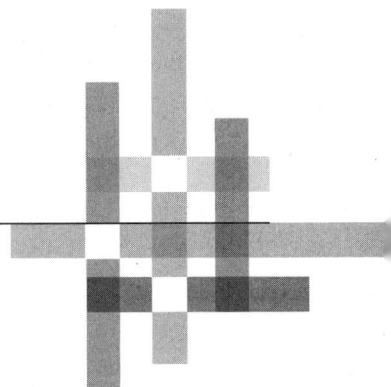

Enhancing Competitiveness

Raj Nallari

The concept of competitiveness can be applied at different levels: firm (micro), sectoral (industry), regional, national, and city. Competitiveness is defined as the efficiency or productivity with which a firm, industry, or nation uses its factors of production (such as labor or human capital, physical capital, land or natural resources, and energy) to produce a unit of output. In other words, productivity is the efficiency in converting inputs to outputs. It is also called total factor productivity and is measured as a residual—the difference between outputs and a set of inputs (for example, labor; capital; and intermediate goods, including energy, land, and buildings). Measurement problems plague both inputs (for example, how do you account for quality of labor or capital?) and outputs.

At the global level, a country is said to be competitive if it is able to hold or increase its share of products (exports) in the world economy. Because of this definition, nations prefer to undervalue or devalue their currency vis-à-vis other currencies to gain a competitive advantage or have their governments use industrial policies to increase their exports with use of such policies as subsidies, tariffs against substitutable imports, depressed wages in export industries, and aid for trade. All these policies are shortsighted and not sustainable for long. The need to keep wages low or to follow a two-track wage structure (one for cheap exports and a higher one for domestic consumption and the like) reveals a lack of true competitiveness and holds down the nation's average standard of living. Similarly, government subsidies for preferred industries and sectors burden public finances, drain national income, and bias choices away from the most productive use of the nation's resources. Undervaluation and devaluation of the exchange rate implies a collective national pay cut by discounting the products and services sold in world markets while raising the cost of the goods and services imported from abroad. Therefore, in a dynamic world, the best policy is to have in place measures that continually increase productivity at the microeconomic level (farms and firms) and at the macroeconomic or national level.

Macroeconomic growth and development of nations have thus far been seen as determined by market orientation, stable economic and political institutions, sound macroeconomic policies (including prudent public budgets, interest rates, competitive wages, and exchange rates), and so forth. As such, sound fiscal and monetary policies, a trusted and efficient legal system, a stable set of institutions, and progress on social conditions contribute greatly to a healthy economy.

At the microeconomic or firm level, the same principle holds. Output and wealth are created at the microeconomic level. The principle is not whether output is produced for domestic consumption or exports, or whether firms are domestic or foreign owned, or whether they are government owned or privately owned; rather, it is the nature and productivity of the economic activities taking place among firms in a particular country. Purely local industries also count for competitiveness because their productivity not only sets their wages, but also has a major influence on the cost of doing business and of living in the country. Operation of farms and firms creates productivity and wealth. "More than 80 percent of the variation of GDP per capita across countries is accounted for by microeconomic fundamentals. Unless microeconomic capabilities improve, macroeconomic, political, legal, and social reforms will not bear full fruit" (Porter 2005, 3).

Competitive Regions and Cities

Regional development occurs due to the availability of natural resources (as in many African countries) as well as to firms producing things to meet local demand for goods and services. Average wages are likely to be lower for workers producing for local needs. In contrast, firms and clusters producing for trade across regions and countries tend to have higher average wages. Globalization has made regions, port cities, and inner cities hubs of economic activity—particularly in manufacturing, commerce, and services sectors. Therefore, regions and metropolises now play a key role in the competitiveness agenda. For example, apart from traditional industries, business support services, high-tech and bio-tech parks, industrial clusters, and information communications technology centers are all springing up to take full advantage of the agglomeration effects and globalization. Regions and cities are now competing with other regions and cities in both the North and the South to attract domestic and foreign firms.

Mobile factors of production of capital and labor, in addition to the ever-increasing movement of goods and services across geographic boundaries, are leading to rapid urbanization and bringing in their train the need for green spaces, smart spaces (research and development firms, universities and colleges for high-skilled workers), support services, essential infrastructure, and affordable housing. The competitiveness agenda has now shifted to spatial development, which includes stepping up urban governance; improving location advantages; and ensuring availability of high-skilled workers, managers, and entrepreneurs.

What Policies Matter for Competitiveness?

Policies and programs that affect schools and education, roads and infrastructure, interest rates and financial markets, wages and exchange rates, costs of production and technological innovation, product quality, and many other elements matter for competitiveness. Among other things, a country's economic, social, and governance institutions; people's work ethic and culture; and geographic location and climate conditions impact competitiveness and pose special challenges for improving competitiveness. So improvement in one and all aspects of competitiveness is important and takes a long time (which can involve uneven changes characterized with fits, starts, stops, and reversals).

Labor quality (in terms of higher education, training, and tenure at the firm), capital quality (for example, recent vintages of machinery; higher investment in information technology, especially on account of organizational decentralization and decisions to adopt new technologies), and firms with research and development spending and learning by doing (that is, innovation and new processes) all do better. Narrowly specialized firms are more competitive.

The competitiveness game is about a country achieving production capabilities through self-discovery, learning from others, and interacting with alternative paths of capability creation. Pursuit of technological innovation for the modernized knowledge economy is therefore a national policy for developing countries that start behind and want to catch up. Interfirm rivalry and demand for goods and services drive creation of capabilities through innovation that is expected to lower costs and improve product quality in the industry and thereby increases industry demand. In other words, the world is more integrated now, firms are less independent than they were, and efforts to promote competitiveness through innovation can rarely be understood in isolation from what others are achieving at the same time. This applies across countries, sectors, and individual enterprises. As such, there is a sharing of knowledge among firms and evolution of technology as adapting firms gain more than original innovators. There is a public-good aspect to technology and innovation, and it justifies a growing role for governments and other noncorporate institutions in knowledge development and transfer.

Spillovers from strong input markets, agglomeration effects, and knowledge transfer are among the external factors that affect productivity. Export firms have higher productivity relative to firms operating only in domestic markets. Foreign direct investment and use of newer "foreign" technologies and heightened market competition as reflected by a large number of firms in inputs and outputs also have a positive impact. Theoretically, models using heterogeneous-productivity firms show that trade policy impacts across producers and depends on their productivity levels. For example, trade liberalization in 1970s in Chile showed a substantial jump in productivity at the microeconomic level. Similarly, deregulation of electricity showed an increase in productivity in Romanian plants. Labor market flexibility (lower unionization) shows a positive impact on productivity.

Competitiveness and Corporate Social Responsibility

The concept of corporate social responsibility (CSR) applies where companies integrate social and environmental concerns in their business strategies and operations—including interaction with their stakeholders primarily on a voluntary basis, but sometimes in response to legislation. The concept of CSR has been primarily developed for large companies and not so much for small and medium-size enterprises.

According to Milton Friedman (1970), "there is one and only one social responsibility of business—to use its resources and engage in activities designed to increase its profits so long as it stays within the rules of the game, which is to say, engages in open and free competition without deception or fraud" (p. 6). Effective CSR requires enterprises to "voluntarily" integrate social and environmental responsibilities into their operations, interacting regularly with their stakeholders (customers, trade unions, the local community, and so forth). CSR spills over as a responsibility of the enterprise at the workplace, the marketplace, the environment, and the local community.

CSR could have positive and negative economic effects on competitiveness. For example, at the firm level, the economic effects of CSR can be felt on the cost structure, human capital, sales to customers, innovation, risk and reputation, and financial performance. Do the costs of CSR outweigh the benefits? Maignan and Ralston (2002) examine CSR in businesses from the United Kingdom, the Netherlands, the United States, and France, comparing the extent and content of businesses communication about CSR. They find mixed results, with costs and benefits being small compared with the total operating costs of the companies. But it appears that, in the 21st century, most large companies want to at least pay lip service to CSR because the risk of a loss in reputation is quite high and costly in an age of mass media. CSR could contribute to national, regional, or city-level competitiveness by generating higher levels of trust between the business and the citizens and stakeholders. The more credible the CSR practices of any company, the higher likelihood that society responds with trust and wants to be associated with the company in all its facets of recruitment, sales, innovation, and profit seeking.

In Conclusion

Competitiveness matters for economic growth and development. It matters at the microeconomic (firm) level and at the macroeconomic level. Coordination of macroeconomic policies and stable economic and political institutions underpin competitiveness. Corporate social responsibility should contribute to firm-level competitiveness with positive externalities for the economy by generating higher levels of trust between the corporation and its stakeholders.

References

Friedman, M. 1970. "The Social Responsibility of Business Is to Increase Its Profits." *New York Times Magazine* September 13.

Maignan, I., and D. A. Ralston. 2002. "Corporate Social Responsibility in Europe and the U.S.: Insights from Businesses' Self-Presentations." *Journal of International Business Studies* 33 (3): 497–514.

Porter, M. 2005. "What Is Competitiveness?" *Notes on Globalization and Strategy* 1 (1).

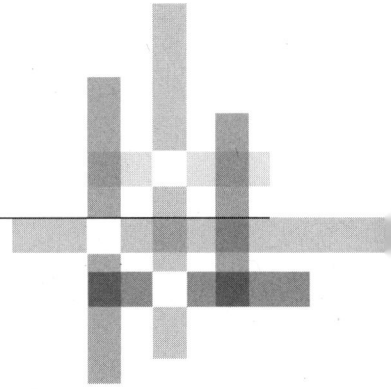

Land Policy and Effective Use of Natural Resources

Breda Griffith and Raj Nallari

Using land effectively is of critical importance to the poor, particularly in rural areas. It represents a means of increasing productivity, increasing household income, and contributing to national economic growth. How-ever, inequality in access to and ownership of land is a serious problem in most developing countries and has been shown to affect three key aspects of economic development—namely, education, institutions, and financial development. Government plays a key role in establishing rights to own and exchange land and in protecting those rights. It may also have a role in addressing the poverty and stifled economic growth stemming from land inequalities.

Secure tenure remains beyond the grasp of the majority of the rural poor, with formal tenure covering only 2–10 percent of the land in Africa, for example (Cotula, Toulmin, and Quan 2006, 20). The remainder is held under a system of customary tenure that often lacks legal recogni-tion. The results in many developing countries are an unequal distribu-tion of land and a large landless population. Granting legal recognition to informal land tenure arrangements with insufficient institutional capacity to administer and implement these laws falls short of the mark. Economic growth is constrained when land rights are insecure. Figure 22.1 indicates the positive social and economic opportunities when land titles are secure. Landowners are more likely to invest in their holdings when they have tenure and to reap rewards from investment when they sell their holdings. Furthermore, individuals have greater access to credit when they can use their land as collateral.

Landownership for women in developing economies is often insecure, but the economic consequences for many areas are far reaching. Many women acquire their land rights through their husbands or male relatives and often have only indirect access to land. In geographic areas where women are the main cultivators, where male emigration is high, where control of productive assets depends on gender, or where high adult mortality rates and unclear inheritance regulations undermine

Figure 22.1 Initial Land Distribution and Growth, by Economy, 1960–2000

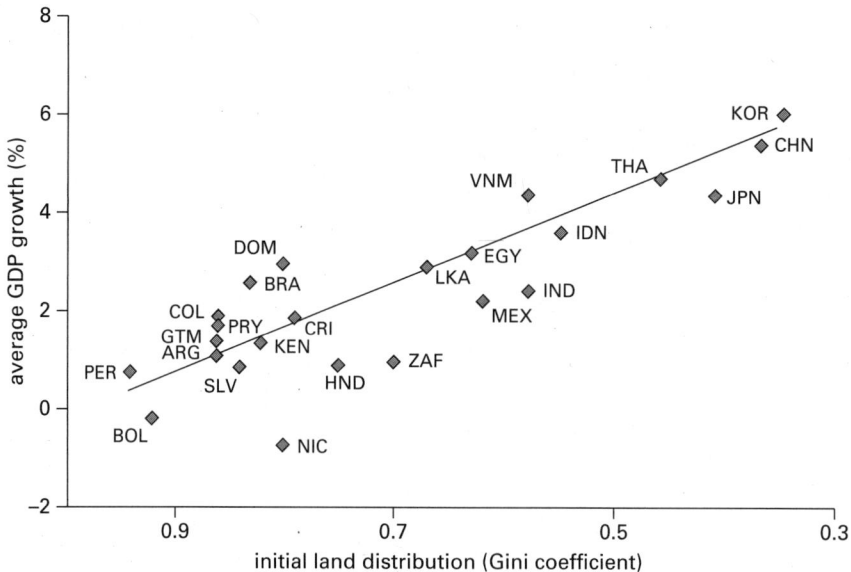

Source: Deininger 2003, 18.

Note: The Gini coefficient measures the degree of concentration (inequality) of a variable in a distribution of its elements. It compares the Lorenz curve of a ranked empirical distribution with the line of perfect equality. This line assumes that each element has the same contribution to the total summation of the values of a variable. The Gini coefficient ranges between 0, where there is no concentration (perfect equality) and 1, where there is total concentration (perfect inequality).

Frontiers in Development Policy

widows' livelihoods (Nallari and Griffith 2011), there are clear economic benefits from females having secure land rights.

Who Owns the Land?

Adding further ambiguity to issues of ownership and access to land is land owned by communities, land passed down through the generations through primogeniture, and land taken over by the state. Indeed, in many countries, the state continues to own large portions of valuable land. This scenario is often accompanied by issues of mismanagement, corruption, and underutilization of resources.

One of the principal obstacles to secure land rights is the absence or insufficient institutional capacity to support land tenure. Property rights are often imposed from outside forces or local elites with little interest in promoting landownership for local inhabitants. Lack of institutional arrangements for land titling exacerbates the situation. Where institutional arrangements exist, they are often ill defined with unclear guidelines for how land rights are defined, how ownership and possession are determined, and how conflicts are resolved (Nallari and Griffith 2011). As noted above, the scope for economic growth is limited where land tenure is not secure or property rights are poorly defined. Easterly and Levine (2003) show that natural resource endowments affect growth through institutions. They cite three scenarios. The first involves a minority landholder class that quickly develops political and legal institutions to protect its large plantations. For other inhospitable environments, colonists established extractive institutions to exploit natural resources. In environments that were more hospitable—for example, with less disease—colonists established institutions that were favorable for economic growth and that endured even after the colonists left.

Role of Government

Government in developing countries has been active in establishing and protecting property rights as a series of first-generation reforms for greater economic liberalization. Property rights in land should have the characteristics noted in table 22.1.

Following the establishment of property rights to land, it is crucial that government implements a system of registration and titling. These

Table 22.1   Characteristics of Property Rights for Land

- The time frame for securing land rights should be long enough to ensure an adequate return on investment. The potential for investment in urban areas is greater than in rural areas, so the time frame should reflect this. Although property rights given for an indefinite period are the best option, long-term rights that can be renewed automatically are the next-best alternative.

- Property rights should be defined in a way that makes them easy to observe, enforce, and exchange. This requires the existence of recognized institutions that are accessible by the general populace and that render decisions backed by the power of the state. The need for universal legitimacy is particularly evident in Africa, where rights to 90 percent of the land are determined outside the legal system. Informal institutions of land administration cannot offer universally recognized mechanisms for enforcing property rights. However, formal institutions make little difference to the lives of ordinary people if their scope is limited.

- If the government is engaged in land allocation reforms, it must decide whether it is more appropriate to confer property rights on individuals or on groups. Group rights are more appropriate in situations characterized by economies of scale in resource management and high-risk markets. While a group system of property rights may be advantageous in the early stages of development, the likelihood of technical progress and demographic changes suggests that one should expect property rights to become individualized over time. This is not an automatic evolution, however, but one that will be shaped by political and economic factors.

Source: Nallari and Griffith 2011.

second-generation reforms tackle insecurity of land rights, which is a plague on growth and development. A system of formalized land ownership delivers large productivity gains. This is especially true in environments where land tenure systems are weak, where the potential return of investment in land is high, and where collateralized lending is the norm. Land titling in Latin America has been largely positive, but a number of writers have questioned its benefit for Africa (see, for example, Atwood 1990; Migot-Adholla et al. 1991; Carter, Weibe, and Blarel 1997; Place and Migot-Adholla 1998; and Jacoby and Minten, 2005). Imposing formalized arrangements on the unsecured, indigenous tenure system that prevails in most of Africa may be disadvantageous and open up opportunities for economic rent seeking.

In Conclusion

Land policies should be cognizant of history and traditional customs, and their objective should be to provide security of tenure to improve the welfare of the poor. A government land policy can also achieve more socially desirable land allocation and utilization such as occurred with farm restructuring in the countries of the former Soviet Union and as part of a postconflict land policy in some East and West Africa states. Land policy should also aim for sustainable land use.

References

Atwood, D. A. 1990. "Land Registration in Africa: The Impact on Agricultural Production." *World Development* 18 (5): 659–71.

Carter, M., K. Weibe, and B. Blarel. 1997. "Tenure Security for Whom? Differential Effects of Land Policy in Kenya." In *Searching for Land Tenure Security in Africa*, ed. J. Bruce and S. Migot-Adholla, 215–22. Dubuque, IA: Kendall/Hunt.

Cotula, L., C. Toulmin, and J. Quan. 2006. *Better Access for the Rural Poor: Lessons from Experience and Challenges Ahead*. London: International Institute for Environment and Development.

Deininger, K. 2003. *Land Policies for Growth and Poverty Reduction*. Policy Research Report. Washington, DC: World Bank.

Easterly, W., and R. Levine. 2003. "Tropics, Germs, and Crops: How Endowments Influence Economic Development." Working Paper 9106, National Bureau of Economic Research, Cambridge, MA.

Jacoby, H., and B. Minten. 2005. "Is Land Titling in Sub-Saharan Africa Cost-Effective? Evidence from Madagascar." Working Paper No. 19, World Bank, Washington, DC.

Migot-Adholla, S. E., P. Hazell, B. Blarel, and F. Place. 1991. "Indigenous Land Rights Systems in Sub-Saharan Africa: A Constraint on Productivity?" *World Bank Economic Review* 5 (1): 155–75.

Nallari, R., and B. Griffith. 2011. *Understanding Growth and Poverty: Theory, Policy, and Empirics*. Washington, DC: World Bank.

Place, F., and S. E. Migot-Adholla. 1998. "The Economic Effects of Land Registration on Smallholder Farms in Kenya: Evidence from Nyeri and Kakamega Districts." *Land Economics* 74 (3): 360–73.

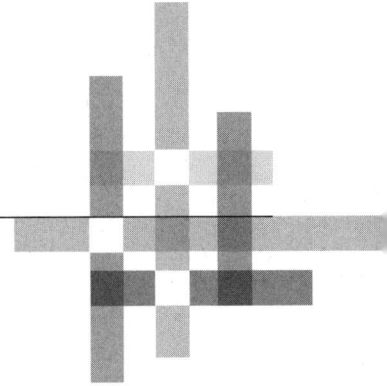

Cities as Engines of Growth

Shahid Yusuf

The advanced countries are highly urbanized, and urban populations are expanding ceaselessly in virtually all of the middle- and low-income countries, irrespective of economic performance. A global urbanization rate of 50 percent in 2009 is expected to reach 70 percent by 2050 (UN-Habitat 2009, 1).

Cities are where most of the world's population will live. They are and will remain the engines of all national economies and the leading consumers of energy and water (on a per capita basis). Urban design is emphasizing compactness, sustainability, and a low carbon footprint. The formation and growth of cities entail many decisions that can be exceedingly costly to undo, in part because cities embody certain long-lived assets. There is much in the current characteristics and geographic distribution of urbanization and in current trends that are unsuited for a warming and more densely populated world. The need to reduce carbon emissions, husband water supplies, and conserve nonrenewable resources runs counter to the largely unchecked and unplanned urbanization now ongoing. And yet, few governments—national or subnational—are gearing up for the challenge posed by long-term sustainable urbanization under far more severe environmental and resource constraints.

Urban Development

Research on urban development has focused on the significance of scale and "urbanization economies."[1] This research suggests that large cities with a diversified mix of industries enjoy a productivity advantage over their smaller cousins. Large diversified cities can more easily weather economic shocks and evolve new activities as existing ones wind down or migrate. A sizable local market well supplied with services encourages entry by new firms, facilitates the testing of new products, contains risks for producers, and is a superior launching pad for penetrating other markets.

Public investment in urban infrastructure, low-income housing, and public services provides the foundation for urban development and can crowd-in private investment in productive activities. In many cities, such types of investment are shared with the private sector, but they can also lie exclusively in the public domain.

The volume of public investment is an important part of development. Municipal leadership and public investment can serve as catalysts, and public investment puts in place some of the essential furnishings of a modern urban system; but economic performance and its sustainability are in the hands of private investors. Their actions are a critical verdict on the worth of local leadership, strategy, and governance.

The research on the subnational investment climate and ranking of cities with reference to their "business friendliness" offers a partial and subjective assessment. Interestingly, although Mumbai is ranked low and Beijing also does quite poorly, both are cities commanding the attention of domestic and foreign investors (see table 23.1).

Policy Dimensions

A brief recapitulation of the policy options can help delineate the scope for policy action; and, at the same time, it can indicate the limits to policy making, given the existing state of knowledge, of implementation capacity, and the slow turnover of assets in most cities. It can also point to the challenges for which answers must continue to be sought.

Geography of Urbanization

To a degree, governments can manage the growth of existing urban centers and the in situ expansion of small towns into cities through investment in

Table 23.1   Business Friendliness

City	Higher-education population	E-readiness (tech-savvy population)	International tourists to the city	Diverted recycled waste
Beijing	6	2	11	12
Chicago	17	20	4	10
Dubai	5	7	15	3
Frankfurt	12	11	9	20
Hong Kong SAR, China	7	16	17	19
Johannesburg	2	6	1	4
London	14	13	20	11
Los Angeles	16	20	8	8
Mexico City	1	5	10	9
Mumbai	3	3	3	7
New York	19	20	16	13
Paris	18	8	19	7
São Paulo	4	4	5	1
Seoul	9	10	14	15
Shanghai	10	2	13	17
Singapore	8	14	18	16
Sydney	13	15	7	14
Tokyo	11	9	6	5
Toronto	20	12	12	18

Source: PricewaterhouseCoopers 2009.

Note: 20 indicates the highest rating and 1 indicates the lowest rating.

transport and other infrastructure and through regulations and land-use rules that strictly control whether a piece of land is developed and for what purpose it is developed. For example, the urbanization of high-risk flood plains, coastal areas, steeply sloped areas, earthquake-prone areas, and regions where water will be increasingly scarce could be tightly regulated; and existing habitation could be gradually scaled back through tax policies and other actions that fully reflect the costs of insuring against risks. Such actions will undoubtedly face intense opposition.[2] Awareness-raising programs coupled with a gradual tightening of implementation is probably the only way forward. This is not a knowledge-gap problem; it is one arising from the unwillingness to write off sunk costs; the continuing attractions of coastal regions and long-settled urban areas; legacy transport infrastructure; and, in developing countries, the combined pressures exerted by population growth and urban migration. The great challenge will be in winning sufficient political support from a majority of the stakeholders and implementing a partial deconstruction and rebuilding of cities. This is a project for the long term—something politicians are rarely inclined to tackle, leaving it to future generations to worry over.

Design of Urban Centers

Land-use planning and zoning laws, real estate taxes, floor-area ratios, and the urban transport infrastructure are among the instruments governments can use more effectively to build low-carbon, sustainable cities that grow vertically. But few are doing so, and awareness of the need for raising urbanization to a new level to avoid future crises is spreading slowly. It goes without saying that starting the process of constructing "smarter cities" now while there is time has many advantages with regard to planning and execution. Whether the threat of climate change and resource constraints will triumph over scientific illiteracy, denial, and procrastination to strengthen implementation remains to be seen.

Sustainability

Reinforcing urban design with measures to reduce carbon emissions can conserve water and minimize heat-island effects. This is a necessity, not an option. Large gains are possible from better harnessing of tested and cost-effective technologies that remain underused because of inertia, ignorance, and the desire to avoid initial costs even when they can be rapidly recouped. Pricing policies (especially for energy and water), codes and standards for buildings and appliances, incentives for new technology adoption and research, road pricing, and other measures can achieve dramatic results. Information communications technology now permits the building of integrated electricity and water use systems that can monitor use, differentiate prices by time period and user, and reward frugality. However, the experience of even advanced countries in phasing in codes, standards, and road pricing, for example, can be a salutary reminder of how stoutly a raising of standards and monitoring is opposed and of the slow-acting and slippage-prone nature of localized enforcement (especially under decentralized conditions).

Urban Industrialization

Economic sustainability is key. Urban location and macroeconomic and social stability are among the preconditions to be met. Other well-rehearsed requirements subject to policy control include adequate infrastructure (now including information technology), a skilled workforce, serviced land (including technology parks and incubators), affordable housing, connectedness to other cities, acceptable levels of congestion and pollution, decent public services, a business-friendly environment, and so forth. This is a long and familiar checklist. The reason so many cities are falling short of their desired benchmarks is because leadership, governance capacity, and resources are all too frequently lacking. Again, there are no easy answers to the issues enumerated above.

Fiscal Sustainability

This also is well-traveled ground, with few innovations to report. The local tax and pricing tools, the center-local fiscal arrangements, and the avenues for raising capital from financial markets are all familiar. So also are budgeting, accounting, and auditing procedures for efficiently allocating funds and minimizing leaks. Adequate municipal financing (which derives from a buoyant, broad-based economy) and fiscal discipline, nationally imposed and municipally reinforced, are inseparable from long-run urban sustainability.

Urban Services

Financing and governance are two vital ingredients of adequate and efficient services delivery. But they are not all; an effective schooling system, health services, and law enforcement also require leadership that is dynamic and open to innovative methods for delivering quality results at competitive prices. In addition, it depends on the engagement of an informed public seeking results.

Innovativeness

The competitiveness of manufacturing or, in rare cases, tradable services (for example, information technology–enabled services, business services, and software) is a function of factor costs, the quality of the workforce, and connectedness. Municipalities can influence these through the setting of rental rates and charges for power, water, sewerage, and other services. Incentives—and locally sponsored technical and consulting entities—can enhance the supply of skills. But lower-middle- and middle-income urban centers must look beyond the low-cost model of competitiveness and derive more of their edge from technological prowess and innovation. Building innovation capability is widely viewed as the quickest route to prosperity because the intense competition squeezes much of the profit out of standardized commodities. Only through ceaseless differentiation of products and innovation will suppliers earn the quasi rents that can fuel rapid growth. Innovative urban economies are also better able to cope with fluctuations in demand and to recover from shocks by evolving their product mix and attracting new activities.

In Conclusion

Cities with their opportunities, their innovations, and networks of services promote capital accumulation. Whether it is financial capital or human capital, the urban environment is richer in incentives for accumulating both and it offers multiple avenues for effectively using the capital. And capital is the major source of growth through the building of physical assets, productivity gains arising from technology embodied in equipment, and the knowledge infrastructure underpinning technological change.

Notes

1. The advantages of scale are well known; those of "urbanization" derive from the opportunities for new departures, unexpected synergies, and technological crossovers arising from the presence of diverse industries, services, and skills in a city. Urbanization economies are usually juxtaposed with localization economies—referring to the gains from industrial specialization more common in small and medium-size cities with labor and skills catering to a few particular activities. The literature has been unable to establish the clear primacy of one over the other in terms of urban productivity advantages.

2. In full awareness of the risks of living in flood plains and building homes on steeply sloped hillsides, people are undeterred. After each disaster, the rebuilding begins.

References

PricewaterhouseCoopers. 2009. "Ranking Cities for Business Friendliness." *View* Spring: 8–9.

UN-Habitat (United Nations Human Settlements Programme). 2009. *Global Report on Human Settlements 2009. Planning Sustainable Cities*. New York: UN-Habitat.

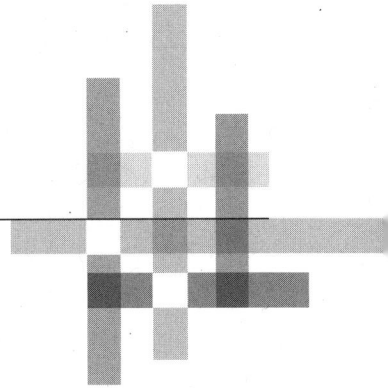

Rethinking Macroeconomic Theory

Raj Nallari

The failure of economics as a profession to anticipate the global financial crisis has brought about renewed interest in Keynesianism among academics and policy makers, particularly in Keynes's views on multipliers. The Keynesian multiplier is the effect of traditional macroeconomic policies, such as an increase in government spending, that is multiplied by boosting private consumption by households and capital investment by firms as they receive income from the initial round of fiscal stimulus. The multiplier effects are important to assess the strength and speed of economic recovery in a country.

Governments have misused the traditional Keynesian model of depression economics, in which increasing government spending could stimulate the economy for decades (particularly in developing countries) during the period of the 1950s to 1980s. The result was the "commanding heights," which expanded the role of the public sector in production, distribution, marketing, and job creation in almost all economic activities. Low economic growth and high rent seeking by bureaucrats (through regulations and licensing systems) in developing countries were recorded during 1960–85.

Macroeconomics and the Recent Crisis

The more recent version of Keynesianism (which searched for market failures and missing markets, with an emphasis on wages and prices adjusting slowly to shocks to the economic system) also provides a rationale for government intervention in various markets, albeit relatively limited intervention when compared with that of traditional Keynesianism. Keynesian economists believe that the capitalist system deviates from the path of prosperity from time to time and needs the steady hand of a strong government to monitor, regulate, and intervene to bring it back on the rails. The recent global financial crisis has exposed government weaknesses in developed and developing countries, both in regulating the financial system and in not maintaining prudent macroeconomic policies. Moreover, government is not a monolith; politicians have an interest in staying in power, the bureaucracy has its own interests, and the military may have a totally different objective.

The new classical framework asserts that economic agents, such as households and businesses, form expectations about the future in a rational way and then follow up by acting rationally to maximize utility. Markets, if left to operate on their own, will function efficiently and will "revert to mean" if they deviate too much from the fundamentals. However, the recent crisis belies this assumption of rational expectations because financial firms and individuals exhibited more of a herd behavior by assuming that housing values and asset prices would continue to increase forever. The demand and supply of housing and assets did not adjust to price changes. Moreover, the crisis revealed that interest rates, exchange rates, energy prices, and commodity prices, among other factors, are largely influenced by governments, financial markets, and large institutional investors in those markets. The forgotten lines of Keynes—that expectations about the future are uncertain and, therefore, economic agents fall back on raw emotion or "animal spirits"—are now resurgent (Akerlof and Shiller 2009). Sudden stops in capital flows across countries, as evidenced during the 1997–98 Asian crisis and the 2008–09 global crisis, vouch for the existence of animal spirits.

The Austrian economics school is of the view that Keynesian stimulus measures are likely to have short-term benefits but, in the medium to longer term, they may be counterproductive—especially if the adjustment between production (supply) and demand for goods and services is impeded by short-term policies. Moreover, failure to adjust quickly could cause fiscal stimulus to lead to a surge in aggregate demand (with supply being slow to adjust) and could quickly feed into inflationary pressures.

Monetary policy affects the economy through the quantity of bank reserves and, thereby, bank credit. Yet, modern macroeconomics does not incorporate the role of financial intermediaries. Financial firms create financial instruments, particularly during a boom, that provide credit to finance the boom.

State-of-the-art economic models (such as dynamic stochastic general equilibrium) include rational expectations and the "sticky price and wage" hypotheses—the new Keynesian-neoclassical synthesis version—and assert that private consumption and investment depend on income and asset values (wealth in the form of housing and stocks among other assets).

Since the mid-1980s, fiscal policy as a countercyclical policy tool faded, in part, because it resulted in excesses of government; but it also faded because financial sector development in the Western world coincided with more use of monetary policy in economic management. Moreover, fiscal policy was estimated to have long lag times (12–18 months), whereas monetary policy took less time to influence output.

In line with this new synthesis, the monetary policy rule (the so-called Taylor rule) is based on the deviation of actual inflation from expected inflation—the output gap (deviation of the current output from its natural or potential level). Monetary policy targeted inflation with the policy interest rate as the key instrument (that is, the short-term interest rate that the central bank can directly control through open market operations). The objective was to keep inflation low and stable with the expectation that such a policy would keep the output gap small. In line with this approach, inflation targeting of 2 percent or so was considered optimal, and the real effects of policy were assumed to occur through market interest rate and asset prices. As long as the economy had enough liquidity, there was no problem. Deflation was considered a distant possibility.

An augmented version of the Taylor rule could include the central bank reacting to housing prices, stock prices, and credit friction. The idea behind credit friction is that the optimal monetary policy rule should be designed in such a manner that the policy interest rate should be lowered when credit spreads increase. This approach avoids the potential increase in credit spreads from effectively tightening monetary conditions, which are not justified by the deviation of the inflation expectations, the output gap, and the other variables included in the monetary policy rule.

In addition, the recent crisis showed that (1) countries also use monetary policy for stabilizing exchange rate volatility and, therefore, the Taylor rule needs to have exchange rate stability in its objective function; and (2) asset prices tend to deviate from fundamentals, not for liquidity purposes but as a result of heightened speculation.

Policy Implications

In short, economic theory is incomplete but still evolving as more and more structural, institutional, and behavioral characteristics are incorporated to depict a modern economy. Basic assumptions about human behavior and globalization have to be understood and rethought, and policy functions have to be improved to reflect a modern economy. Modern macroeconomic theorists are embroiled in debating a false dichotomy and theoretical issues while neglecting to incorporate practical realities such as financial intermediaries and their regulation in their macroeconomic frameworks. Also important to consider are political economy constraints, such as state capture by elites, where policy is an outcome of a collusion between big business and finance on the one hand and big government on the other.

Inflation targeting need not be as stringent as previously thought. There is merit to maintaining a more relaxed inflation target. The cost to reducing an already low inflation rate has been shown to be expensive (Blanchard, Dell'Ariccia, and Mauro 2010). Furthermore, it is unclear how much greater economic benefit arises from tightening monetary policy further.

Should monetary policy deal with asset price booms and excessive credit or leverage ratios? The policy interest rate is a blunt tool for dealing with housing and asset price booms, and it requires prudential regulations. Such policy will require close coordination between the regulatory authorities and central bank authorities.

To minimize credit bubbles in the future, policy makers must develop a system of monitoring leverage ratios among financial firms. In addition, they may need to regulate pockets of leverage for certain firms or types of transactions, including by ensuring more capital for such highly leveraged firms or by increasing margin requirements or restricting the use of loan-to-value ratios for housing loans.

Rethinking exchange rate regimes and the use of capital controls is another area for study. Much needs to be done to upgrade macroeconomic theory and policy.

In Conclusion

Since the financial crisis, there has been renewed thinking in macroeconomic policy as economists are starting to recognize the importance of human behavior in decision making. Consequently, there needs to be a balanced approach toward fiscal and monetary policy to effectively regulate and protect against any potential pitfalls.

References

Akerlof, G. A., and R. J. Shiller. 2009. *Animal Spirits: How Human Psychology Drives the Economy and Why It Matters for Global Capitalism.* Princeton, NJ: Princeton University Press.

Blanchard, O., G. Dell'Ariccia, and P. Mauro. 2010. "Rethinking Macroeconomic Policy." Staff Position Note 10/03, International Monetary Fund, Washington, DC.

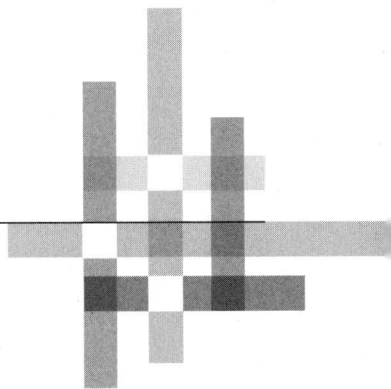

Macro-Fiscal-Monetary Policies

Breda Griffith and Raj Nallari

The recent global crisis has exposed government weaknesses in developed and developing countries, both in regulating the financial system and in not maintaining prudent macroeconomic policies. The 2008 global financial crisis has caused macroeconomists to rethink their tools and to question their approach before the crisis and in a postcrisis world.

The recent crisis belies the assumption of the rational expectations model in which households and businesses form expectations and act rationally to maximize utility and in which markets (if left to operate on their own) will function efficiently and will "revert to mean" if they deviate too much from the fundamentals. In reality, financial firms and individuals exhibited more of a herd-like behavior, assuming that housing values and asset prices would continue to increase forever. The demand for and supply of housing and assets did not adjust to price changes.

Krugman (2008) explained the current financial crisis, using the approach of Calvo (1998) and Kaminsky, Rinehart, and Vegh (2003). Contagion spreads through balance sheet effects on financial intermediaries. Many episodes of financial crisis during recent decades involved a "leveraged common creditor" where different countries were connected financially. The issue is not one of liquidity but one of undercapitalization. For example, when the financial crisis hit the Russian Federation in

1998, hedge funds that had large exposure in Russia plugged massive amounts in Brazil as well, thereby creating financial problems in Brazil.

During the recent crisis, highly toxic assets such as mortgage-backed securities were held by several highly leveraged financial institutions in Brazil, China, and the United States, and in Europe and elsewhere. A large decline in housing prices reduced the general public's demand for mortgage-backed securities (assets), and leveraged institutions had to cut back sharply on the supply of those securities. This initial effect was magnified as the falling asset prices forced the leveraged institutions to further contract their balance sheets, leading to a further fall in asset values. When housing prices declined—not only in the United States but also in a large number of countries in Western and Eastern Europe and several emerging economies—the global financial multiplier was further magnified in a vicious spiral downward.[1]

Precrisis Monetary and Fiscal Policy

For most advanced economies, the 20 or so years before the crisis was a period of economic stability in which the tools of macroeconomics had achieved a "decline in the variability of output and of inflation" (Blanchard, Dell'Arriccia, and Mauro 2010, 1). Macroeconomic policy was oriented toward controlling interest rates because they were a good short-term tool to balance inflation. Assuming that the market has liquidity, monetary policy was considered to be an efficient tool.

Fiscal policy that held sway in the 1950s and 1960s was given equal footing with monetary policy in the 1970s and 1980s, but then fell by the wayside. Because fiscal policy takes longer to permeate and bring substantive results (12–18 months), monetary policy was emphasized more. Additionally, because fiscal policy required a stronger government presence, it was further overlooked.

Blanchard, Dell'Ariccia, and Mauro (2010) summarize five arguments from the academic literature for the demise in fiscal policy. First, there was doubt about the effects of fiscal policy. Second, it was seen as redundant in the context of the output gap where monetary policy had more to offer, especially when "financial market developments increased the effectiveness of monetary policy" (p. 5). Third, there was a priority among advanced economies to stabilize and reduce high debt levels. Fourth, there was the view that fiscal measures were likely to take too long to implement and were thus irrelevant in an environment of short recessions. Fifth, fiscal policy was more "likely to be distorted by political constraints" (p. 6) than was monetary policy. The reality, however, was a little different; and policy makers would resort to fiscal stimulus in periods of "normal recessions" (p. 6). Discretionary fiscal spending was tolerated in emerging markets where automatic stabilizers were not well developed.

What Can Macroeconomics Learn from the Crisis?

Macroeconomics is an evolving field that needs to reevaluate its policy outcomes on the foundation of "real" factors like political economy (such as state capture) and the importance of financial intermediaries in regulation policy. The inherent expectations about the logical behavior of individuals also need to be reconsidered in light of the global financial crisis.

Developing countries should continue to restrain the role of government in productive activities; however, they need to ensure some fiscal space at all times to deal with exogenous shocks, such as the food, fuel, and financial crises of 2006–09. More important, governments in developing countries need to expand the coverage of social protection, including automatic stabilizers to protect the poor and the vulnerable. Fiscal policy as a tool needs to be reasserted. Premature withdrawal of fiscal stimulus policies could reverse an economic recovery and increase unemployment rates.

Blanchard, Dell'Ariccia, and Mauro (2010) highlight five lessons for macroeconomics stemming from the crisis. These lessons are the following:

1. Stable inflation may be necessary, but is an insufficient condition.

2. Low inflation limits the scope of monetary policy in deflationary recessions.

3. Financial intermediation matters.

4. Countercyclical fiscal policy is an important tool.

5. Financial regulation has macroeconomic implications.

Lessons from the crisis suggest that inflation is poorly understood. Even when all looks well—stable and low inflation, stable output gap—the composition of output and other price and credit aggregates may be less desirable[2] and cause fluctuations in the macroeconomy at a later date.

Central banks decreased their policy rate in 2008 in response to falling aggregate demand. Given the low level of the rate, there was limited scope for reduction because of the zero-bound nominal rate. Had the inflation rate been higher and, thus, the nominal interest rate, there would have been more scope to reduce it, less of a reliance on fiscal policy (and larger deficits), and less cutting of output.

Modern macroeconomics does not incorporate the role of financial intermediaries in its models. The structure of banks and financial intermediaries does not matter in current economic models. Banks use deposits (which the government protects through deposit insurance) as a base to generate loans and provide credit.

Minsky (1982) outlines that, at the beginning of the credit cycle, the duration of the loans is longer; but it gets shorter and shorter during later stages of this credit cycle as new loans are basically given to service the interest on previous loans (the so-called greening of loans). In such a way, the Minsky-Kindleberger theories emphasize irrational myopia and herd-like behavior, causing endogenous cycles as greed and fear dominate banking and investment behavior rather than rational, long-term projection of fundamentals. Whereas greed leads to underpricing of risk, fear leads to overpricing of risk. Although fear and greed partly explain the U.S. mortgage crisis, they do not explain the timing of the crisis, the duration of the credit cycle in the United States and why the duration of the credit cycle varies in different countries, or the ultimate length of a financial collapse.

Fiscal policy returned to center stage after the crisis. Monetary policy had reached its limit, and the recession was expected to be deep and long lasting. Discretionary fiscal policy before the crisis left a lot of advanced and some emerging market economies in a weak macroeconomic position. Countries with weak fiscal space have had limited scope to pursue countercyclical fiscal policy.

Financial regulation was confined to individual institutions, and the implications for the macroeconomy were not explored. For most advanced countries, financial regulation was not a macroeconomic tool.[3] This was less true of some emerging markets that had regulatory rules designed with macroeconomic stability in mind. One of the main lessons from the crisis is that financial regulation, or the lack thereof, has implications for the macroeconomy. The most fundamental problem of the crisis was the widening gap between financial intermediaries' assets and liabilities. For example, the housing prices declined steeply during the run-up to the 2008 financial crisis in the United States and Europe and led to the subprime crisis, which was exacerbated by high leverage ratios and liquidity demands. How can regulation avert or minimize the losses arising from future financial crises?

Three regulatory paradigms coexist in the financial world today. First, under the *agency paradigm* the managers of financial intermediaries (agents) intentionally or unintentionally take risks as they focus only on private benefits and costs and not on the impact on society (that is, externalities are not considered). The market failure here is that managers would be betting with someone else's money, be it the money of principal depositors or taxpayers because there are implicit or explicit guarantees. In the case of the subprime crisis, the managers who originated special investment vehicles and credit default swaps to distribute risks had no skin in the game. They were the masters for all the profits and not liable even for 1 percent of the risks. The solution is for agents to bear the burden of the risks and align the incentives with potential losses arising from the managers' actions. Risks should be priced, and supervisors and securities commissions should serve as "crime police" to prevent abuse.

Second, under the *collective welfare paradigm* the managers have difficulty understanding the internal workings of modern finance (for example, the quantification of securitization and associated risks). Here the managers of most financial institutions engage in a behavior that is opportunistic to them but detrimental to society. There is a "free-rider" problem in all collective actions. As such, there is a certain amount of "systemic herding" behavior, and the "financially innovative" instruments are marketed as the best thing that happened to the world since sliced bread. The solution is to internalize the externalities, but pricing of this possible "wide-spread failure'" is like insuring against a 100-year flood: it is a rare tail-risk event.

Third, under the *asymmetric information paradigm*, at the level of the whole financial system, information on the solvency situation of financial intermediaries and their management is of value to depositors and investors but is kept out of the public domain. Informational asymmetry limits rationality to one of bounded rationality. Moreover, there are insufficient incentives and penalties on owners of financial firms and banks, and their boards of directors and supervisors are likely to raise moral hazard problems that result in nonperforming loans and bank failures. The financial system is an elite club that tends toward oligopoly in its structure as potential entrants are kept out because of information barriers, and there is a need to limit competition to have larger profits and to limit risk. Information is a public good; the regulatory agency should push for full disclosure, tame the excess creativity and profits, and limit the oligopolistic structure.

The bottom line is that the three paradigms lead to different policy prescriptions that are often inconsistent. No matter which paradigm the financial regulators appear to be operating in, the fundamental problems of tail-risks, free-riders, informational asymmetry, and Knightian uncertainty about unknown-unknowns remain to be addressed. Systemic risk can be minimized by limiting regulatory arbitrage but imposing the same regulations on all financial firms that take deposits or borrow in the marketplace. Intermediaries should not be regulated differently. Unregulated firms should be allowed only to borrow from regulated firms. A liquidity tax should be considered that penalizes short-term borrowing or lending, not one that penalizes the mismatches as is commonly proposed. The herding behavior has to be contained by countercyclical prudential norms that the central bank fine-tunes, depending on the circumstances in each country at that time.

In Conclusion

To summarize, we might ask what the macro-fiscal-monetary mix might look like going forward. Blanchard, Dell'Ariccia, and Mauro (2010) suggest that monetary policy should continue to target a low and stable inflation rate that will ensure a stable output gap. This should be accompanied by regulation tools that policy makers can use to respond to the composition of output, the behavior of asset prices, and the leverage of different agents. Monetary and regulation policy should be accompanied by the design of better automatic stabilizers for fiscal policy. There is renewed interest in Keynesianism among academics and policy makers, particularly in Keynes's views on multipliers.[4] The multiplier effects are important to assess the strength and speed of economic recovery in a country.

Notes

1. The same multiplier can also work in a virtuous cycle such as when the next great financial innovation occurs—for example, when life insurance policies, pension funds, or some other asset replaces mortgage-backed securities.
2. Blanchard, Dell'Ariccia, and Mauro cite "too high a level of housing investment, too high a level of consumption, or too large a current account deficit" (2010, 8).
3. The exceptions are Spain and Colombia, which introduced rules relating provisioning to credit growth (Blanchard, Dell'Ariccia, and Mauro 2010, 6).
4. The Keynesian multiplier is the effect of traditional macroeconomic policies, such as the increase in government spending that is multiplied by boosting private consumption by households and capital investment by firms as they receive income from the initial round of fiscal stimulus.

References

Akerlof, G. A., and R. J. Shiller. 2009. *Animal Spirits: How Human Psychology Drives the Economy and Why It Matters for Global Capitalism*. Princeton, NJ: Princeton University Press.

Blanchard, O., G. Dell'Ariccia, and P. Mauro. 2010. "Rethinking Macroeconomic Policy." Staff Position Note 10/03, International Monetary Fund, Washington, DC.

Calvo, G. A. 1998. "Capital Flows and Capital Market Crises: The Simple Economics of Sudden Stops." *Journal of Applied Economics* 1 (1): 35–54.

Kaminsky, G. L., C. Reinhart, and C. A. Vegh. 2003. "The Unholy Trinity of Financial Contagion." Working Paper 10061, National Bureau of Economic Research, Cambridge, MA.

Krugman, P. 2008. "The International Finance Multiplier." Unpublished manuscript. Princeton University, Princeton, NJ. http://www.princeton.edu/~pkrugman/finmult.pdf.

Minsky. H. P. 1982. *Can "It" Happen Again? Essays on Instability and Finance*. Armonk, NY: M. E. Sharpe.

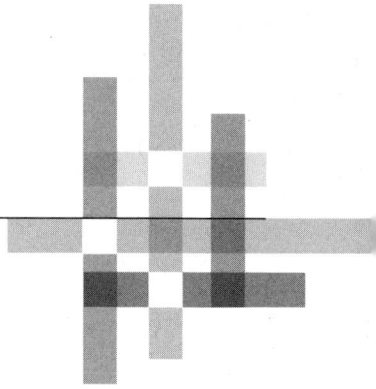

Fiscal Activism

Raj Nallari

The challenge of raising aggregate demand is now a global phenomenon. To get an understanding of the underlying processes, take the case of the United States. Here, the fall in the stock market and in owner-occupied real estate values led to more than a $10 trillion erosion of household wealth. This drop in value led to an estimated decrease in aggregate demand of about $600 billion annually, or about 3 percent of gross domestic product (GDP), because of falls in household spending and production (about $400 billion and $200 billion, respectively). Automatic stabilizers (such as a decrease in personal and corporate income taxes) cushioned the fall in aggregate demand by about a third, but still left a net GDP gap of about $400 billion annually. So the present challenge in the United States alone lies in establishing policies that could potentially raise aggregate demand by about $400 billion annually (Feldstein 2009, 557).

Given the extent of the downturn and the limits to monetary policy action,[1] fiscal policy is regarded as crucial in providing short- and medium-term support to the global economy. However, though a fiscal response across many countries may be needed, not all countries have sufficient fiscal space to implement it because expansionary fiscal actions may threaten the sustainability of fiscal measures. This section discusses the possible fiscal policy goals, options, and long-term outcomes.

Consumption declines following a crisis because of decreases in income or wealth and tighter credit and increased savings.[2] Therefore, there is a need for government interventions that will shore up aggregate demand. Not everyone is convinced about fiscal activism during a downturn. For example, Taylor (2009) and others point to the ineffectiveness of the $150 billion in the first stimulus package provided through tax rebates during the summer of 2008 under President George W. Bush. The stimulus did not prevent recession—which began in December 2007—from deepening during 2008 and beyond. These analysts also believe that government intervention could worsen and prolong the recession. Reinhart and Rogoff (2009), citing eight centuries of financial crises worldwide, worry about fiscal activism leading to the large deficits, debts, and defaults that invariably seem to have occurred following financial panics. They also point out that, on average, public debt of over 60 percent of GDP is likely to lead to a sovereign debt crisis (Reinhart and Rogoff 2011, 43). For example, in February 2010, the government of Greece was under pressure to default on its debt payments and needed the support of the European Union as a contingency measure.

Fiscal Policy Goals

Fiscal measures today are aimed at getting the financial system back to health, increasing aggregate demand, raising consumer confidence, and improving economic growth. As many as 40 countries have responded to the global crisis by announcing fiscal stimulus packages. The International Monetary Fund (Scott 2008) recommends that for the fiscal stimulus package to be effective, it should be all of the following:

1. *Timely*, because the need for action is urgent. But there is a trade-off between timeliness and quality of a fiscal program. For example, in a rush to implement a fiscal stimulus package, project cost-benefit analysis and procurement procedures may be ignored.

2. *Temporary*, so that fiscal sustainability is not jeopardized and unintended consequences of programs are avoided. In practice, politics makes it difficult for programs to be unwound once economic recovery takes hold because vested interests will fight for continued funding of programs.

3. *Targeted*, so the resources go to the areas and people who are affected most. This goal would require very good data for formulating programs

and for monitoring the impact of those programs. In developing countries, inadequate data constrain effective use of resources. For example, mismatches often occur when unemployment is high and public works programs are put in place that do not correctly target the source of unemployment.

4. *Large*, because the drop in demand is large. But large packages must be implemented carefully. Countries with limited fiscal space (such as India and several Eastern European countries) quickly run into issues of fiscal sustainability in the face of large fiscal deficits. Moreover, large fiscal packages could also lead to misallocation of resources within the government, thus encouraging corruption at all levels of government. The bulk of resources may end up protecting industries and jobs—not for efficiency reasons but for political reasons.

5. *Lasting*, in terms of the package's economic effects, because the recession will likely last for some time.

6. *Diversified*, because there is uncertainty regarding which measures will be most effective.

7. *Contingent*, because this will indicate that further action will be taken, if needed.

8. *Collective*, because all countries that have the fiscal space should use a fiscal stimulus package, given the severity and global nature of the downturn. This objective is aimed at avoiding a free-rider problem among major countries of the world.

9. *Sustainable*, to avoid debt explosion in the long run and adverse effects in the short run.

Protecting the poor and vulnerable relies on social protective measures, such as safety nets[3] and labor[4] programs.

Potential Long-Term Outcomes

Two of the most visible spin-offs of the gargantuan fiscal stimulus packages are (1) growing public debt that compromises intergenerational equity and economic performance and (2) fiscal sustainability. There is also the potential risk in a prolonged and deepening recession of antimarket and protectionist industrial policies.[5] Furthermore, a protracted and deep recession has adverse consequences for government revenues and the operation of automatic stabilizers. In a prolonged recession, the impact on the sustainability of public finances would be far more severe.

Policy makers have to balance the two opposing risks of high debt and fiscal sustainability. One is the risk of prolonged depression and stagnation if efforts to boost aggregate demand are not large enough. The other is the risk of a loss of confidence in government fiscal solvency and the larger long-term impacts of a rising debt burden. The trade-off between these two risks will depend on country-specific circumstances. Not all countries can afford big fiscal stimulus packages; and, in this respect, projected debt levels and indicators of fiscal vulnerability will be less relevant in making policy choices. However, in countries with more fiscal room, such trade-offs can exist and can be improved if governments credibly clarify their strategy to ensure fiscal solvency. The International Monetary Fund (IMF 2008) suggests that a fiscally sustainable and credible path could be achieved by following some key principles:

1. Fiscal stimulus packages should consist, as much as possible, of *temporary measures,* or measures that have clear sunset clauses contingent on the economic situation.

2. Governments should have a *precommiment* to unwinding stimulus measures either at a specific date (such as lowering value-added tax for just two years, as the United Kingdom recently did) or on a contingent basis (such as reversing the value-added tax cut once GDP growth has risen above a certain level).

3. The stimulus package should increase the scope of *automatic stabilizers* (such as unemployment benefits) which, by their nature, are countercyclical.

4. It should improve *procurement and expenditure procedures* to ensure that stepped-up public works spending is well directed to raise long-term growth potential.

5. Policies should be cast within *medium-term fiscal frameworks,* supported by fiscal responsibility laws, fiscal rules, or independent fiscal councils. They should cover a period of four to five years and should ideally include accurate and timely projections of government revenues and expenditures, a government balance sheet reporting data on government assets and liabilities, and a statement of contingent liabilities and other fiscal risks.

6. Policies should strengthen *fiscal governance* by increasing fiscal transparency to reduce the public's perception of possible political biases.

7. General *wage increases* in the public sector and general *price subsidies* should be avoided because such measures are distortionary.

In Conclusion

The global scale of the financial crisis makes international coordination and cooperation more important than ever to avoid measures that distort international competition or effectively shift the problem to other countries (that is, the free-rider problem in which some countries benefit at the expense of others).

Needless to say, the challenge for fiscal policy is to find a way to balance the competing goals of (1) stimulating economic recovery and growth and (2) protecting the poor and vulnerable. Fiscal stimulus will also involve several trade-offs—for example, going for large and lasting actions rather than fiscal sustainability. Figure 26.1 identifies the various fiscal options.

Figure 26.1   Balancing the Fiscal Options

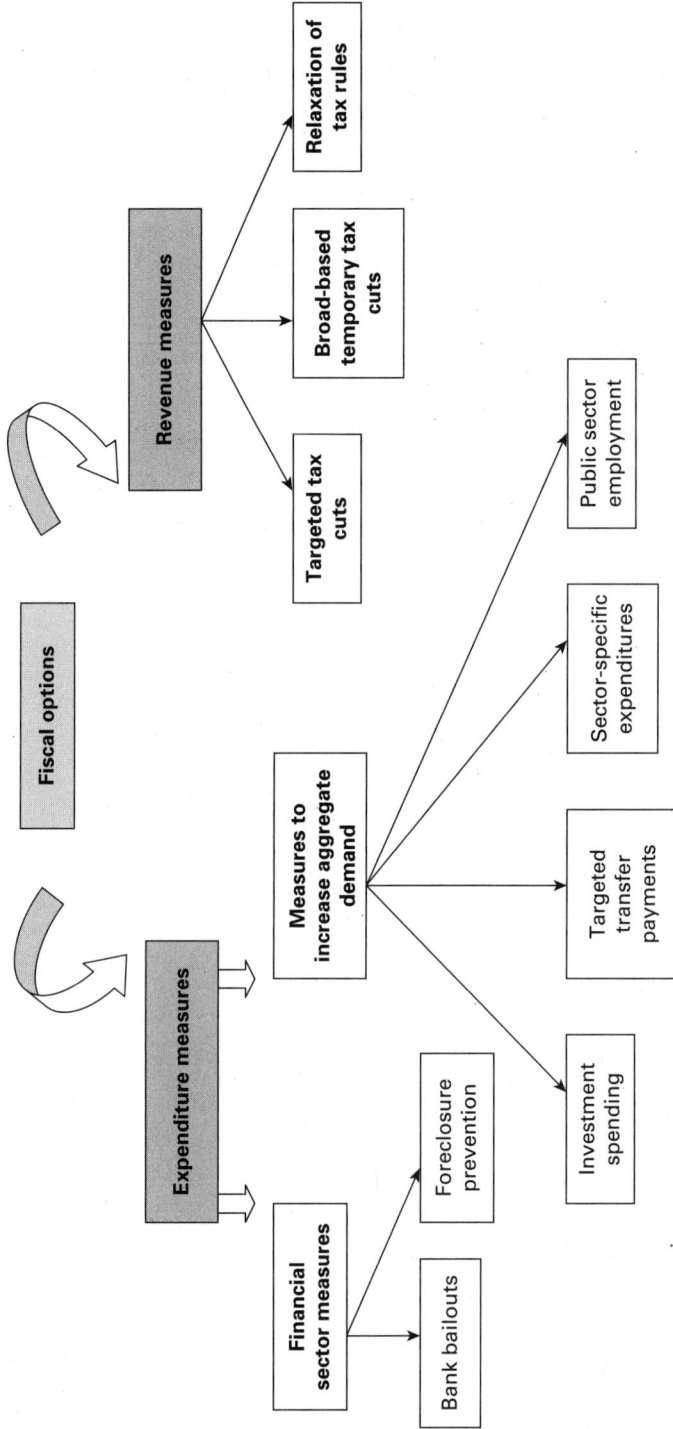

Source: Author's illustration.

Notes

1. Interest rates in many of these countries are already at historically low levels, leaving little leverage for further use of this instrument. Central banks in many developing economies have lowered rates cautiously to maintain incentives for capital inflows and external stability.
2. Between October 2008 and March 2009, savings by U.S. consumers increased from negative 3 percent of GDP to 5 percent of GDP.
3. Safety nets include unconditional or conditional cash transfers, food transfers and school food programs, public works, and waivers of fees for essential services.
4. Labor programs include industrial policies, expansion of unemployment benefits, and training programs with income stipends.
5. A slide toward trade and financial protectionism would have cross-border ramifications and be hugely damaging to the global economy, as learned from the experience of the beggar-thy-neighbor policies of the 1930s.

References

Feldstein, M. 2009. "Rethinking the Role of Fiscal Policy." *American Economic Review* 99 (2): 556–59.

Reinhart, C. M., and K. S. Rogoff. 2009. "The Aftermath of Financial Crises." Working Paper 14656, National Bureau of Economic Research, Cambridge, MA.

———. 2011. "A Decade of Debt." Working Paper 16827, National Bureau of Economic Research, Cambridge, MA.

Scott, A. 2008. "Making Fiscal Stimulus Effective During Downturns." *IMF Survey Magazine*. http://www.imf.org/external/pubs/ft/survey/so/2008/res100208b.htm.

Taylor, J. 2009. "The Financial Crisis and the Policy Responses. An empirical Analysis of What Went Wrong." Working Paper 14631, National Bureau of Economic Research, Cambridge, MA.

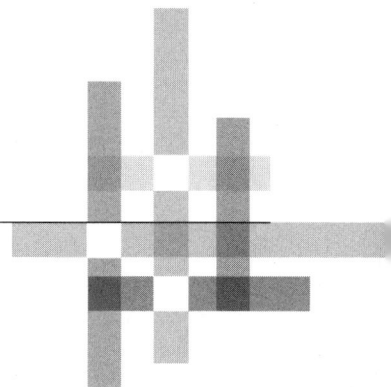

Fiscal Multipliers

Raj Nallari

Keynes is best known for suggesting fiscal stimulus policies and programs to increase aggregate demand to get out of a deep recession. Since the marginal propensity to consume is positive and less than one, the bigger it is, the larger the fiscal multipliers will be and the faster we will get out of a recession. Conventional Keynesian multipliers are meant for closed economies and do not consider the total debt position of a country. More generally, the fiscal multipliers of an expansionary fiscal policy will be bigger if the leaks are minimized through an accommodative monetary policy, and the fiscal position of the country is sustainable after the initial change in fiscal policy. Historically, multipliers on government spending are estimated to be in the range of 1.5 to 2.0, whereas tax-cut multipliers can be much smaller (between 0.5 and 1.0).

The recent global crisis highlighted the global interdependence and openness of economies. We expect that the various multipliers are likely to be much smaller because of leaks in the form of higher imports. Also, the various multipliers may work at cross-purposes, and the cumulative effect may be much smaller (as shown in Ilzetzki, Mendoza and Vegh 2009). The full effect of the fiscal policy multipliers in the first round is smaller in models that incorporate a sensitivity of private investment in the interest rate. Public investment might crowd out private investment when expansionary fiscal policy causes the interest rates to increase, making financing more expensive for private investors.

Fiscal policy is usually deployed with other policies; and many factors come into play at the same time, making it difficult to estimate the size of the multiplier. Moreover, the impact of fiscal policy can be felt over many years, by which time other policies and factors may have changed as well. There is a lengthy body of literature on the empirics of multipliers, particularly for advanced economies. Focusing on recent studies, one could summarize the following:

1. Government spending in recessions, rather than tax cuts, has to do the heavy lifting[1] because multipliers on government spending are historically higher than those for tax cuts. Taylor (2009) points out that the May 2008 tax rebates of $300–$600 per person by the Bush administration did not avert an economic recession in the fourth quarter of 2008. The small and insignificant effect of tax rebates in 2001 and 2008 conforms to the permanent income and life-cycle theories of consumption in which temporary increases in income are predicted to lead to small increases in consumption.

2. In contrast, Moody's economy.com model indicated that the multiplier for low-income and liquidity-constrained consumers is 1.73 for unemployment benefits, 1.64 for food stamps, and 1.36 when money is transferred to the states.

3. In Ilzetzki, Mendoza, and Vegh (2009), fiscal multipliers tend to be lower for advanced or high-income countries than for emerging or developing ones, are bigger for countries following fixed exchange rate regimes than for those adopting flexible regimes, and tend to be bigger for closed economies than for open economies.

4. When credit markets are impaired, tax cuts as well as income earned from government spending on goods and services will not be leveraged by the financial system to nearly the same extent, resulting in (much) smaller multipliers.

Although the structure of the economy and dynamics behind the multiplier is more complicated than the standard textbooks indicate, it is crucial to understand important factors (such as the role of housing and stock in households' wealth and in firms' balance sheets). Also, understanding credit frictions or lending rates is very important because those rates affect not only firms' investments but also the optimal monetary policy of any central bank.

**Table 27.1 Spending Multipliers of the United States and
Other Country Groups**

Country Group	Impact Multiplier
Group of Seven	0.40
High income	0.36
Emerging countries	0.60
Developing countries	0.70
Predetermined (fix)	1.06
Flexible regime	0.11
Open economy (more leaks)	0.73
Closed economy	0.43

Source: Ilzetzki, Mendoza, and Vegh 2009.

The estimates of Ilzetzki, Mendoza, and Vegh (2009) in table 27.1 explain the so-far-weak impact of the large U.S. fiscal stimulus package of over $757 billion during 2009, and they explain why the Bush administration's tax refunds of $150 billion in mid-2008 did not prevent a U.S. recession in the latter half of 2008.

In Conclusion

The world is a drastically changed place, owing to the global financial crisis. In fact, the various multipliers are likely to be much smaller because of leaks in the form of higher imports from the rest of the world. Also, the various multipliers may work at cross-purposes, and the cumulative effect may be much smaller. The full effect of the fiscal policy multipliers in the first round is smaller in models that incorporate a sensitivity of the private investment to the interest rate. Public investment might crowd out private investment in implementation of fiscal stimulus packages. The crowding-out is the result of an expansionary fiscal policy causing the interest rates to increase, thereby reducing private investment as financing becomes expensive.

Note

1. Feldstein (2009) estimates that the marginal propensity to consume out of disposable income is 0.70, whereas the marginal propensity to consume out of reduction in taxes and tax rebates is only 0.13.

References

Feldstein, M. 2009. "An $800 Billion Mistake." *Washington Post,* January 29.

Ilzetzki, E., E. G. Mendoza, and C. A. Vegh. 2009. "How Big Are Fiscal Multipliers?" Policy Insight No. 39, Center for Economic Policy Research, London.

Taylor, J. 2009. "The Lack of an Empirical Rationale for a Revival of Discretionary Fiscal Policy." *American Economic Review, Papers and Proceedings* 99 (2).

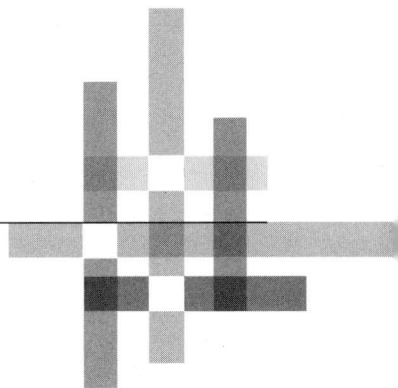

Preventing Future Credit Bubbles

Raj Nallari

Several institutions (such as the U.S. Federal Reserve Bank, the Bank of England, the Bank for International Settlements, and the International Monetary Fund) as well as private consulting firms (such as McKinsey) have presented their opinions on how credit bubbles can be prevented in the future. Here is what we know from their writings.

There is now a broad consensus that developed countries' monetary policies had focused almost exclusively on inflation targeting (or, in the United States, on a very narrow definition of price stability) and they neglected the speculative bubbles that were jeopardizing financial stability. The correct policy response during 2002–08 should have been higher policy interest rates and containment of the credit-driven asset booms. But the identification of bubbles and credit booms is fraught with problems. Should credit growth of 1.5 times the nominal GDP be considered a credit boom?

How Monetary Policies Should (or Should Not) Respond to a Boom

The consensus before the 2008 crisis was that monetary policy should focus on keeping inflation low (because low inflation is conducive to growth).

Asset prices should be monitored for information related to the economic situation but never targeted by central banks. For example, most emerging market economies experienced a boom in stock prices, but seldom did their central banks attempt to contain the "irrational exuberance." This narrow focus of monetary policy is based on the view that it is difficult to differentiate between a speculative boom and episodes of rational decisions by individuals. Moreover, monetary policy may be a blunt instrument to stop a boom, and it may end up doing more harm to the whole economy while trying to contain a boom. For example, during booms, the expected returns on assets may be so high that small changes in the policy interest rate may have little or no effect on investors' decisions. However, higher interest rates can lower demand for and supply of bank loans and could have mitigated the U.S. and European housing booms. Similarly, raising reserve requirements can sometimes be effective in limiting credit growth in domestic currency. As will be discussed, flexible prudential regulations and tightened supervision may be better tools in managing a boom.

How Growth in Credit and Financial Leverage Should Be Monitored for Systemic Risk

The ratio of credit to GDP and its growth is a useful warning bell for boom conditions and leverage. Other leverage indicators could be data on borrowers and analysis of firms' balance sheets for exposures. Details of capital accounts in balance of payments could provide useful information about unsustainable leverage positions and could provide an early warning about so-called good and bad booms. In addition, housing and real estate price booms typically involve a high degree of borrower leverage. Depending on individual country circumstances, central banks should develop a range of firm-specific measures to assess systemwide risks, including leverage and foreign exposures.

What Policy Makers Should Do in the Future

The 2008–09 financial crisis was due, in part, to unusually high overleveraging (ratios of 40 to 1) by financial firms in the United States and Europe. Credit flows to real estate were way too high, compared with credit flows to small and medium-size enterprises in those countries, partly because of tax incentives (low interest rates and tax deductions for mortgage interest) and the politicization of housing (the so-called American dream to own a house). The ongoing global crisis necessitates deleveraging—at least for the next two to three years—rising deficits, debt, and default; and reregulation. At the same time, the danger of premature withdrawal of fiscal stimulus and of monetary easing may send the economies into another tailspin. To minimize credit bubbles in the future, policy makers should take the following steps:

- Develop an international system to monitor leveraging by banks and financial institutions (particularly the large ones), including leveraging among the various sectors in different geographic areas. Developing such a "heat map" is necessary because central banks are usually unable to identify credit bubbles but can monitor leverage ratios at micro- and macrolevels.

- Encourage banks to develop risk models that include leverage ratios and internal risk-adjusted weights in each of the real sectors. Can private sector risk managers do it by themselves? Not really. The private sector has invested heavily in risk management tools and progressed quite a bit in its use of quantitative and qualitative tools; but private sector risk managers would need the help of global institutions, which have an advantage in comparing and contrasting across countries, sectors, and firms. Stress testing by the private sector has failed. The behavior of financial firms and their counterparts has been disappointing during this crisis because the best risk management would have been for the credit agencies to insist that mortgage originators have a stake in the debt instruments at all times.

- Regulate pockets of leverage (for example, trade brokers in certain institutions), by ensuring more capital for such highly leveraged firms, by increasing margin requirements, or by imposing restrictions such as loan-to-value ratios for housing loans. Capital requirements are necessary but not sufficient.

- Phase out the distortions arising from bias in terms of directed credit and tax exemptions for real estate.

In Conclusion

Booms and busts have been the norm for quite some time. They will continue to be the norm in the near future. The answer is not to move to the repressed markets of the past. We have been there and done that!

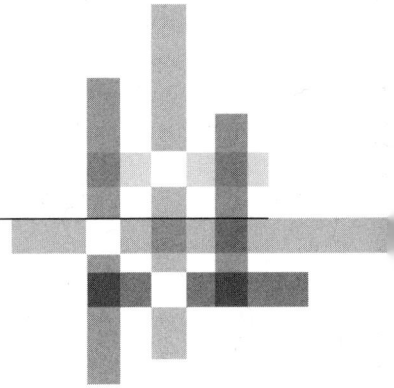

Revisiting Exchange Rate Regimes

Raj Nallari

Countries with fixed exchange rate regimes are highly vulnerable to sudden movements in capital flows. In the early 1990s, as transition economies joined the world economy, they pegged to the deutsche mark, while the East Asian countries pegged to the U.S. dollar. The Mexican crisis of 1995, the East Asian crisis of 1997–98, the Russian Federation ruble crisis of 1998, and the collapse of long-term capital management in 1998 revealed that the capital account crisis in these countries was the result of a sudden stop or reversal in capital inflows. By 1999, two views of exchange rate regimes were evident. First, in countries where credibility of the fixed exchange rate regime was low (for example, Argentina), a monetary union was thought to better exhibit commitment and discipline. At the other extreme, some Asian countries where the macroeconomic fundamentals were strong both before and after the 1997–98 crisis were advised to move to a freely floating exchange rate regime as their economies became more and more integrated into a global economy.

In practice, countries preferred intermediate exchange rate regimes, where the exchange rate was relatively rigid but not pegged to a single currency. Calvo and Reinhart (2000) show that emerging economies are in fear of floating and de facto maintain a managed float. The fear arises because, when the value of their local currency declines significantly, governments worry about the imported inflation and balance sheet effects of foreign currency borrowing (by both the private and the public sectors) as the costs of debt servicing go up. However, when the value of local currency rises, there is a loss of competitiveness, which lowers growth.

Central banks are now cognizant that a fixed exchange rate regime brings benefits in terms of low inflation and lower nominal and real exchange rate volatility. However, such regimes are more prone to overvaluation (because currency depreciation is politically sensitive, it can take months for government to announce a new depreciated rate), and this overvaluation erodes competitiveness and likely lowers growth. In contrast, full floating regimes, though avoiding overvaluation, do not yield lower inflation or reduce exchange rate volatility. Growth performance is shown to be best under intermediate exchange rate regimes because such regimes avoid too much overvaluation.

Eastern European countries that had an intermediate arrangement with the euro enjoyed strong growth in the years leading up to the global crisis of 2008, but they did build up large external imbalances, which made them vulnerable to the crisis. Moreover, they did not have fiscal room to implement countercyclical macroeconomic policies.

Global Financial Crisis

What has happened since the global crisis of 2008? At the time of the crisis, most large developing countries had established more flexible exchange rate regimes. Local currencies depreciated sharply during the period from August to October of 2008; but, on average, the depreciation was in the range of 8–10 percent. But the currencies of Brazil, Chile, Colombia, Hungary, Mexico, Poland, South Africa, and Turkey experienced much larger depreciation in the initial months of the crisis. Some central banks intervened heavily to slow down this depreciation—and lost large reserves in doing so. The apparent immediate response by developing countries during those three months was to target policy more to address domestic conditions than to defend exchange rate levels. Since the early months of the crisis, expansionary fiscal policies and monetary easing in more than 40 countries have been put in place to avert a serious economic downturn. These measures will put additional pressure on specific currencies to depreciate against the U.S. dollar and other major currencies.

In Conclusion

For almost a decade, international economic observers have advised governments that the world needs a major adjustment. Sustained global growth requires that the United States cut back on its domestic demand and let the dollar depreciate to increase net exports, which will enable the United States to improve its current account balances. Conversely, China and other Asian countries should stimulate domestic demand and let their exchange rates appreciate. These steps would rebalance aggregate demand from the United States and toward China, which would help sustain a global recovery. If this rebalancing does not happen quickly, global growth may be flat.

With the United States at the epicenter of the financial crisis, fast-growing developing countries such as Brazil, Russia, India, and China (the so-called BRIC countries) and oil–producing countries with large foreign exchange reserves primarily in U.S. dollars began to worry about the efficacy of the dollar as the main reserve currency. Although the euro is a major challenger to the U.S. dollar as the world's currency, it is still widely used only in Euro Area countries. The yen is even more limited in its use around the world. Therefore, the euro and yen may find it hard to dislodge the dollar as the reserve currency, and the yuan is hampered by China's closed capital account. The rising U.S. public debt is reaching unsustainable levels, however, and that puts a lot of pressure on the U.S. dollar as the world's currency. The worst-case scenario will come to fruition if surplus countries such as China, Japan, and the Republic of Korea move away from dollar-denominated treasuries in favor of the accumulation of gold or alternative currencies. For example, some of the BRIC countries met in Russia in early 2009 to think about pressuring the International Monetary Fund to make special drawing rights a reserve currency.

Reference

Calvo, G. A., and C. M. Reinhart. 2000. "Fear of Floating." Working Paper 7993, National Bureau of Economic Research, Cambridge, MA.

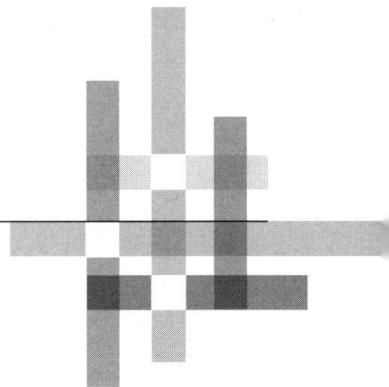

Reexamining Trade Policy

Raj Nallari

Trade theory rejoices in partial equilibrium analysis. Over the past few decades, a large number of emerging markets (for example, Japan in the 1970s, the Republic of Korea and other Asian Tigers during the 1980s, and China since the 1990s) aimed to maximize their exports while restricting imports because foreign exchange is more expensive to them ("heads I win, tails you lose" trade policy while professing allegiance to an "export-led growth model"). Trade theory seldom incorporates power relationships between countries through examining trade as a form of foreign policy, for example; or deals with the oligopolistic nature of the globalized world (for example, much of trade is in the hands of large multinational companies, which also wield power directly or indirectly through their host governments). For example, oil is one of the major traded goods in the world; but trade specialists and organizations pretend that there is no "cartel pricing," and oil's export price is as freely set as the price of Mali's cotton exports. Yet it was always thus. Trade policy has always been an instrument of foreign policy. Seldom do trade specialists explain how in the name of trade East India (Trading) Company was able to colonize an entire subcontinent of India or how six Dutch East Indies trading companies politically dominated Indonesia and its islands.

The current consensus is that free trade is good and losers should be compensated. Lawrence Summers, in reference to China at the recent Davos Forum, stated that free trade is not possible when one of the trading countries is following "mercantilist policies." Other commentators—Samuelson (2004), Gomory and Baumol (2000), Ronald Reagan's supply-sider economist Paul Craig Roberts, Blinder (2009), and Palley (2006)—have expressed concerns about U.S. losses in recent trade relations resulting from China's productivity increases. Losses have been especially visible in goods and services where the United States historically has had a comparative advantage. China and other emerging economies are adding to global production and supply and driving down world export prices. This means that prices received by U.S. exporters are constantly being lowered (that is, worsening U.S. terms of trade and reducing U.S. gains from trade).

Rapid globalization forces firms to be at the technological frontier all the time. Trade policies are about unit costs: either reducing a home firm's unit costs or increasing unit costs of foreign firms at the same time. In the earlier version of trade theory, a country's comparative advantage was dependent on its climate, natural resource endowments, and the technology used in converting raw materials into exportables. Krugman (1984) introduced strategic trade policies based on increasing returns to scale and imperfect competition that could help countries scale up and gain a comparative advantage and ensure higher gains from trade.

More recently, improvements in human capital, the business environment, trade facilitation, technology and productivity, and outsourcing have been used to reduce unit costs for the home firm. Industrial policies in the form of input subsidies, export promotion programs, and government-sponsored research and development are an effort to reduce the unit costs of production and exports. Increasing foreign firms' unit costs and, therefore, their export price is done through domestic tariffs, quotas, and quantitative restrictions. Adding also to the export prices are costs emanating from antidumping duties, labor, hygiene and environmental standards, carbon-footprint labeling, and other nontariff barriers.

Unit costs of production at the firm or industry level can be decreased through adoption of new technologies, through increasing returns to scale, and through internal or external economies of scale (agglomeration effects). National health care policies are but one example of reducing unit costs of production to companies. Another example is when firms move to low-cost countries. These positive effects can bring about a comparative advantage and global leadership in certain goods and services, resulting in a redistribution of gains from trade.

In the context of globalization, there is an issue of alignment of national interests with interests of large corporations. For example, outsourcing by American companies will transfer technology and comparative advantage to trading partners while expanding markets and securing foreign profits for American firms. However, U.S national interest may be hurt by technology transfer to the trading countries—especially if it is "frontier" technology. For instance, while China using American know-how expands on its exports to the United States, the United States can regain its technological leadership by encouraging immigration of foreign scientists and skilled workers to accelerate its own comparative advantage. In this way, global corporations rapidly transfer new innovations and processes to all economies that are open to trade.

Trade theory has to be integrated within a macroeconomic framework. Undervaluation of exchange rates gives a country comparative or perhaps even absolute advantage relative to the other trading partners. This is especially true of products that rely on abundant, cheap labor. Such a country can expand its market share in these products, destroying foreign firms. It is beggar-thy-neighbor policies and increasing returns to scale that enable a labor-surplus economy to first gain in trade share and then lock in its comparative advantage, at least for the short to medium term. As China accelerates its export growth, its domestic income increases; but government policies (for example, inadequate social protection and health care means that the Chinese must maintain precautionary savings) keep consumption low and foreign exchange restraints restrict imports. Thus, China's trade policy is an active instrument of its foreign policy.

Several countries that are embarking on production-sharing, export diversification and upgrading their production base have a large pool of cheap and skilled labor (such as China, India, and several emerging countries) with capabilities from production to marketing. Trade is handled increasingly by large, multinational corporations, and that makes it difficult for smaller firms in a particular sector engaging directly in international trade.

In Conclusion

The recent global crisis has revealed that production and trade is now handled by extensive global supply chains, where components (particularly durable goods) are made and traded a number of times before the final good is assembled and produced. For example, 30.9 percent of total trade in fiscal 2006/07 in developing East Asia was trade in components and parts (up from 13.8 percent in fiscal 1992/93) (Athukorala 2010, 38). Moreover, these global chains need trade finance for longer periods of time before they can be repaid for their value added. The credit crunch has affected trade finance, so trade volumes in almost all the countries have declined sharply during the global downturn. Trade models need to capture these dynamics.

References

Athukorala, P. C. 2010. "Production Networks and Trade Patterns in East Asia: Regionalization or Globalization." Working Paper Series on Regional Economic Integration No. 56, Asian Development Bank, Manila, Philippines.

Blinder, A. S. 2009. "How Many U.S. Jobs Might Be Offshorable?" *World Economics* 10 (2): 41–78.

Gomory, R. E., and W. J. Baumol. 2000. *Global Trade and Conflicting National Interest.* Cambridge, MA: MIT Press.

Krugman, P. 1984. "Import Protection as Export Promotion: International Competition in the Presence of Oligopoly and Economies of Scale." In *Monopolistic Competition in International Trade,* ed. H. Kierzkowski, 180–93. Oxford, U.K.: Oxford University Press.

Palley, T. 2006. "Rethinking Trade and Trade Policy." Public Policy Brief No.86, Levy Institute, Bard College, Annandale-on-Hudson, NY.

Samuelson, P. 2004. "Where Ricardo and Mill Rebut and Confirm Arguments of Mainstream Economists Supporting Globalization." *Journal of Economic Perspectives* 18 (Summer): 135–46.

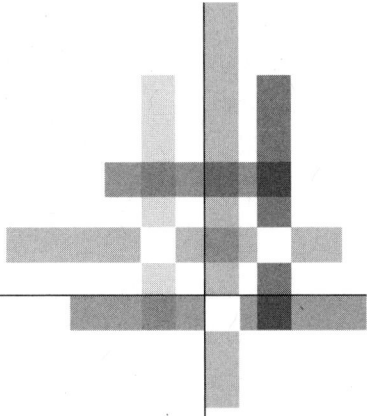

Part IV

HUMAN DEVELOPMENT POLICIES

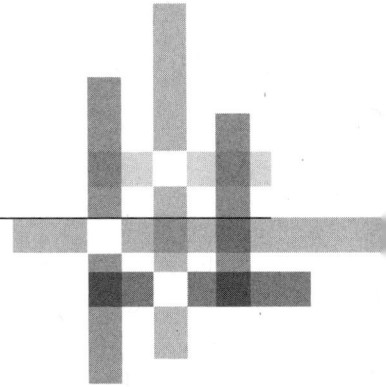

Overview

Raj Nallari

Human development policies are about expanding an individual's choice-set to live a long and healthy life. They embrace issues such as early childhood development, education, and employment. Additional aspects such as political freedom, guaranteed human rights and self-respect also form part of human development policies. In the past, human development policies took a back seat in developing economies as macroeconomic stabilization policies and a focus on gross national product held sway. The United Nations launched the *Human Development Report* 1990 with the aim of putting people back at the center of development. More recently, the Millennium Development Goals brought the pursuit of human development policies to the fore.

Research in the areas of early childhood development, education, health, and the labor market highlights the importance of human development and its link to economic growth and poverty reduction.

In early childhood development, issues such as nutrition, maternal health, and education have a strong bearing on the individual's potential development.

Education is correlated with economic growth, and the relationship works both ways. For many of the world's poor, education remains out of reach. Research indicates that investment in primary education is critical for growth and development. Completion of five to six years of schooling is sufficient to maintain lifelong literacy and numeracy skills. Significant progress has been made in providing education for all. The focus is beginning to shift toward achieving greater quality in education. Here the focus has been on test scores. While there is debate about this measure, higher test scores in mathematics and science are indicative of higher-order skills that, in turn, are positively associated with national income.

A healthy population contributes positively to economic development. Health policy in developing economies is particularly difficult to achieve and implement. This is primarily a result of the lack of information on issues relating to the health sector. There is a paucity of information with regard to best practice in advanced economies, information about drug trials, and what works and what does not work in health policy. There are many different markets in the health sector, all subject to market successes and market failures. In sum, a sustainable health policy requires a combination of regulation and competition with financing from the public and private sectors and institutions that facilitate this.

The labor market is always changing, and examining some of the trends with regard to participation, unemployment and underemployment, gender disparity, and the working poor is instructive. Globalization has helped shape these trends, and we examine its effects in this part of the report.

Academic research on the labor market is well subscribed, with broad agreement on the factors that impact employment. The World Bank has identified five such factors and developed a framework for the analysis of these factors. The five factors are macroeconomic performance, investment climate, labor market policies and institutions, education, and skills and social protection for workers (the MILES framework). Together, the macroeconomic performance of an economy and its investment climate coupled with labor market policies approximate the demand side of the labor market; policies, education, and social protection summarize the supply side.

Focusing on labor market policies and institutions, the material in the following sections identifies and examines the effect of various active labor market policies that aim to increase employment and wages or reduce unemployment. We also look at labor market institutions and the issue of deregulation in the labor market.

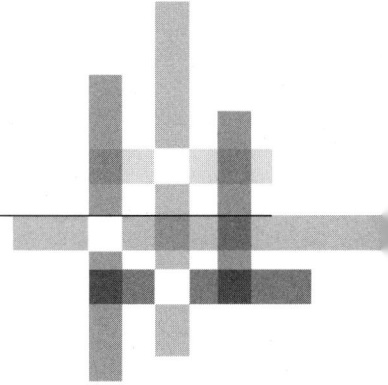

Early Childhood Development: The First Thousand Days Are Most Important

Raj Nallari

The World Bank estimates that more than 1.4 billion people in the world live below the poverty line of $1.25 per day (Chen and Ravallion 2008, 22). What happens to children born in poverty as we follow them from womb to tomb over their entire life cycle? We now have several countries with detailed information in the form of living standards measurements and other surveys. There is a lot of country-by-country variation, but the trends are unmistakable.

We know from Subramanian and Deaton (1996, 134), the poorest people—the ones in the bottom decile of per capita expenditure—consume, on average, slightly less than 1,400 calories a day, which is almost half of that recommended by poverty specialists. Women—particularly pregnant women—still suffer from undernourishment, iodine and other deficiencies, and lack of prenatal care (despite the advances made in maternal mortality and prenatal care in recent years).

Children of the poorest are disadvantaged from conception. Medical research has shown that nutrition, cognitive stimulation, and nurturing care before birth through age 6 strongly influence a child's achieving his or her full potential (Young 2002). For example, rapid brain development occurs during the first few years of life, and early childhood experiences have life-long effects. The number of brain cells and the interconnectedness among them is determined quite early. Because failure to grow and thrive occurs almost exclusively during the intrauterine period and in the first two years of life, prevention of stunting or anemia is needed. This means that to avoid poverty and to improve the standard of living of all people, policies and programs have to be developed to deal with equitable access to and quality of prenatal care and early childhood development.

The harmful effects of deficient early childhood development outcomes can be long lasting, impacting academic achievement, educational attainment, social integration, and welfare participation (Vegas and Santibáñez 2010).

The poor spend very little on education. The expenditure on education generally hovers around 2 percent of household budgets (Banerjee and Duflo 2007, 150). The reason spending is low is that children in poor households typically attend public schools or other schools that do not charge a fee (Banerjee and Mullainathan 2008). The mother's education level also determines whether her offspring attend school. Three- and 4-year-old children of mothers with no education are 10 times less likely to attend preschool programs in Burundi, Niger, and several African countries; and 4 times less likely in India, the Dominican Republic, and Zambia (Nonoyama-Tarumi, Loaiza, and Engle 2009, 390).

Test scores of a 3-year-old child in the poorest decile in Ecuador in 2003–04 approximated those of a 3-year-old in the fourth decile in the same country (Paxson and Schady 2005, 16). The standardized test scores are around 90 for each child (p. 13). But within the next two years, the test scores tend to deviate, with the scores of the relatively richer child increasing and those of the poorest child falling sharply at the fourth and fifth year. At the end, a 5-year-old child from the poorest decile has a 40 percent lower test score compared with the relatively richer 5-year-old child (p. 19). We know that the higher the test score at an early age, the higher is the earning advantage for an individual. Richer kids are likely to go to better schools, and that exacerbates the gap in test scores even further.

Standardized tests show a huge disparity between children from developed countries and those from developing countries. A difference of 1 standard deviation in test score performance was related to 1 percentage point difference in gross domestic product per capita growth per year (Basic Education Coalition n.d., 2).

When the poor come under economic stress, their form of "insurance" is often eating less or taking their children out of school. For example, Jacoby and Skoufias (1997) find that poor children leave school in bad years. Rose (1999) finds that the gap in mortality of girls relative to boys is much larger in drought years (but only for the landless households who are not able to sell land or borrow to weather the crisis). They also are less likely to get medical treatment for themselves or their children.

In Conclusion

Issues of nutrition, maternal health, and education impact early childhood development as well as income and poverty. In turn, early childhood development affects health, education, employment prospects, and overall growth and development.

References

Banerjee, A., and E. Duflo. 2007. "The Economic Lives of the Poor." *Journal of Economic Perspectives* 21 (1): 141–67.

Banerjee, A., and S. Mullainathan. 2008. "Attention and Income Distribution." *American Economic Review* 98 (2): 489–93.

Basic Education Coalition. n.d. "Building Economic Growth through Basic Education." Washington, DC. http://www.basiced.org/wp-content/uploads/Factsheets/Economic_Growth.pdf.

Chen, S., and M. Ravallion. 2008. "The Developing World Is Poorer Than We Thought, But No Less Successful in the Fight against Poverty." Policy Research Working Paper 4703, World Bank, Washington, DC.

Jacoby, H., and E. Skoufias. 1997. "Risk, Financial Markets, and Human Capital in a Developing Country." *Review of Economic Studies* 64 (3): 311–35.

Nonoyama-Tarumi, Y., E. Loaiza, and P. Engle. 2009. "Inequalities in Attendance in Organized Early Learning Programmes in Developing Societies: Findings from Households Surveys." *Compare* 39 (3): 385–409.

Paxson, C., and N. Schady. 2005. "Cognitive Development among Young Children in Ecuador: The Roles of Wealth, Health, and Parenting." Policy Research Working Paper 3605, World Bank, Washington, DC.

Rose, E. 1999. "Consumption Smoothing and Excess Female Mortality in Rural India." *Review of Economics and Statistics* 81: 41–49.

Subramanian, A., and A. Deaton. 1996. "The Demand for Food and Calories." *Journal of Political Economy* 104 (1): 133–62.

Vegas, E., and L. Santibáñez. 2010. *The Promise of Early Childhood in Latin America and the Caribbean*. Washington, DC: World Bank.

Young, M.E., ed. 2002. *From Early Child Development to Human Development: Investing in Our Children's Future*. Washington, DC: World Bank.

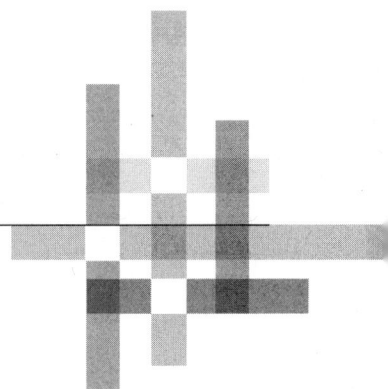

Education Access and Quality: What We Know and Don't Know

Raj Nallari

Educational attainment is correlated with economic growth, but cause and effect are more difficult to isolate. For example, richer countries invest a higher proportion of their income in education, and countries with higher education levels are likely to grow faster than those without. Furthermore, higher educational attainment may hide a high incidence of repeat students, disparities in family income, gender issues, and geographic location. Nevertheless, the World Bank's *Growth Report* (the Spence Report) found that investments in human capital (economist's term for workers' education and skills) was one of the main contributors to sustained growth over a 25-year period for a group of seven developing countries (Commission on Growth and Development 2008). Education levels correlate with a country's savings rate, health indicators, technological adaptation, innovation, and increased productivity. All of these factors are instruments of economic growth. For many of the world's poor people, however, educational attainment remains out of reach.

A number of global efforts have taken up the challenge of achieving education for all. In 1990, Education For All (EFA) was launched, committing the global economy to provide education for all of its citizens by 2015. The most recent initiative is, of course, the Millennium Development Goals (MDGs). MDG 2 calls for the achievement of universal primary school completion,[1] and significant progress has been made on that front. To date, primary school completion reaches 86 percent across developing countries as a whole, with rates of 93 percent for middle-income countries and 65 percent for low-income countries. Furthermore, significant progress has been made in relation to MDG 3, gender parity in primary and secondary education. Almost two thirds of developing countries have reached gender parity in primary education, with progress on track for 2015 for gender parity in secondary education (Go, Harmsen, and Timmer 2010, 8). The impetus to improve enrollment and completion rates in education extends beyond economics. Education affects child and reproductive health and enhances human skill and capital; it is critical to the success of the other MDGs (Nallari and Griffith 2011). It underlies all of the other MDGs—poverty reduction, gender equity, child and maternal health, lower rates of HIV/AIDS and other communicable diseases, and environmental stability.

The focus on completion rates stems from the research findings that there is a weak correlation between enrollment rates and completion rates in developing economies. There are a number of reasons that we might expect this to be the case. First, family circumstances may play a role in keeping children out of school or failing to complete school. Illness, lack of resources, or being required to work on the land can all prevent children from attending school. Second, children and, particularly, females from rural areas are less likely to attend school; rural boys are also at a disadvantage. Third, gender differences have traditionally favored boys attending and completing school. As noted, MDG 3 seeks to redress this, and progress has been achieved. The reasons for achieving gender equality in education and increasing the participation of females are compelling. Women who are educated are more likely to send their children to school and keep them there, child mortality is lessened, fertility rates are lower, female participation and productivity in the workplace is increased, and per capita income is increased.

Investment in primary education is critical for economic development and growth. Completion of five to six years of primary school is imperative for sustaining lifelong literacy and basic numeracy skills. This period is roughly equivalent to the primary-school cycle in most countries. From the 1980s, the World Bank has advised that countries invest in primary education. More recently, research (Hanushek 2005; World Bank 2007) has indicated that the rates of return on investing in education do not fall over time (that is, there are no diminishing returns); rather, they increase as each additional year of education achieved from primary to tertiary education results in higher individual incomes. For example, earnings of college-educated people everywhere in the world have been rising relatively faster than those who are less educated. This partially explains why there is a shortage in college-educated teachers because teaching pay scales are lower than in other private and public sector jobs. So the policy implication is that the salaries of teachers should be equal to or higher than those of nonteachers in any given country.

Having achieved "quantity" in education, governments are now turning to issues of quality. Educational quality, as measured by what people know, positively affects individual earning levels as well as economic growth. This relationship holds for both developed and developing economies, although the data are much richer for the former. Hanushek and Kimko (2000), in their cross-country study, find that differences in school test scores in mathematics and sciences across developing countries are strongly linked to economic growth. For example, East Asian countries during 1960–90 scored consistently higher in test scores. That could be why they grew more rapidly. Difference in test scores of 1 standard deviation was associated with a 1 percent difference in growth rate of per capita GDP annually (Basic Education Coalition n.d., 2). The focus has therefore shifted toward quality of education, but there may be an issue of reverse causality—countries that are growing rapidly have more resources to improve schooling and thus test scores. Better performance could be the result of GDP growth—not the other way around. But there is no doubt that better proficiency in mathematics and sciences is conducive for skills development; and this, in turn, contributes to higher income growth.

How then to improve test scores among students? Most educational interventions are considered successful if they increase test scores, which implies higher cognitive ability. Higher test scores in school imply gains in higher earnings later on, and this is one reason for emphasis on measuring test scores. However, random evaluations conducted across countries show that too much importance on test scores may be counterproductive as well because it could suppress the students' creativity and ability for critical thinking. So noncognitive outcomes could also be important. A new paper by Krishnan and Krutikova (2010) measures psychosocial skills, such as self-esteem and efficacy among poor households in Mumbai, India, and finds that such skills directly correlated with wages and that these skills can be improved through appropriate program interventions. While cognitive outcomes are eroded quickly over time, noncognitive improvements persist and become more salient over time.

Community control of public schools is one solution to improving access and quality of public education, and parent-teacher associations are another way to monitor quality. However, in rural areas, parents are less educated and may be unable to monitor teacher performance or standard test scores. Conditional cash transfers for going to school and for test-based scores while in school are another way to improve access to and quality of education. A voucher system that gives the parents the school choice may be another method.

In Conclusion

Education is one of the key aspects of human development. Participation in education has repercussions for an individual's growth and well-being as well as for the overall economy. Five to six years of schooling have lifelong impacts for literacy and numeracy. The simultaneous relationship between education and income is difficult to extrapolate, and we now know that quantity and quality of education matter.

Note

1. There is a weak correlation between enrollment and completion rates in education in developing economies.

References

Basic Education Coalition. n.d. "Building Economic Growth through Basic Education." Washington, DC. http://www.basiced.org/wp-content/uploads/Factsheets/Economic_Growth.pdf.

Commission on Growth and Development. 2008. *The Growth Report. Strategies for Sustained Growth and Inclusive Development*. Washington, DC: World Bank.

Go, D. S., R. Harmsen, and H. Timmer. 2010. "Regaining Momentum: Progress on the Millennium Development Goals Has Been Slowed by the Crisis. The Rest of the World Has to Help." *Finance and Development* 47 (3): 6–10.

Hanushek, E. A. 2005. "Why Quality Matters in Education." *Finance and Development* 42 (2): 15–19.

Hanushek, E. A., and D. D. Kimko. 2000. "Schooling, Labor Force Quality, and the Growth of Nations." *American Economic Review* 90 (5): 1184–208.

Krishnan, P., and S. Krutikova. 2010. *Skill Formation in Bombay's Slums*. Cambridge Working Papers in Economics No. 1010, Cambridge, UK.

Nallari, R., and B. Griffith. 2011. *Understanding Growth and Poverty: Theory, Policy, and Empirics*. Washington, DC: World Bank.

World Bank. 2007. *Education Quality and Economic Growth*. Washington, DC: World Bank.

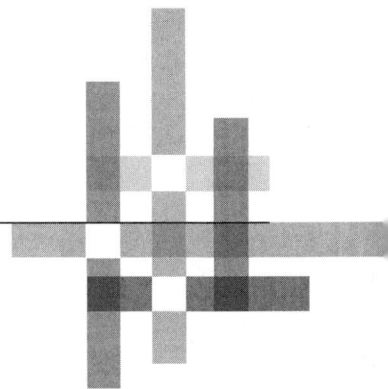

Health Care Policy

Raj Nallari

A healthy population contributes much to human development and, therefore, to economic prosperity. Poor health—whether it is obesity or aging populations in advanced economies or the rapid spread of HIV/ AIDS or other communicable diseases—adult illness and malnutrition in poorer countries reduce GDP per capita. The growth in GDP per capita is restricted and reduced by a lower ratio of workers to dependents. Poor health restricts or reduces labor productivity, investment in physical and human capital, access to natural resources and the global economy, and schooling and cognitive capacity. Treatment commandeers resources from households, private employers, and governments. Competitiveness and income are reduced at the individual and country levels.

Formulating sound health policy in developing economies is made difficult by the lack of information on issues relating to the health sector. Hsiao and Heller (2007) suggest the creation of an agency to disseminate knowledge.[1] Policy for health does not follow a free-market strategy. The health sector has many different markets, all of which are susceptible to failure. Health policy requires a combination of regulation and competition, financing from the public and private sectors, and an institutional framework that facilitates all of this. Policy for health care should consider the following points:

- Health care is not like any other good or service. Serious illness can cost many families their livelihoods in developing countries. International law guarantees the basic human right to receive health care.

- There are serious market failures. An asymmetry of information exists between the health care professionals, the insurance companies, and the individual patient. Adverse selection means that those who cannot afford health care and who are in most need of it are dropped from coverage and service provision, while the affluent have better access. This, in turn, leads to moral hazard as those who have insurance tend to overuse medical services while those who cannot afford insurance or are denied insurance because of preexisting conditions tend to underuse the medical system. In addition, competition is limited among medical practitioners as a sick and dying patient will not be shopping around for best price and quality of service. Moreover, patent laws in most advanced countries provide for patent protection and monopolistic pricing. The big insurance companies usually collude among themselves and with big pharmaceutical firms to create a health care industry with unusually high profits.

- Different countries at different stages of development are faced with different health problems. But all nations are faced with rising per capita health costs.

- Advanced economies are faced with aging populations and low fertility rates, which translate to a high-dependency ratio. In addition, obesity and chronic diseases are on the increase. The result is that costs are ever rising because keeping people alive is requiring newer and more expensive technologies and investment in pharmaceuticals. The fiscal burden shows up as a rising proportion of resources being allocated for health care in households' and firms' balance sheets and in government budgets.

- Middle-income countries such as China also face aging populations with low fertility rates, in addition to a double disease burden. As Hsiao and Heller (2007) point out, " as a nation's economy develops and matures, it has more knowledge and resources to address problems of clean water, sanitation, malnutrition, communicable diseases, and basic health care. As infectious diseases and infant and maternal mortality decrease in a nation, middle- and higher-income urban households suffer more from chronic illnesses while lower-income households and the rural population continue to suffer primarily from infectious diseases. Moreover, as a nation's economy grows larger, policymakers and the public become more aware of the disparity in the availability of health care and the reality that the burden of unforeseen health expenditure has been a critical factor leading to impoverishment" (p. 30).

- In contrast, low-income countries are not doing well in reaching the Millennium Development Goal targets related to health: reducing infant, child, and maternal mortality rates; reducing malnutrition and stunting; and providing clean drinking water and ensuring sanitation. In addition, many low-income countries have a high incidence of HIV/AIDs. The issue is one of access to basic primary health care for which a system of primary health centers is needed. The situation is even worse in 34 fragile and conflict-affected countries where the basic health care system has collapsed or is collapsing, and where international nongovernmental organizations have to attend to basics such as vaccination and immunization (Hsiao and Heller 2007, 34).

As can be seen in the above discussion, resources allocated for health care need to aim for equity among all segments of the population, protection of the whole population against health risk, and a means to ensure a high level of public satisfaction for the services provided. In other words, both efficiency and equity have to be achieved while ensuring universal access and high quality of care and keeping unit costs low to a demanding public.

Any discussion of costs and benefits or cost-effectiveness is fraught with contradictions and complexities. Benefits of good health care policies are, primarily, increased labor productivity leading to higher GDP growth. Costs of health care could be manifold: costs arising from increased pressure for higher health spending as the population increases and grows old, as newer diseases come to the fore, and the pressure from health care professionals to use newer and more expensive drugs and technologies. Few developing countries have the financial resources and both quantity and quality of health care professionals to satisfy people's needs and wants in health care.

Consequently, health care has to be rationed—either by price or by access. Health care is a necessity of life, and access and equity concerns are key factors that lead most people to rely on insurance because they fear illness will impoverish them. Mandated health insurance favors large oligopolistic insurance companies with stringent criteria to minimize insurance payouts. Price rationing favors the affluent because they can afford to access it (at home or abroad). For those reasons, most nations provide nearly free basic health services or cover their citizens under social health insurance programs. As a result in the real world, price is not used as the primary rationing tool. Queues, waiting time, travel distance, and lesser quality and outright unavailability of service frequently serve as effective rationing tools. The distortions arising from rationing and overpricing by monopolistic insurance companies, among other issues, create an atmosphere of social and political dissatisfaction (as in the United Kingdom, Canada, and the United States recently).

How a country arranges the financing of health care will influence spending and outcomes. Key questions are these: What proportion of total costs of health care should be out-of-pocket payments by households or by social insurance that could be paid by employer, employee, and government? Should government be operating the health system—financing, regulating, as well as enforcing health policy? These and other issues lead to differential impacts. Hsiao and Heller (2007) analyze a number of different country models that range from centrally planned (Cuba and Vietnam) to national health service (as in the United Kingdom) to free-market, voluntary health insurance (the United States).

In Conclusion

First, government must play a strong role in financing health care to ensure equity. Second, the efficiency and quality of health care can be improved by introducing competition and incentives and by efficiently organizing a two- or three-tier system. Third, a hard budget constraint for the health sector should be put in place by the government to contain inflation. Fourth, a government may seek to influence the demand by education campaigns, capping medical insurance benefits, and establishing mandatory medical savings. Demand-side measures such as direct patient payments have been ineffective in containing health care inflation. Developing country governments do not have the capacity or resources to finance health care; to provide medical services to the satisfaction of the masses; to organize and manage a multitier health system of hospitals, health centers, and rural clinics that caters to the affluent, the middle class, and the poor; or to regulate the private sector involvement in health insurance and service provision.

Note

1. Knowledge here refers to information about best practice in other countries—what has and has not worked, how issues have been resolved, and information on drug tests and trials and the costs and benefits associated with new drugs.

Reference

Hsiao, W., and P. Heller. 2007. "What Should Macroeconomists Know about Health Care Policy?" Working Paper 07/13, International Monetary Fund, Washington, DC.

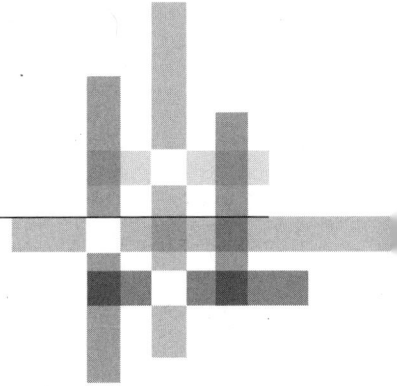

Labor Market Trends

Raj Nallari

Economic growth is about increases in productivity through an appropriate combination of physical capital, labor employment, and other factors of production (including efficient management of all resources). Labor employment enables a rise in household incomes and real wages—which, in turn, stimulate demand for goods and services. Growth is about accelerating this virtuous cycle and constantly moving the frontier of production. Long before the recent global crisis interrupted this process, globalization had been shaping the trends in labor force participation, formal and informal employment and un(der)employment, income inequality, and labor movement within and across countries. The following labor market trends (as described in various International Labour Organization [ILO] reports) are noteworthy events over the past 15 years.

Emergence of a Global Labor Market

Between 2000 and 2009, the world's labor force is estimated by the ILO to have increased from 2.74 billion to 3.21 billion, with well over half of the world's workers (56.3 percent) located in Asia, and four out of five workers living in the developing countries (ILO-IMF 2010, 7). The concentration of workers in the global labor market will be primarily in developing countries (medium-income developing countries and least-developing countries taken together), and less than 15 percent will be in developed countries. China and India, particularly, will be home to 40 percent of the world's labor force. In stark contrast to much of the developing world, most industrial countries are moving into a period of population stagnation or fall, with the consequent effect of an aging workforce and a rise in dependency ratios. Globally, there were 205 million unemployed people in 2010, a level unchanged from the previous year and above the level at the start of the crisis (177.4 million in 2007) (ILO 2010, 61). Table 35.1 further shows the breakdown of the global labor market.

Impact of Trade

Before trade and capital liberalization in the developing world, workers in these areas were hardly affected by global changes. Now, because the creation of a final good requires the assembly of several intermediate goods, there is a requirement of involving workers from different parts of the world. Thus, the increased connectivity through trade inevitably affects labor markets. Freeman (2007) had argued that liberalization by these countries in effect doubled the size of an emerging global labor market. Inevitably, the global financial crisis has taken a toll on international trade,

Table 35.1   Labor Supply Trends, by Region

Region	Working-age (15–64) population (millions) 2006	Average annual labor force growth (%) 1990–2006	Average annual population growth (%) 1990–2006	Average annual population growth (%) 2006–16	Share of women in labor force (%) 1990	Share of women in labor force (%) 2006
East Asia and Pacific	1,317.8	1.4	1.1	0.8	44.1	43.5
Eastern Europe and Central Asia	317.3	−0.1	0.1	0.0	45.7	44.7
Latin America and the Caribbean	356.5	2.6	1.5	1.1	33.9	40.8
Middle East and North Africa	195.7	3.4	2.0	1.7	22.9	28.0
South Asia	928.1	2.0	1.8	1.4	29.7	29.3
Sub-Saharan Africa	419.0	2.7	2.6	2.3	43.0	42.2
High-income countries	691.6	0.9	0.7	0.4	41.4	43.4
World	4,223.6	1.6	1.4	1.1	39.7	39.9

Source: World Bank 2008.

Frontiers in Development Policy

Table 35.2 World Merchandise Imports and Exports, by Region, 2008–09
percentage change over preceding year, based on dollar value

Region	Exports		Imports	
	2008	2009 (Jan–Sept)	2008	2009 (Jan–Sept)
World	15	–30	15	–30
Western Europe	11	–30	12	–32
Asia	14	–24	20	–27
North America	11	–27	8	–30
South/Central America	21	–25	30	–32
Commonwealth of Independent States	35	–45	32	–41
Africa and Middle East	31	–50	26	–21

Source: Jansen and von Uexkull 2010, 31.

and occupations prevalent at the base of the pyramid have been most affected (low-skilled jobs). Sectorally, world merchandise trade had dropped by almost 30 percent in the first three quarters of 2009 (Jansen and von Uexkull 2010, 31). The drop was most sharp in the Commonwealth of Independent States and in Africa and the Middle East (see table 35.2).

And in manufacturing, trade in automotive products suffered the steepest decline at the end of 2008 and the first half of 2009, thus affecting countries like Japan and Germany. In comparison, the service industry did not suffer as much. While there was some decrease seen during the first half of 2009, this was relatively short lived (skilled jobs continue to have a higher demand). Similarly, those industries affected with the highest jobs losses and decreased salaries concentrate on employing low-skilled workers.

Agriculture, forest and fishing, mining, manufacturing, and construction are businesses that have seen the highest job losses globally; wholesale and retail trade, health, and education have seen the highest job gains. While many of these job losses have been in the Americas and Europe, the spillover effect of these low-skilled jobs will be inevitable nonetheless.

Gender Participation in the Labor Market

During 2000–09, labor force participation among men was more or less steady, and female labor participation slightly increased. Though the global employment level for women has changed only slightly between 2000 and 2008, there has been a slight increase in countries that had low levels of female participation (in comparison to the median) and countries

Table 35.3   Female and Male Labor Force Participation, by Region, 2007 and 2009
percent

Region	Women 2007	Women 2009	Men 2007	Men 2009	Total 2007	Total 2009
World	51.6	51.6	77.8	77.7	64.7	64.7
Developed economies	52.8	52.9	69.1	68.6	60.7	60.5
Central and Southeastern Europe (non–European Union) and Commonwealth of Independent States	50.5	50.6	69.2	69.0	59.3	59.2
East Asia	66.8	66.5	79.6	79.4	73.4	73.1
Southeast Asia and Pacific	57.2	57.4	81.9	82.0	69.4	69.5
South Asia	34.8	34.9	81.7	81.6	58.9	58.8
Latin America and the Caribbean	51.0	51.7	80.1	79.7	65.2	65.4
Middle East	24.8	25.4	75.1	75.3	51.2	51.5
North Africa	27.3	27.4	75.5	76.4	51.3	51.8
Sub-Saharan Africa	61.9	62.6	81.1	81.2	71.4	71.7

Source: ILO 2010, 50.

Note: Figures for 2009 are preliminary estimates.

with high levels of female participation (in comparison to the median) have seen a slight decrease. Thus, the gap between the countries has reduced as well. This trend is identified by a U-shaped line where countries with low and high income tend to have low female rates of participation and countries with mid-level income tend to have a higher rate of female participation. Table 35.3 shows the regional labor force participation rate (LFPR) for men and women for 2007 and 2009. Globally, the LFPR is estimated to have remained steady for women and declined marginally for men. Across regions, the estimated increase in the LFPR for women is highest in Sub-Saharan Africa, the Middle East and North Africa, and Latin America and the Caribbean (a 0.6–0.7 percentage point increase). The increase for the other regions is marginal (0.1 percentage point), with a decrease projected in East Asia (0.3 percentage point). For men, LFPRs fell, except in Southeast Asia and Pacific, the Middle East and North Africa, and Sub-Saharan Africa—all of which showed marginal projected increases of 0.1 percentage point.

Unemployment Rates

Global unemployment until the 2008 global crisis averaged around 6 percent in the formal sector. In 2010, more than 209 million out of an

Table 35.4   Unemployment Rates for Both Sexes, by Region, Selected Years 1999–2009
percent

Region	1999	2000	2004	2005	2006	2007	2008	2009
World	6.4	6.2	6.4	6.3	6.0	5.7	5.8	6.6
Developed economies and the European Union	7.0	6.7	7.2	6.9	6.3	5.7	6.0	8.4
Central and Southeastern Europe (non-European Union) and Commonwealth of Independent States	12.4	10.6	9.7	9.4	9.0	8.3	8.3	10.3
East Asia	4.7	4.5	4.2	4.2	4.0	3.8	4.3	4.4
Southeast Asia and Pacific	5.1	5.0	6.4	6.5	6.1	5.4	5.3	5.6
South Asia	4.3	4.5	5.2	5.3	5.1	5.0	4.8	5.1
Latin America and the Caribbean	8.5	8.4	8.4	8.0	7.4	7.0	7.0	8.2
Middle East	9.3	9.5	9.3	10.0	9.5	9.3	9.2	9.4
North Africa	13.1	14.0	12.3	11.5	10.4	10.1	10.0	10.5
Sub-Saharan Africa	8.2	8.3	8.2	8.2	8.2	8.0	8.0	8.2

Source: ILO 2010, 46.

Notes: Figures for 2009 are preliminary estimates.

estimated global labor force of 3.21 billion were unemployed—a rise of more than 31 million since 2007. With annual force growth of 1.6 percent adding more than 5 million job seekers per year to the global labor force, the challenges exacerbated by the crisis are unlikely to diminish. In the next 10 years, more than 440 million new jobs will be needed to absorb new entrants to the labor force (ILO-IMF 2010, 591). Table 35.4 outlines the unemployment rate over 1999–2009.

Working Poverty

Before the financial crisis, the share of people falling below the poverty line, $1.25 a day, was on a declining trend. Those living on less than $1.25 a day had decreased by 16.3 percentage points between 1998 and 2008, and the working poor had decreased by 17 percentage points during the same time. Nonetheless, even in 2008, the number of people considered to be working poor was a surprising 633 million workers. In 2009, there was a small decrease in the number of working poor; but this pattern is only a continuation of the past trends. The financial crisis can put 7 percent of workers at risk of falling under the poverty line (another 215 million workers). The largest impact is expected to be in South Asia, Southeast Asia, and Sub-Saharan Africa. In the case of Sub-Saharan Africa, more than two thirds of workers are at risk of falling below the extreme poverty line in a worst-case scenario (ILO 2010, 22).

Rise of Insecure Work

Globalization and the associated need to constantly improve productivity and competitiveness to maintain market share are also reflected in an increased intensity of work characterized by tighter deadlines and faster production processes, overly flexible (for example, part-time, casual work, short-term, flexible hours and employment arrangements) and sometimes insecure work arrangements (such as consultancies, self-employment, frequent furloughs, and so forth) that are affecting work life balance. These workers do not have many of the rights and benefits that apply to regular employees doing the same types of work, such as remedies for unfair dismissal, redundancy pay, sick pay, or maternity pay. They also often have less protection with regard to occupational health safety, social security, freedom of association, and collective bargaining. Oftentimes, when workers lose their jobs and have limited opportunity, they shift to insecure or vulnerable jobs.

The number of workers in vulnerable forms of employment has seen a recent increase in Sub-Saharan Africa and South Asia. While tracking the number of people working in vulnerable jobs is difficult, economists speculate that, between 1998 and 2008, there was a decreasing trend for people in vulnerable jobs (ILO 2010, 18). However, since 2008, this number has increased drastically. The largest impact is estimated to have occurred in Central and Southeastern Europe, the Commonwealth of Independent States, and the Middle East and North Africa regions, where vulnerable employment may have increased by 5 percentage points (ILO 2010, 17).

High Youth Unemployment

The youth labor force grew to 619 million by 2009, an increase of 6 percent over the previous 10 years (ILO 2010, 16). Despite a decade of high global growth, youth unemployment has remained stubbornly high—at around 12 percent. Informal employment among youth is on the rise. Long-term employment among youth was already a concern before the crisis and has only increased since. Many youth have a job search period that exceeds a year. Decreasing youth labor force participation rates in some countries suggest that many young men and women have become discouraged by a fruitless search for work. Unless educational enrollment increases to match declines in labor force participation, future growth will suffer from a weakened skill base. Interestingly, most of the young population now resides in developing economies. As table 35.5 shows, the distribution of young workers is much higher in developing countries.

From the data in table 35.5, it is clear that, as the number of young people continues to grow in developing countries, there needs to be an increased focus on honing labor skills. Suffering primary education and limited availability of vocational and other higher-education institutes are increasing the labor skills mismatch in developing countries. In some developing countries—such as Pakistan—the failure to establish efficient primary school education means that, from the beginning, youth lack the skills to be competitive in the labor market. This often makes capitalizing on the potential and productivity of young people harder. In other situations, the lack of vocational schools or higher-education institutes makes recruitment harder. In transitioning economies—such as India and China—there is an increasing need to produce quality managers. However, the quality of higher education in these countries is poor (with the exception of a few universities), so retraining recruits becomes important for employers. As outsourcing and globalization increase, identifying the demand of the labor market and matching it with an appropriate labor supply will become critical for economies.

Table 35.5 Youth Unemployment Rates, by Region, Selected Years, 1999–2009
percent

Region	1999	2000	2004	2005	2006	2007	2008	2009
World	12.6	12.5	13.0	13.0	12.4	11.8	12.1	13.4
Developed economies and the European Union	13.9	13.2	14.4	14.1	13.0	12.2	13.1	17.7
Central and Southeastern Europe (non-European Union) and Commonwealth of Independent States	22.7	19.9	19.6	19.1	18.5	17.5	17.1	21.5
East Asia	9.2	8.9	8.5	8.4	8.2	7.8	8.7	9.0
Southeast Asia and Pacific	13.1	13.2	17.0	17.9	17.2	14.9	14.4	15.3
South Asia	9.8	10.2	10.3	10.4	10.0	9.9	9.9	10.7
Latin America and the Caribbean	15.6	15.5	16.5	16.1	15.1	14.1	14.3	16.6
Middle East	20.5	21.1	20.8	22.6	21.6	21.4	21.7	22.3
North Africa	27.3	29.9	27.2	26.8	24.2	23.6	23.5	24.7
Sub-Saharan Africa	12.6	12.6	12.6	12.4	12.4	12.3	12.3	12.6

Source: ILO 2010, 47.

Note: Figures for 2009 are preliminary estimates.

Domestic and International Migration Patterns

Over the past few decades, there has been a shift from agriculture to industry and services. Populations and jobs moved to urban areas. This migration averages around 30 million women and men each year (ILO-IMF 2010, 61). "For example, in 1997–2007, China, a country that has experienced very high levels of rural–urban migration, grew at an average of 9.6 percent a year, but only just managed to stay ahead of the demand for new jobs as employment expanded by only 1 percent a year" (ILO-IMF 2010, 61). India, conversely, has not been able to provide as many jobs for its population. Because most of the businesses are capital intense in the region, job availability for low-skilled workers is relatively harder to come by. As in most developing economies, China and India have some regions that produce jobs for low-skilled workers, and mass migration takes place to those regions. For example, the infrastructural development in a metropolitan city often means the arrival of laborers from rural sections of the country.

Similar to domestic migration, international migration is also significant and rising—although labor movements remain subject to strict controls. By 2010, 214 million people or 3.1 percent of the world's population lived outside their country of birth, according to United Nation's estimates. Some 60 percent of immigrants are in advanced countries, where 10.3 percent of the population is foreign born; in developing countries, 1.5 percent of the population is foreign born (Makina 2010, 35). The ILO estimates that a little under half are economically active in their country of destination.

College Wage Premium

In most countries, the average worker with a college degree earns almost twice as much as a high school–educated worker. The wage premium fluctuates a lot, depending on the supply of college graduates. And women with college degrees, on average, earn less than men with similar qualifications.

Three trends were observed: (1) rising college and postcollege wages; (2) stagnant and falling real wages for those without a four-year college degree; and (3) the stabilization of the wage gaps among workers with some college, high school graduates, and high school–dropout workers. The wage returns to schooling have become increasingly convex (quadratic) in years of education, particularly for males.

Information Technology Has Polarized the Labor Market

Since the early 1980s, coinciding with the information technology revolution and the introduction of computers at the workplace, employment in occupations such as secretary, salesperson, bank clerk, supervisor, and the like declined as a share of total employment. David Autor of the Massachusetts Institute of Technology and David Dorn of the Centre for Monetary and Financial Studies in Madrid used U.S. Department of Labor data on occupations, classified jobs vulnerable to automation, and found that job polarization between the 1980s and 2005 was "indeed most marked where jobs vulnerable to automation initially predominated" (Economist 2010). Several other studies find that industries using higher information technology and research and development spending had fastest growth in demand for the most educated workers and the sharpest declines in demand for people with mid-level education and skills. Adoption of technology itself is a process of technology; therefore, openness to trade and information technology adoption are closely related.

Offshoring and Outsourcing of Jobs

Outsourcing has capitalized on the talent in developing economies and spurred innovation and creativity in developed economies. Technological innovation has made it possible to outsource such jobs as those of call center workers, medical technicians, and researchers to countries that will provide cheap labor. Employment in developing markets has also given birth to burgeoning middle-classes who have become avid consumers of such goods. A combination of increased productivity and growth in consumption has led American businesses to thrive and reinvest in the national economy. The effective reinvestment of profits in the national economy should lead to increased innovation.

India and China have become economic giants in less than two decades, with the support of foreign direct investments. Now, rather than seeking out medium- to low-skilled jobs (that require routine interactions), these economies crave more creative professions that would allow them to further tap into their talents. Jeffrey Garten, dean of Yale School of Management, has predicted that the outsourcing of jobs would eventually result in developing economies to become the innovation hub (Lowenstein 2004).

Having been exposed to the technology and potential of developed economies, workers in India and China soon will also want to compete with them for innovation rather than low-paying service sector jobs. However, the weak infrastructure of developing economies has, so far, inhibited much innovation. Developed countries, too, have not been efficiently incentivizing their workforce to develop and grow. While the financial crisis has pushed the Obama administration to emphasize the importance of retraining and going back to school, the scientific and technological aspects that were once the strength of the American economy have not been reinvigorated.

Rising Corporate Profit

In recent years, there has been a marked decline in wage shares of total income in many developed and developing countries. A joint ILO–International Monetary Fund report titled "The Challenges of Growth, Employment and Social Cohesion" (2010) showed that "with real wages growing, on average, by only 0.75 percent for every 1 percent expansion of GDP, there has been a marked decline in wage shares in many developed and developing countries in recent years" (p. 11). Technological change and trade liberalization are important causes in this fall in wage shares. One possible explanation for the link between increased trade and lower wage share is that the intensification of competition—particularly the presence of large low-wage exporters in the market for labor-intensive products—has worked as a wage moderation factor. A lower wage share had also been found to be associated with a more unequal distribution of income.

Short-Term Challenges for Economic Policy

The financial crisis and the ensuing loss of jobs with inadequate social protection programs in emerging and developing countries and the high fiscal deficits and debt-to-GDP ratios in some countries have created a situation of heading toward another "perfect storm" that can explode with social unrest and violence across developed and developing countries. Ensuring that well-sequenced, coordinated, short-term exit strategies and deficit reduction policies are linked to a progressive recovery of the real economy and jobs and the protection of the most vulnerable people is vital. Measures should be tailored to specific country situations. There are significant differences between and within European countries, other developed countries, emerging economies, and least-developed countries. It is essential to put in place multilateral policies to support an orderly, long-term management of debt repayments and cost sharing at a pace that does not damage recovery.

Long-Term Challenges for Economic Policy

Looking toward the long term, sustainable growth requires structural change and productivity growth. A common feature of sustainable job-rich growth in many countries is investment in industries characterized by economies of scale and potential productivity of growth as well as strong production and technological links throughout the economy.

For a number of developing countries, the industrial sector has historically been a key driver of overall productivity and employment growth. More recent work has also demonstrated that the service sector has contributed positively to total productivity growth for the rapidly growing regions. This combination characterized the most successful and dynamic late-developing countries (concentrated in East Asia), which relied heavily on exports to generate output growth. A combination of structural change, productivity, and employment growth that leads to substantial real wage increases is possible with the quantity and quality of employment increasing at the same time. Growing inequality and declining wage shares in many developed and developing countries suggest, however, that workers in many countries have not shared significantly in productivity gains in recent years. At the same time, the declining employment intensity of growth is a cause of growing concern. That is, any given increase in GDP translates into fewer jobs today than in the past. With a continued large increase in the labor force in the years ahead and the existing stock of unemployed workers, this is troubling for many countries.

In Conclusion

The counterpart to a decline in the employment intensity of growth is a rise in the contribution of productivity to growth. This can lead to a broad increase in living standards, provided that increases in labor productivity are accompanied by increases in wages and household incomes. However, if wages lag behind productivity growth for prolonged periods, that and declining employment intensity of growth will lead to a relatively weak increase in household incomes. In such circumstances, economies have to rely on either their exports or increased household borrowing to sustain consumption as drivers of effective demand. But exporting cannot be a global strategy, even if it can be important for individual countries; and the crisis has demonstrated starkly that debt-fueled economic growth is not sustainable. The mechanisms through which productivity gains are allocated are, thus, an important component of policies to support a sustainable growth path.

References

The Economist. 2010. "Economics Focus. Automatic Reaction: IT Spending Has Hollowed Out Labour Markets to the Detriment of Middle-Income Workers." September 9. http://www.economist.com/node/16990700?story_id=16990700&CFID=153458776&CFTOKEN=19267969.

Freeman, R. 2007. "Labor Market Institutions around the World." Working Paper 13242, National Bureau of Economic Research, Cambridge, MA.

ILO (International Labour Organization). 2010. Global Employment Trends 2011: The Challenge of a Job Recovery. Geneva: ILO.

ILO-IMF (International Labour Organization–International Monetary Fund). 2010. "The Challenges of Growth, Employment, and Social Cohesion." Discussion document prepared for the Joint ILO-IMF Conference in Cooperation with the Office of the Prime Minister of Norway, Oslo, Norway, September 12–13. http://www.osloconference2010.org/discussionpaper.pdf.

Jansen, M., and E. von Uxekull. 2010. Trade and Employment in the Global Crisis. Geneva: International Labour Organization.

Lowenstein, R. 2004. "Jobs." New York Times, September 4. http://query.nytimes.com/gst/fullpage.html?res=9B0CEEDF1431F936A3575AC0A9629C8B63&pagewanted=all.

Makina, D. 2005. "The Impact of Regional Migration and Remittances on Development: The Case of Zimbabwe." Open Society Initiative for Southern Africa, Washington, DC. http://www.osisa.org/resources/docs/PDFs/Openspace-Oct2010/The_Impact_of_Regional_Migration_and_Remittances_on_Development.pdf.

World Bank. 2008. World Development Indicators. Washington, DC: World Bank.

Labor Market Policies

Raj Nallari

The MILES Framework

The overall economic efficiency of a country is crucial for growth and job creation. In a high-growth country, labor may have to be quite mobile in moving between jobs as more-productive and high-wage jobs are created and less-productive jobs disappear. In contrast, one finds that in stagnating economies, labor regulations and other practices act as barriers to employment creation in the formal sector and push job seekers to less-productive informal sector jobs or to underemployment or unemployment. Ultimately, workers may become discouraged and leave the labor market—and even possibly migrate to other countries.

The World Bank has developed a framework for the analysis of the main factors impacting employment. Five factors are identified: (1) macroeconomic performance, (2) investment climate, (3) labor market policies and institutions, (4) education and skills, and (5) social protection for workers. MILES, the name of the framework, is the acronym summarizing these five determinants of job performance (table 36.1). The first two factors deal with job creation, and labor market institutions are important here, too. Labor market institutions are also important for labor supply together with education and skills and social protection.

Table 36.1 MILES framework

Factor	Policy Issues
Macroeconomic conditions	• Conditions for growth
	• Macroeconomic stability
Investment climate	• Regulatory environment
	• Government transparency
	• Taxes
	• Financing
	• Infrastructure
	• Legal Environment
Labor market policies and institutions	• Labor market regulation
	• Wage setting
	• Nonwage costs
Education and skills	• Basic education
	• Higher education
	• Training and lifelong learning
Social protection	• Social risk management programs
	• Social insurance

Source: World Bank.

Thus, the framework brings together demand and supply in the labor market. By assessing all of the factors, the analysis can determine the binding constraints to the creation of more and better jobs, and thus identify policy priorities.

Countries need to ensure that (1) the overall macroeconomic environment is conducive to growth (that is, low inflation, low interest rates so firms can access finance); (2) the investment climate is conducive for private sector investment (that is, the cost of doing business is affordable with balanced regulations, service provision is available at reasonable prices, law and order exists, property rights are protected, there is free entry and exit of firms for job creation, and the judiciary is effective and efficient); (3) the labor market is functioning, including provision of employment services, to create an adaptable labor market (that is, a market where employers have incentives to hire workers, and workers have incentives and skills to take up available jobs); (4) an educated labor force with appropriate skills is needed to respond to the demand for labor in a high-growth country; and (5) there is social protection with adequate safety nets for workers, especially for those who are willing to work.

Labor Market Policies and Institutions

Labor market policies comprise active and passive measures and labor regulations. The interaction of these policies in developing countries yields very mixed results for employment and earnings. In addition, labor market institutions (such as collective bargaining arrangements and the degree of labor unionization) affect labor market outcomes. This is further compounded by the fact that labor policy research and evaluation work is fraught with inadequate data. These issues are discussed below.

Active labor market policies are defined as those that aim to increase employment or wage earnings or reduce overall unemployment. Examples of active policies are (1) public spending on job training, (2) assistance for job search, and (3) job subsidy programs to create jobs in public and private sectors or even subsidies for self-employment.

Public job-training programs are widespread across developing countries, and their analysis reveals the following findings:

1. The amount of spending on active programs is positively related to the unemployment rate. In the short term (at best, for one to two years), there is some positive impact of active program on job creation, but there is very little evidence on the long-run effects of active programs in terms of increase in future earnings and employment prospects of participating workers. Nor is there any evidence of social benefits, such as reduced crime, better health, or less drinking or drug use among workers who participated in active programs.

2. There is almost no evidence on which types and content of training programs work best. Do skill-enhancing activities (for example, classroom training or on-the-job training) work best; or must they be combined with personal counseling, job-search assistance, and mentoring services to work?

3. Government-run training programs form the bulk of active labor policies in the developed and developing world. In general, these programs are estimated to have yielded low or even negative rates of return when benefits on earnings or employment are compared with the cost of these programs. More disaggregated data for the United States is shown to have more positive effects on adult women when compared with adult men (Friedlander, Greenberg, and Robins 1997; Stanley, Katz, and Krueger 1998), and almost no program seems to have worked for out-of-school youths. So, tight targeting of training programs in necessary.

4. Most of the gains took the form of improved employment opportunities rather than higher hourly earnings. Even for those groups for whom participation in the programs yielded a positive rate of return, the estimated annual earnings gains were typically not large enough to lift most families out of poverty. The question still remains that research does not tell us why any program works or does not work.

5. Such training programs need to be small in scale and to have a strong on-the-job component (not just classroom training). Local private employers should be involved in design of programs so that there is a strong link with industry. At the same time, training programs that have strong links with local employers are likely to encourage displacement, as participants of job training programs tend to get jobs at the expense of individuals who did not participate in the program or those who are already working and who are experienced with higher wage rates.

Job-search assistance (such as public employment service agencies) conduct initial interviews with job seekers, provide job placement services and in-depth counseling at various stages of unemployment periods, set up job fairs, and so forth. Such services are usually the least costly of active labor market programs. Furthermore, evaluations of these programs show consistently positive outcomes, reflected in higher morale and getting the unemployed back to work faster. A job assistance program that is quite successful in Japan, the Republic of Korea, and several states of the United States is reemployment bonuses, where cash payments are provided to unemployment insurance recipients who find a job quickly and keep it for a specified length of time. This program reduced the average duration of unemployment significantly. But there could be a downside—workers with a high probability of finding a new job quickly may arrange with their employers to be laid off to collect the bonus. For avoidance of such an abuse, several safeguards (including monitoring the behavior of bonus claimants and employers) are needed, and this incurs additional costs.

Youth unemployment programs designed to increase jobs for youth (for example, apprenticeships, technical vocational training, seed money for self-employment, special education, and job training programs) have shown negative evaluation results. Grubb (1999) finds that, in the United States, successful youth jobs programs had a close link to local firms—particularly larger firms with relatively higher earnings, strong employment growth and good opportunities for advancement—and contained a mix of academic education, occupational skills, and on-the-job training. Early and sustained interventions for disadvantaged youth (such as early childhood development, improving attitudes to work, and ensuring secondary and tertiary education) were found to be important.

Subsidies to private sector employment may be designed not only to create additional jobs, but also to ensure that individuals are in regular contact with employers and the world of work, ensuring continuous labor supply and giving priority to the long-term unemployed (even if this is done at the expense of the short-term unemployed). Evidence from wage subsidies in Australia, Belgium, Ireland, and the Netherlands found that, for every 100 jobs, only 10 jobs were net gains in employment (Martin 2000, 97). There is a stigma attached to being long-term unemployed, and wage subsidies only compound that problem.

To summarize, five principles stand out. These are (1) in-depth counseling; (2) job-finding incentives (for example, reemployment bonuses) and other low-cost job-search assistance; (3) small-scale public job-training programs that are targeted to the needs of job seekers and local employers; (4) early interventions, reaching back to preschool, can be helpful to disadvantaged youths, but they must be sustained to ensure that school dropout numbers are minimized and attitude to work is improved; and (5) wage or employment subsidies should be for a short duration, targeted, and closely monitored.

In Africa, South Asia, and Europe, and Central Asia countries, the much larger informal labor markets and weaker capacity to implement programs may limit what some programs can achieve in terms of creating formal employment or increasing wages. On the other hand, some other programs (such as youth training programs, job counseling programs, or guaranteed public works employment) have much more positive impacts than are seen in industrial countries. Such programs in these labor markets may have more potential because abundant supplies of skilled workers are not available.

While active programs aim to help job seekers in finding jobs, unemployment compensation or benefit systems provide income support to the unemployed and may act as a disincentive for the unemployed to get back to work sooner. Paying attention to the interactions between active measures and unemployment benefit systems is important. In Organisation for Economic Co-operation and Development countries, the available evidence suggests that replacement rates are sufficiently large to have potentially significant effects on work incentives and on wage-setting behavior. This, in turn, has led to attempts in recent years to curb the so-called unemployment trap.

There is a close interaction between active and passive measures that is central to the trade-off between equity and efficiency. If the unemployment benefit system is generous and poorly managed, it is very difficult to operate active programs in ways that increase labor market efficiency and reduce structural unemployment. Conversely, if active measures are used on a large scale and mainly serve to reestablish benefit entitlements, they risk becoming a de facto passive measure. So, an integrated, "one-stop-shop" approach is needed to ensure, among other things, a close coordination between active and passive policies so that the unemployed can acquire the attributes, skills, and education necessary to fill available job vacancies. Other issues are (1) to make passive income support as "active" as possible by using instruments like reemployment bonuses, in-work benefits, regular contacts of claimants with the public employment service, job fairs, and the like and (2) to make income support conditional on participation in active programs after a certain minimum duration of unemployment (say, six months). For all the above reasons, policies to deal with the unemployment problem yield mixed results, and there is no magic bullet.

Labor regulations determine the minimum wage, mandated benefits, dismissal costs, unemployment insurance, and the framework for settling industrial disputes. These regulations impact the functioning of the labor market. The extent to which firms and workers in developing countries are affected is difficult to ascertain because of inadequate data, differences in definitions and methodologies, weak compliance with and enforcement of regulations, and the existence of informal labor arrangements.

Labor Market Institutions

Labor market institutions operate in the formal sector, the size of which ranges from about 30 percent of the workforce in low-income African countries to less than 5 percent in middle-income countries in other regions. Organized or unionized labor is mainly active in protected sectors, such as the civil service and public utilities (including banking, in the urban informal sector, and mining companies). Even in the formal sector, only permanent workers are covered by collective bargaining between workers and employers. Available information suggests a trade-off between labor regulations and union density—more extensive government involvement in the labor market seems to have undercut organized labor. Casual observation suggests that this government involvement tends to make labor market outcomes more predictable, with a positive impact on productivity.

Deregulating the labor market may not improve labor market flexibility in developing countries. Whatever benefits are derived from labor market flexibility could be negated by increasing union density. Countries with well-coordinated collective bargaining tend to have less wage dispersion than other countries, and countries with high bargaining coverage tend to be associated with relatively higher wages and overall poor macroeconomic performance. In the informal sector, the rules of the game are imposed neither by the government nor by the unions; but by the traditional values of community, ethnicity, and trust. There is some evidence that foreign direct investment is deterred by strong labor regulations and lack of an institutional framework. Hence, formalization of the labor market is a desired policy path.

In Conclusion

A comprehensive strategy of more and better growth through sound macroeconomic and investment climate policies, better-educated labor force with skills that are adaptable to rapidly changing work force needs, and microeconomic measures that are effective to cut unemployment significantly are needed in addition to an appropriate mix of active and passive labor measures and labor regulations. Firm-level findings indicate that small firms are higher net job creators, and these small firms are established in almost all sectors of the economy. Self-employment and entrepreneurship should be encouraged, including through active labor market policies.

References

Friedlander, D., D. H. Greenberg, and P. K. Robins. 1997. "Evaluating Government Training Programs for the Economically Disadvantaged." *Journal of Economic Literature* 35 (4): 1809–55.

Grubb, W. N. 1999. "Lessons from Education and Training for Youth: Five Precepts." In *Preparing Youth for the 21st Century: The Transition from Education to the Labour Market*. Paris: Organisation for Economic Co-operation and Development.

Martin, J. P. 2000. "What Works among Active Labour Market Policies: Evidence from OECD Countries' Experiences." OECD Economic Studies 30, Organisation for Economic Co-operation and Development, Paris. http://www.oecd.org/dataoecd/31/35/2732343.pdf.

Stanley, M., L. Katz, and A. Krueger. 1998. "Developing Skills: What We Know about the Impacts of American Employment and Training Programmes on Employment, Earnings, and Educational Outcomes." Working Paper H-98-02, Malcolm Weiner Center for Social Policy, John F. Kennedy School of Government, Harvard University, Cambridge, MA.

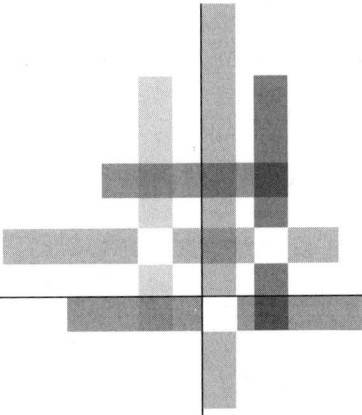

Part V

MANAGING RISKS

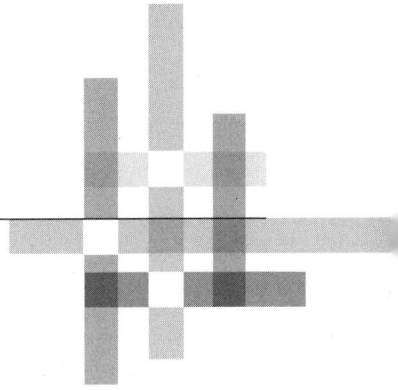

Overview

Raj Nallari

This section highlights three key international issues that are at the fore-front of developer's minds. These are climate change, macroprudential policies, and global capital flows. Fostering growth in developing econo-mies needs to be done in a sustainable manner, and developed economies need to look to their footprint on the environment to ensure its sustainabil-ity. Managing greenhouse gases and global climate change is a challenge for all countries. A number of approaches are put forth in assessing the eco-nomic impact of climate change. Fiscal policy, in terms of expenditure and taxes, has a large role to play—as does technology.

The recent global financial crisis highlighted the interconnectedness of the world economy. It became quickly apparent in 2008 that the regulation and supervision of the financial sector in most advanced countries was tar-geted to the individual firm, with little appreciation for the links these firms had forged nationally and internationally. Macroprudential tools deal with the systemic risk or soundness of the entire financial system. We examine some of these tools below.

Increasing globalization and the removal of barriers to resource flows and private capital flows resulted in unprecedented capital flows to developing countries. These flows have waxed and waned favoring some developing countries over others. In the run-up to the global financial crisis, capital flows to developing economies as a whole peaked at $1.2 trillion in 2007, subsequently declining to $707 billion in 2008 (Imparato and Sharma 2009, 29). How can developing countries cope with this boom-and-bust cycle of capital flows? What are the risks posed by this volatility in flows, and what policy measures can governments use to make best use of financial integration? These questions are discussed in the sections that follow.

Reference

Imparato, N., and S. Sharma. 2009. "The World's Poorest Nations and the Global Financial Crisis." *World Economy* 10 (4): 25–44.

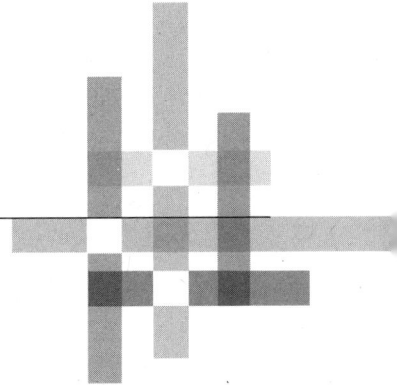

Managing the Climate Crisis

Raj Nallari

How to Manage the Climate Crisis

Economic growth among the developing countries will need to be fostered in an environmentally sustainable way if greenhouse gases (GHGs) are to be effectively stabilized. Despite much progress on this subject, the world is quite unsure about the effects of climate change and their magnitude on economic performance. The challenge is to disentangle the impact of several mechanisms through which climate could influence economic outcomes. The complex relationship between climate and economic outcomes involves several causes and effects, including on agricultural output, fisheries, fresh water access, storm frequency, and tourism, among others. In addition, there appears to be a link between increase in temperatures (as a result of climate change over decades) on labor productivity, on child and adult mortality, on incidence of crime, and on drought conditions and related conflict occurrence—all of which have direct and indirect effects on economic activity.

Given the numerous transmission channels mentioned above, the approach thus far has been to estimate the overall economic impact of climate change using an integrated assessment model. The model takes different mechanisms, one by one, and estimates each mechanism's effect; it then adds up all the effects to assess the full economic impact of climate change (see, for example, Mendelsohn, Dinar, and Williams 2006 and Nordhaus and Boyer 2000). However, this integrated assessment approach requires a large number of assumptions and combines direct and indirect effects.

Dell, Jones, and Olken (2008) take a more direct approach and construct a cross-country database (using historical economic growth data) of fluctuations in temperature and precipitation for the period 1950–2003. With relatively few assumptions, their results show that (1) in poorer countries, a rise of one degree centigrade in temperature in a given year is likely to reduce growth by about 1.1 percentage points; (2) in rich countries, changes in temperature have little or no effect on growth; (3) temperature influences growth by impacting the level of agricultural yields and hence output, and it affects productivity of labor; (4) by varying the lags of temperature, an examination of temporary and permanent effects revealed that, in poorer countries, there is some persistent impact on economic output. Further, estimates using the overall change in climate from 1970 to 2000 (rather than yearly changes) indicated larger negative estimates on output in poorer countries. Other things remaining equal and on the basis of these results, it is possible that continuous climate change may significantly widen income gaps between rich and poor countries.

The Bali Action Plan (Carpenter 2008) examines ways to mitigate climate change. Dramatic changes in lifestyles will help reduce carbon emissions significantly, but this will take a long time. A second way is to put a price on actions causing GHG emissions, either through a carbon tax or cap-and-trade program that creates a market for transferable emissions licenses. The underlying logic is that taxes and prices for licenses would not translate to price increases on the products demanded by the consumers, and therefore firms would look for technology and innovation to reduce emissions. This, in turn, would need private and public investments in research and development spending. Moreover, how the carbon tax and licenses market works is very uncertain as we know that markets may not always be efficient in their allocation, especially in global public goods, as averted GHG emissions are beneficial to the world at large.

Public goods management is faced with the problem of government "knowing" best where to set the tax rates or the cap on various forms of GHGs and the "free-rider" problem resulting in an underreduction of emissions. Should tax rates and caps change on an annual basis or frequently, or should they be automatically linked to market conditions. What if these licenses are used for financial speculation and form the basis for derivatives? In an age of "too-big-to-fail" firms, energy-intensive companies, and a plethora of government agencies mandated to deal with GHG emissions, envisaging a smooth functioning of the whole process is hard.

In both developed and developing countries, fiscal policy will play an important role in facilitating a sustainable use of natural resources and in safeguarding the environment. For example, harmful subsidies and inappropriate tax policies that lead to the excessive exploitation of natural resources will need to be phased out. The prices of energy products will have to reflect their social costs. Subsidies for pesticides and fertilizer use—which contributes to overfarming of land—will need to be eliminated and replaced with government expenditure programs that more directly benefit small farmers. At the same time, industrial countries must implement similar policies to ensure that the world's environmental resources are not overexploited.

Another way is for governments to stimulate the search for new technologies and knowledge by publicly funded programs. This sort of spending (especially during a fiscal-financial crises) is inherently risky and the results unpredictable. One way to complement this process is to let both public and private companies compete because the challenge involves the creation and timely diffusion of new technologies.

Damages caused by forest fires, ecological disasters (oil spills), hurricanes, tornadoes, and the like could lead to actions that increase GHG. There is a need for knowledge and research and development spending in geoengineering to explore options for reducing the vulnerabilities of structures and people to extreme weather.

Existing technologies define the speed with which we can move to greener solutions. For example, a coal-fired power plant emits higher levels of carbon emissions and the plant itself lasts about 30 years. So governments and the private sector should be expected to replace coal-fired power plants with newer technologies right away. Given the large research and development efforts, there is a need for global knowledge sharing, adaptation, and the broad diffusion of innovations. This calls for a rethinking on excessive protection of intellectual property rights by the advanced countries. Targeted domains for research exemptions; liability approaches to intellectual property rights infringement; and competition policy adjustments to permit efficient pooling of patent, copyright, and database rights all deserve consideration under this heading. Private investment is unlikely until carbon taxes and cap-and-trade regimes and pricing policies are put in place. Thus, the international community could find itself in a low-effort equilibrium with a chicken-and-egg problem: the government not able to clarify the rules and regime, and the private sector unwilling to invest until the rules are clarified and established.

The Republic of Korea and China appear to be the only countries that used fiscal stimulus funds for dealing with a range of GHG emissions by investing in wind turbines. China is moving away from coal technologies in which it has an advantage because of an abundance of coal and toward greener technologies.

In Conclusion

The economic, engineering, and technological solutions to the GHG problem have to come from both advanced and developing countries, including innovations from the poor in dealing with their day-to-day energy needs. This means that there is a need for international coordination in research and development programs and the sharing of knowledge and resulting technological advances.

References

Carpenter, C. 2008. "The Bali Action Plan: Key Issues in the Climate Negotiations." Summary for Policy Makers. United Nations Development Programme, United Nations, New York. http://www.undp.org/climatechange/docs/UNDP_BAP _Summary.pdf.

Dell, M., B. Jones, and B. Olken. 2008. "Climate Change and Economic Growth Over the Last Half Century." Working Paper 14132, National Bureau of Economic Research, Cambridge, MA.

Mendelsohn, R., A. Dinar, and L. Williams. 2006. "The Distributional Impact of Climate Change on Rich and Poor Countries." *Environment and Development Economics* 11 (2): 159–78.

Nordhaus, W., and J. Boyer. 2000. *Warming the World.* Cambridge, MA: MIT Press.

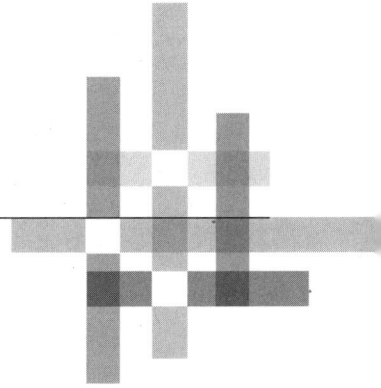

The Role of Macroprudential Regulations

Raj Nallari

The global financial crisis that began in 2008 highlighted the fact that analysis, regulation, and supervision of the financial sector in most countries were aimed at the level of the financial firm (microeconomic level) with the objective of ensuring its stability, but with no heed to the interconnectedness of the world economy. We now know that there is a need to look at the impact of individual-firm behavior on the entire financial system (macroeconomic level).

Securitization enabled the original lender to pass on the loan risk to other institutions through innovative new instruments. There emerged a "shadow" financial system, while the regulations and supervision did not keep pace with this evolution. One agency—perhaps the central bank—should be in charge of ensuring the overall financial stability of the entire system. This systemic regulator would need to collect new data and information on "too-big-to-fail" and systemically important firms.

The second principle is that regulators should use as many tools as possible, with the aim of minimizing the likelihood of bailouts of financial firms by internalizing the costs of potential failure that do not depend on taxpayers. This means that regulators should make sure that capital requirements and buffers are in place, depending on the firms' exposures to risks. These tools will insure against firm losses, but also transfer the risks and losses onto the shareholders. More complex firms should hold more capital.

Rather than rely on the board of directors and stakeholders to discipline the risk taking of executives and firms, regulators should design penalties and costs of failure for management over and above those placed by stakeholders. Banks need to recapitalize by issuing new, hybrid debt with a pre-specified trigger or threshold that, when violated, will automatically be converted from debt to equity. The idea is that bondholders would bear the costs of failure rather than leaving taxpayers on the hook or resorting to bankruptcy. Despite this mode of recapitalization, there will be financial firms that could fail. So firms need to be required to have a "living will" where the complexity of the firm's organizational structure and instruments would be described along with a detailed plan of how they could be dismantled in case of failure.

Basel III, which is still under discussion, has at its center some of the above capital and liquidity elements for banks. It has a common equity buffer of 7 percent, a countercyclical capital buffer, a capital surcharge for systemically important financial firms, newly introduced liquidity requirements, and a leverage cap. These elements focus on "loss absorbency" and appear to emphasize the unstable short-term funding and short-term foreign currency debt as the main vulnerabilities. It does not consider what is happening to household savings (core liability) and systemic risks arising from the interconnectedness of banks and how that contributes to asset growth during a lending boom. During a lending boom, retail deposits by households may not keep pace with lending (asset) growth. Noncore deposits and liabilities (including foreign currency liabilities) increase, and cross-holding among financial intermediaries also increases rapidly during a lending boom. Lending booms occur because of lower interest rates or lower lending standards. During a lending boom, capital ratios (Tier 1) tend to be at their peak and even forward-looking provisioning (as in Spain) appears not to be sufficient. A tax or levy on noncore liabilities may also be considered.

Macroprudential Tools

Microprudential regulation is about the soundness of individual banks and is, therefore, partial equilibrium analysis. For example, a bank with an asset of $100 and a capital ratio of 6 percent may lose money in year 1, which means its capital-to-asset ratio may be reduced (say to 4 percent). The regulators want to restore stability of the bank and insist that the bank managers raise more capital (back to 6 percent or more) or call back its loans from the $100 to a level that matches with the capital-to-asset ratio. All that the regulators are interested in is raising new capital or shrinking assets to restore individual bank soundness.

Macroprudential regulation, however, deals with systemic risk or soundness of the entire system. Each bank, by acting in its own self-interest, may jeopardize the entire system. If every bank in the economy is faced with the problem of shrinking assets—say, resulting from a common shock—the whole economy will suffer for want of credit. The costs to society when many banks shrink their assets simultaneously are credit crunches and fire sales of assets. Individual banks cannot raise new capital to correct the situation because their balance sheets are impaired and raising new capital in the market is expensive or difficult—especially during bad times. Also, banks do not keep capital buffers during good times because they are interested in maximizing lending and, therefore, profits. Keeping additional capital voluntarily is not in the interest of the individual bank.

What Should Be the "Field of Vision" of the Financial Regulators?

One macroprudential tool is for regulators to impose a higher capital-to-asset ratio in good times, compared with the ratio that is imposed by the market in bad times. During bad times, markets place a premium on "wobbly" banks.

A second tool is the quality of capital. For example, banks A and B both begin with total assets of $100 each and total capital of $6 each. But A's capital is composed entirely of equity, where B has $2 of equity and $4 of preferred stock. Now suppose both banks lose $3. In an effort to avoid shrinking their assets, they would like to raise new capital. Suppose they do so by trying to issue equity. This will be harder for Bank B, whose entire preexisting equity layer has been wiped out and whose preferred stock is, as a result, now trading at a steep discount to its face value (for any new equity that B brings in will largely serve to bail out the position of its more senior preferred investors). Common equity is desirable as such.

A third possible tool is to promptly take corrective action. For example, bring the capital-to-asset ratio back to the required ratio, as discussed above.

A fourth policy could be to resort to contingent capital where a debt is automatically converted to equity once a certain threshold of capital-to-asset ratio is not met (as Lloyd's insurance company did in 2009).

Capital insurance is a similar policy instrument that is triggered when the capital ratio falls below a certain level.

Another issue of concern is the short-term versus longer-term funding. In 2009, the Basel Committee on Banking Supervision put forth a set of proposals that requires a financial firm to have a certain amount of long-term funding comprising both equity and debt with a maturity of greater than one year. Deposit-insured firms or banks have to be regulated, as do noninsured financial firms. So the bottom line is that the too-big-to-fail and all other financial firms have to be monitored and regulated.

Credit growth to gross domestic product (GDP) and other traditional measures related to monetary aggregates (for example, M2 money supply) may be helpful as macroprudential indicators to monitor. When a lending boom occurs because of buoyancy in domestic economic and financial conditions, then caps on loan-to-value ratios and debt service-to-income ratios may be additional administrative measures. Measures of cross-exposure across financial intermediaries such as covariance caps on bank leverage may be used as a way to limit asset growth by tying total assets to bank equity.

Macroeconomic Impact of Capital Requirements

There will definitely be economic costs associated with higher capital requirements. These costs will be primarily on financial firm performance and will reflect the true costs of financial services—perhaps making credit more expensive. But there is no point in implicit or explicit subsidies or hiding of the "true costs" by clever arguments.

With the use of macroeconomic models, the Bank for International Settlements simulations found that it is more expensive for banks to fund assets with capital than with deposits or wholesale debt. This suggests that banks facing stronger capital requirements will seek to increase capital levels by retaining earnings and issuing equity as well as reducing nonloan assets. Moreover, they may also increase the interest rates they charge borrowers and reduce the quantity of new lending. Any increase in the cost and decline in the supply of bank loans could have a transitory impact on growth, especially in sectors that rely heavily on bank credit. In the longer term, however, as banks become less risky, both the cost and quantity of credit should recover, reversing the impact on consumption and investment.

The majority of the models assume that tighter capital standards affect the economy as banks respond by increasing their lending spreads. A small number of models also allow for the possibility that banks constrain the supply of credit beyond what is reflected in the increase in spreads. Many models also assume that monetary policy responds to lower output levels and associated reduced inflationary pressures in line with central banks' mandates. Comparing results across the models making these different assumptions offers insights into the potential importance of these mechanisms. Changes in *lending spreads* alone are estimated to reduce GDP relative to the baseline trend by roughly 0.16 percent in the four-year implementation case—about the same as the median decline across all results reported in this section (Macroeconomic Assessment Group 2010, 3).

Estimates of the impact of *credit supply effects* suggest a somewhat larger transitional impact of raising capital standards on aggregate output. Taking account of these effects by incorporating indicators of bank lending standards into models yields a median reduction in GDP of 0.32 percent after four and a half years (again, per percentage point increase in the capital ratio) (Macroeconomic Assessment Group 2010, 3). Models that incorporate the impact of both higher lending spreads and supply constraints tend to yield some of the largest impact estimates, perhaps because they were calibrated based on past data that include episodes when deep recessions coincided with persistent banking sector strains. This underlines the importance of implementing new regulatory requirements in a way that is compatible with the ongoing economic recovery.

An easing of *monetary policy* reduces the estimated output losses. When it is assumed that the central bank responds to the incipient aggregate demand fall and reduced inflationary pressures precipitated by the regulatory changes, the central estimate of the maximum output loss shrinks significantly. Such offsets are especially pronounced in models that incorporate credit supply constraints, for which the GDP loss in the 18th quarter falls from 0.32 percent to 0.17 percent (Macroeconomic Assessment Group 2010, 4).

In Conclusion

For prevention of future financial disasters, it is integral to recognize and put in place various measurement systems that can be implemented through a government entity, such as the central bank. The roles of that entity would be to prevent any such financial issues through monitoring and to include design measures (such as those discussed in this section) to respond to these conditions.

Reference

Macroeconomic Assessment Group. 2010. "Interim Report. Assessing the Macro-economic Impact of the Transition to Stronger Capital and Liquidity Requirements." Bank for International Settlements, Geneva, Switzerland. http://www.bis.org/publ/othp10.pdf.

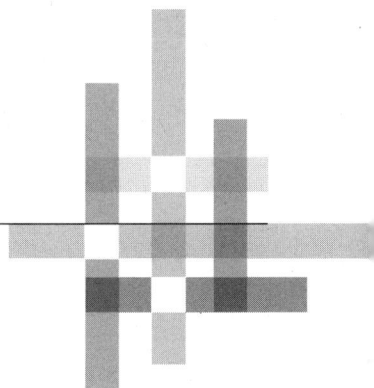

Managing Capital Flows

Raj Nallari and Ababyomi Alawode

For several decades, developing countries have complemented external official sources of funding with private forms of financing to support their development. As increasing globalization led to the removal of barriers to resource flows, cross-border movements of private capital have become an important feature of the global economy and dominate capital flows for many developing countries, especially for emerging markets. But these capital flows have been volatile, with large swings—as when capital flows sharply increased before the East Asian and other financial crises in emerging markets in the mid-1990s and then abruptly declined at the crises onsets.

In the years preceding the recent global financial crisis, there was again a surge in the flow of private capital to developing countries. Between 2003 and 2007, net private capital flows to these countries rose to unprecedented levels, peaking at $1.2 trillion in 2007 (see table 40.1). Strong performance in emerging economies and relatively higher rates of return in these economies were partly responsible for this. As the global financial crisis unfolded, however, many emerging markets experienced substantial capital outflows combined with sharply reduced inflows. It became more difficult and more expensive to access international capital markets as investors became strongly risk averse and sought safe havens in the United States and Europe.

Table 40.1   Net International Capital Flows to Developing Countries, 2005–10

$, billions

Type of Capital Flows	2005	2006	2007	2008	2009[a]	2010[b]
Net private inflows	573.3	732.1	1,223.7	752.4	454.0	589.5
Net equity inflows	349.9	469.0	663.8	536.5	445.9	497.5
Net debt flows	223.4	263.1	559.9	215.9	8.1	92.0

Source: World Bank 2010.

a. Estimate.

b. Forecast.

As a result, net private capital flows to developing countries in 2008 were $752 billion, compared with the $1.2 trillion recorded just a year earlier (table 40.1).[1] For 2010, projections indicate that net private flows will be around $590 billion, 30 percent higher than the 2009 estimates. However, this is still much lower than peak level of 2007. As capital flows begin to recover somewhat, low interest rates in advanced countries are making some emerging markets attractive destinations for international investors for (short-term) investments. Some countries are receiving large capital inflows and having to resort to various measures to mitigate the adverse macroeconomic impacts.

These developments raise the following issues: how can recipient governments of developing countries best deal with the boom-and-bust cycle of capital flows and various risks posed by the volatile capital flows? What policy measures can they use to optimally make use of the opportunities provided by international financial integration? How to mitigate the risks?

Private Capital Flows and Their Benefits and Pitfalls

In developing countries, a common obstacle to raising investment levels is the mismatch between available domestic savings and investment needs. Hence, capital inflows from abroad have often served as a welcome supplement to domestic savings, enabling many countries to undertake much-needed investment. A sustained inflow of foreign direct investment helps, as it can also coincide with technology transfer and management expertise. Evidence shows that countries and firms that open up to international financial flows are increasingly subjected to forces of "market discipline." This translates as an improvement at the level of the macroeconomy and at firm-level management, enhancing both the public sector's and the corporate sector's transparency and governance. Also, increased flows across borders imply closer integration with international capital markets. Such integration gives access to a larger number and a wider range of potential investors, which should make it easier and cheaper for firms to raise funds for viable projects. Firms in developing countries could consequently lower their cost of capital significantly. Domestic financial sector development is also likely to follow with financial integration (see Kose, Elekdag, and Cardarelli 2009 for a review of the costs and benefits of financial integration).

The main pitfall for receiving countries is the susceptibility of such flows to destabilizing boom-and-bust cycles, with surges often followed by sudden stops and substantial reversals in flows. Indeed, there is evidence that capital inflow "bonanzas" raise the probability of economic and financial crises in emerging economies significantly (see Reinhart and Reinhart 2008).

In general, a gush in capital inflows (especially of the short-term variety) tends to fuel domestic lending by banks, increase domestic demand, create asset price bubbles, and increase inflation as the economy overheats. Economic agents (individuals and firms) become highly leveraged and fiscal policies may become strongly procyclical. More abundant credit available often gets directed into less-productive investments. Higher inflows may also cause an undesirable appreciation of the exchange rate, reducing the competitiveness of exports and putting the external accounts under pressure. Governments are often forced to intervene in the foreign exchange market in an effort to minimize the impact of inflows on the exchange rate.

The scenario for a bust has proved to be consistent and predictable over the years and in the recent financial crisis. There is a sudden reversal of flows, leading to a sudden credit crunch and a collapse of asset prices. Nonperforming loans rise as overleveraged domestic borrowers struggle to meet loan obligations. Domestic output contracts and the surge in outflows lead to significant depreciation of the domestic currency. As the crisis unfolds, weak banks may collapse, creating a combination of banking and currency crisis—the so-called twin crisis.

This scenario has played out in numerous episodes of financial and currency crises in developing countries (including the currency crises of the 1990s in Mexico, East Asia, and the Russian Federation), where large capital outflows put pressure on exchange rate regimes, leading to a depletion of international reserves, distress of financial institutions, and severely impaired ability of borrowers to service their debts. In many cases, borrowers had loans denominated in foreign currency, although they generated income or revenue only in domestic currency. That created severe difficulties in servicing debt when exchange rates depreciated and reserves shrank. The experience of several countries during the recent global crisis has also been along similar lines, albeit with less-serious consequences in developing countries.

External Capital Flows: Some Policy Questions

The reversals in capital flows witnessed in the wake of the recent global financial crisis once again served to underscore the potential downside risks of external capital flows for developing countries. And the current large capital flows to some emerging markets show the complexity in managing capital flows so as to avoid a repeat of a boom-and-bust cycle. Consequently, in many policy circles, questions are being raised regarding the best management of capital surges in a globalized and increasingly volatile financial environment (see, for example, Ghosh 2010, IMF 2010, and Ostry et al. 2010). Some key questions being asked are the following:

- *What are the main determinants of private flows to developing countries?* In a globalized financial and economic system, what are the main causes of capital surges into developing countries? What is the relative importance of "push" vs. "pull" factors? What are the implications of causal factors for the management of capital inflows?

- *How do you distinguish between temporary and permanent increases in capital inflows?* As pointed out by Reinhart and Reinhart (2008), policy makers and investors are often lulled "into treating the bonanza as a *permanent* phenomenon rather than a *temporary* shock" (p. 3). However, it is easier to identify temporary bonanzas with the benefit of hindsight. Therefore, how can policy makers in recipient countries differentiate between a temporary shock and a permanent shift in their ability to attract capital inflows?

- *What combination of monetary, fiscal, and exchange rate policies can help best manage capital inflows and the consequences?* In the face of capital inflows, policy makers try to pursue two key macroeconomic objectives: (1) avoiding domestic macroeconomic overheating and (2) avoiding a loss of competitiveness through exchange rate appreciation. In principle, policy makers can deploy a range of monetary, fiscal, and exchange rate policies to pursue these objectives, including allowing the exchange rate to appreciate (if it is initially underval-ued), intervening to manage the exchange rate, or fiscally tightening to counter a boom. The question is whether all of these policies are available in the context of integrated financial markets and what the best policy mix is. How, depending on initial conditions in each coun-try, can policy makers select appropriate macroeconomic policy reac-tions to surges in capital inflows? This involves a number of related questions:

- *Can monetary policy be used to counter asset price bubbles and credit booms?* One prevailing contention regarding the recent financial cri-sis is that monetary policy remained loose for too long, creating abun-dant liquidity, low borrowing rates, and myopia as to the true risk of investments. However, there is no consensus over whether monetary policy should or could be used to counter credit booms and asset price bubbles.

- *Is there a role for fiscal policy?* The prevailing view is that, in the face of large capital inflows, fiscal policy should be less accommodating or even contractionary. But this does not seem to have prevented the problems with exchange rate appreciation and asset price rises in some countries.

- *What exchange rate regime is more conducive to mitigating the ad-verse effects of large capital flows?* Is a fixed exchange rate regime more attractive in the context of large capital flows and close finan-cial integration? Or a pegged or floating exchange rate regime? Should countries build up more foreign exchange reserves?

- *Is it desirable to accumulate substantial reserves in response to a surge in inflows? What is the appropriate level of reserves?* There is evidence that some countries that amassed substantial international reserves were able to cope better with the recent global financial crisis (see Jeanne 2010). Is this a desirable policy option for developing coun-tries in managing capital inflows? What are the costs of maintaining high levels of reserves?

- *How should regulatory policies be coordinated with monetary, fiscal, and exchange rate policies?* There is some evidence that countries with more developed and well-regulated financial systems are better able to deal with influxes of capital from abroad, maximizing the potential benefits while mitigating the risks. Countries with weaker financial systems may see capital inflows directed into relatively unproductive ventures, while leverage in domestic enterprises increases to unsustainable levels (Kose et al. 2010).

○ *Is there a role for prudential regulation and supervision in managing capital inflows?* Prudential regulation and supervision can play two roles: (1) ensuring that financial institutions operate prudently and observe sound principles of risk management in making loans and (2) using countercyclical macroprudential regulations to counter lending booms and prevent credit-induced overheating. The use of prudential regulation to counter booms is little tested, however, and has become an important topic of debate recently.

○ *Is there a role for administrative controls in managing capital flows? Which controls are effective? Should controls be imposed on inflows, outflows, or both?* Controls on capital flows either restrict the amount of capital entering a country (for example, through restrictions on residents borrowing from abroad in foreign exchange) or limit the amount of capital that can leave the country (for example, by preventing residents from holding deposits abroad or limiting the repatriation of profits by investors). Also, controls could be imposed on the *type* of inflows (for instance, by restricting short-term investments to encourage longer-term inflows such as foreign direct investment). While there is evidence that controls generate high administrative costs, tend to work only for a short period of time, and are often circumvented, they remain an important tool for policy makers in developing countries. Policy and academic debates, therefore, have continued on the form and type of controls suitable for managing capital inflows in the current postcrisis environment.

In Conclusion

Capital flows to developing countries have helped increase competitiveness; however, similar to other financial market regulations, there are boom-and-bust cycles that need to be monitored. Additionally, preventive steps for boom-and-bust cycles also need to be created, bearing in mind that capital flows can also adversely affect economies.

Note

1. Equity outflows were notably substantial, jumping to $244 billion in 2008, compared with $190 billion in 2007 (World Bank 2009, 37).

References

Ghosh, S. 2010. "Dealing with the Challenges of Capital Flows in the Context of Macrofinancial Links." *Economic Premise* 19.

IMF (International Monetary Fund). 2010. "Global Liquidity Expansion: Effects on 'Receiving' Economies and Policy Response Options." In *Global Financial Stability Report*, 7–33. Washington, DC: IMF.

Jeanne, O. 2010. "Dealing with Volatile Capital Flows." Policy Brief No. 10–18, Peterson Institute of International Economics, Washington, DC.

Kose, M. A., S. Elekdag, and R. Cardarelli. 2009. "Capital Inflows: Macroeconomic Implications and Policy Responses." Working Paper 09/40, International Monetary Fund, Washington, DC.

Kose, M. A., E. Prasad, K. Rogoff, and S.-J. Wei. 2010. "Financial Globalization and Economic Policies." In vol. 5 of *Handbook of Development Economics*, ed. D. Rodrik and M. Rosenzweig, 4283–59. Handbooks in Economics Series. Amsterdam: Elsevier/North-Holland.

Ostry, J. D., A. R. Ghosh, K. Habermeier, M. Chamon, M. S. Qureshi, and D.B.S. Reinhardt. 2010. "Capital Inflows: The Role of Controls." Staff Position Note 10/04, International Monetary Fund, Washington, DC.

Reinhart, C. M., and V. Reinhart. 2008. "Capital Flow Bonanzas: An Encompassing View of the Past and the Present." Working Paper 14321, National Bureau of Economic Research, Cambridge, MA.

World Bank. 2009. *Global Development Finance: Charting a Global Recovery*. Washington, DC: World Bank.

———. 2010. "Global Economic Prospects, Summer 2010: Fiscal Headwinds and Recovery." Washington, DC.

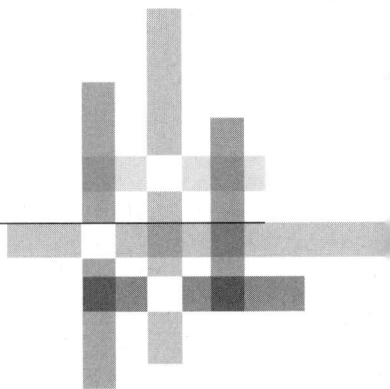

Triple Crisis: Rising Food Prices, Global Financial Crisis, and Climate Change Issues

Raj Nallari and Rwitwika Bhattacharya

Just as the world was settling from the turbulence of the global financial crisis, the political movements in the Middle East and an earthquake in Japan again shook the global economy. A culmination of events in the past years has resulted in the emergence of three major crises: rising food prices, global financial crisis, and climate change issues. Like in most crises, those at the base of the pyramid remain most vulnerable. The global economic crisis had already pushed 53 million people into poverty (World Bank 2009), and the food price hikes are estimated to have added another 44 million (World Bank 2011, 6). As scientists continue to point out the adverse impacts of climate change, it becomes apparent that the poor will be most affected because they have limited capacity to deal with such shocks. Through programs such as conditional cash transfers that can reduce poverty, provide improved education and health, and boost future growth, various aspects of the triple crisis can be overcome.

Rising Food Prices

According to the Independent Evaluation Group of the World Bank (2011), crop yields are growing more slowly than the population for the first time since the green revolution. A combination of increasing population and decreased focus on agricultural productivity has resulted in a mismatch between supply of and demand for food. As a reaction to this prospect, international cereal prices have increased sharply, with export prices of major grains up at least 70 percent (PanArmenian.net 2011). Food accounts for over 50 percent of the household spending at the base of the pyramid. Therefore, any increase in food costs is likely to significantly affect the poor. The 2007 food prices are estimated to have reversed poverty reduction by about seven years.[1]

Lessons from the 2007 food crisis have taught us that there needs to be a stronger social net for the poor. Particularly for vulnerable populations, governments need to have food reserves available. These food reserves would be able to fight hunger and malnutrition. Additionally, for the short term, food-importing countries should not block any food items and should continue trading openly.

In the longer term, the smallholder farmers need to be provided with the tools to increase productivities (especially in Sub-Saharan Africa) so that they are able to produce their own food. To increase productivity, several issues along the supply chain need to be addressed, including land access and property rights; availability of seeds, fertilizers, and other inputs; support for research and technology dissemination; infrastructure improvements in irrigation and rural roads; and access to credit and marketing.

Stressing agricultural productivity is expected to stabilize world food prices; however, the changing global climate is further complicating the existing conditions. With water stresses mounting in many countries and climate change adding to the problem, much of the increase in crop production will need to come from drier and riskier production environments.

Global Financial Crisis

According to the World Bank's Independent Evaluation Group (2010b), the spillover effect of the financial crisis rooted in the North resulted in the setback of years of poverty reduction efforts. From a peak of around $1,200 billion in 2007, net private capital flows to developing countries fell by over a third in 2008, as a liquidity squeeze in advanced economies led investors to pull back from emerging markets (IEG 2010b, 13). Other than the reduced capital flows, though, emerging markets were left relatively unscathed because they weren't exposed to any toxic assets.

Since the global financial crisis, however, there have been few changes to the financial architecture in the North. The institutional stability of a few companies has taken precedence over the need for overhauling the entire structure. To prevent future financial crisis, governments should reform the financial system. Two possible paths are as follow:

1. Create a systemic regulator who can oversee the entire financial system and look out for any "shady" activity. In the last financial crisis, the financial institutions had invented various complex tools to justify their actions.

2. Regulators should construct tools that would ensure that firms failing would need to bail themselves out. Buffers should be in place to ensure against losses and to transfer risks and losses to shareholders.

The global crisis led economists to rediscover "logical" thinking. The financial crisis showed that the markets had not been operating as the economists had suspected. The financial system is subject to human behavior. Therefore, the economics profession must come to grips with these instabilities, not treating finance as a benign veil on the real economy and understanding the interlinks between microeconomic and macroeconomic dimensions.

Climate Change Issues

According to the World Bank's Independent Evaluation Group (2009, 2010a), the global financial crisis had temporarily slowed down green house gas emissions in 2008–09. However, a financial crisis is not the solution to combating climate change. The poor suffer disproportionately from climate change. Particularly people living in deltas and low-lying areas are prone to floods and other natural disasters. The increased frequency of natural disasters in the past few years can be attributed to climate change patterns. Even agricultural productivity has reduced because of hostile climate conditions.

These challenges and their effects are already being felt today, and addressing them will require concerted international action to set limits for greenhouse gas emissions as well as actions at the national level in both developed and developing countries. Some measures could be as basic as adopting new technologies that are energy efficient or incentivizing energy efficiency.

A concerted effort from the public sector, the private sector, and civil society is needed to combat climate change. Unfortunately, the global financial crisis has resulted in decreased investment for research in climate change technology; however, there are various other measures. Following are the five major lessons about climate change that need to be adopted:

1. heightened emphasis on energy efficiency,

2. forest preservation through protected area schemes,

3. appropriate project finance,

4. technology transfer, and

5. accelerated learning.

In Conclusion

Countries can combat the three crises by implementing policies in more than one area. For example, countries can spur growth and address climate change simultaneously through investment in green and carbon-saving technologies. Energy efficiency stands out as offering high domestic returns while also reducing carbon emissions.

Note

1. Data are available at http://www.worldbank.org/ieg/crises_conference/challenges.html.

References

IEG (Independent Evaluation Group, World Bank). 2009. *Climate Change and the World Bank Group. Phase I: Evaluation of World Bank Win-Win Energy Policy Reforms*. Washington, DC: World Bank.

——. 2010a. *Climate Change and the World Bank Group. Phase II: The Challenge of Low-Carbon Development*. Washington, DC: World Bank.

——. 2010b. *The World Bank Group's Response to The Global Economic Crisis*. Washington, DC: World Bank.

——. 2011. *Growth and Productivity in Agriculture and Agribusiness: Evaluative Lessons from World Bank Experience*. Washington, DC: World Bank.

PanArmenian.net. 2011. "PAO: Export Prices of Major Grains up at Least 70%." News Release. http://www.panarmenian.net/eng/economy/news/63116/.

World Bank. 2009. "Financial Crisis Could Trap 53 Million More People in Poverty." News Release, World Bank, Washington, DC. http://web.worldbank.org/ WBSITE/EXTERNAL/NEWS/0,,contentMDK:22068931~pagePK:64257043 ~piPK:437376~theSitePK:4607,00.html.

———. 2011. *Food Price Watch*. February. World Bank, Washington, DC. http:// siteresources.worldbank.org/INTPREMNET/Resources/Food_Price_Watch _Feb_2011_Final_Version.pdf.

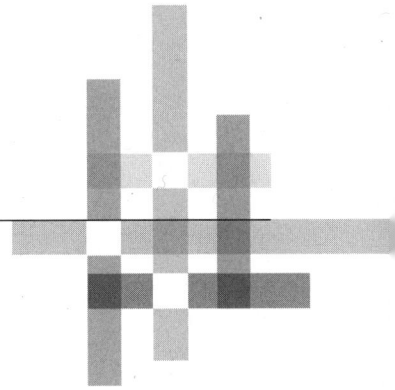

Catastrophes and Economic Growth

Raj Nallari and Rwitwika Bhattacharya

Tragedies such as earthquakes, hurricanes, and tsunamis have now become common. Every time there is a natural disaster, newspaper headlines and television highlights scream about the economic impact of the disaster and the fiscal expansion that is needed to address the adverse impact of any tragedy.

Disasters lead some countries to reconstruct infrastructure and consequently lead to productivity increases and economic growth (see, for example, Skidmore and Toya 2002); however, many other countries (such as Haiti) suffer disasters and never seem to recover. War has similar effects on a country's human and infrastructure assets. On the whole, the growth effects of disasters will depend on the stage of development of the country and the type of disaster.

Poor countries with weak budgetary and political institutions as well as weak implementation capacity that are hit by an economic catastrophe may not have the human or financial resources and organizations and institutions to get back to predisaster growth levels or rates. Such countries may face negative long-term effects because disasters will only set them back farther. Loss of human life—particularly of skilled workers—will take longer time to recover.

Conversely, countries with resources and capacities may bounce back with renewed strength as they upgrade technologies and infrastructure and restore lost stock of capital. There are also small islands and countries that seem to be prone to hurricanes and demonstrate resilience since they recover with little external support. Countries such as Sri Lanka and Caribbean and Pacific islands appear to be in this middle ground of countries able to deal with calamities.

In the case of Japan, the 2011 earthquake followed by a tsunami that resulted in about 15,000 deaths and another 15,000 people unaccounted for will have an immense cost. Barclays has estimated this cost to be about $186 billion, or about 3 percent of Japan's 2010 gross domestic product (*Economist* 2011).

What are the transmitting channels and how would one go about measuring the effects of calamities? There is a stylized approach.

Fiscal Costs

There will be a need for increased government spending on immediate humanitarian relief (food, shelter, warm blankets, and so forth) and for clearing the damage and reconstructing existing capital shock (roads, power, building, houses, and the like). Where private property is damaged, insurance companies will pay for some of the costs suffered. Larger assets such as planes and ships may be insured with companies such as Lloyd's of London for cost recovery. Taking stock of these costs can provide an estimate of fiscal costs.

Additionally, one must also bear in mind that, once the reserve sources such as roads and power supply are damaged, production will temporarily decline and so will revenue intake. Poorer countries may expect some grants and charitable contributions to compensate.

Real Output Loss

Natural disasters and wars are associated with loss of agricultural and manufacturing output because the infrastructure setup is adversely affected. For example, after a natural disaster, there is interrupted supply of electricity, lack of clean water supply, and shortage of food. In some circumstances, physical infrastructure is affected as homes, roads, and buildings are destroyed. As citizens suffer, tourists also choose to refrain from visiting those areas. Therefore, ultimately, the real output loss is affected.

Balance of Payments

As production is disturbed, exports could decline while inputs (humanitarian relief and reconstruction costs) are likely to go up substantially. Taking the existing structure of national accounts, one can easily estimate the impact on the export and import of goods. Within these estimations, considering the hiring of external consultants who can play an important role in the reconstruction process is also important. Because countries are often in disarray after a disaster, seeking the support of external resources for rebuilding may be more efficient.

For citizens living outside the affected country, (that is, a diaspora), disaster often means the possibility of increased remittances (along with donor grants and foreign aid).

On the whole, there are innumerable costs in the medium to long term—costs of loss of outputs, fiscal costs, and impacts at the base of the pyramid.

In Conclusion

While different countries respond to natural disasters in differing ways, there are three macroeconomic areas that are inevitably affected: fiscal costs, real output loss, and balance payments.

References

The Economist. 2011. "Japan and the Economics of Natural Disaster." March 16. http://m.economist.com/democracy-in-america-21016929.php.

Skidmore, M., and H. Toya. 2002. "Do Natural Disasters Promote Long-Run Growth?" *Economic Inquiry* 40 (4): 664–87.

INDEX

Boxes, figures, notes, and tables are indicated by *b, f, n,* and *t,* respectively.

A

adverse selection, 232
alternative energy investments, 262
asset prices
  credit bubbles and, 205–207
Accra Agenda for Action (2005),
  35*n*12, 151, 153
Acemoglu, D., 27, 51, 56, 57, 59
advanced materials innovations, 92*n*5
Africa. *See* Middle East and North Africa;
  Sub-Saharan Africa; *specific countries*
Afsa, C., 10
agency paradigm, 189
aging populations, 232, 236
agriculture, 121, 237, 278, 284
aid. *See* foreign aid
AIDS and HIV, 32
Akamatsu, K., 55
Alawode, Ababyomi, 269
Angola, economic growth in, 4
ASEAN (Association of Southeast Asian
  Nations), 56, 56*f*
Asia. *See* East Asia and Pacific; Europe and
  Central Asia; South Asia; *specific*
  countries
asset prices
  global financial crisis and, 62, 63*f*
  monetary policy and, 273
Association of Southeast Asian Nations
  (ASEAN), 56, 56*f*
asymmetrical information, 189, 232

B

Aterido, R., 112
Australia, wage subsidies in, 251
automobile industry, 91, 92*nn*6–7
Autor, David, 243

balance of payments, 285
Bali Action Plan (2008), 260
Bank for International Settlements, 205, 266
Bank of England, 205
bank regulation, 111–114, 206–207,
  257, 265–266
Barth, J. R., 113
Basel Committee on Banking Supervision,
  264, 266
Baumol, W. J., 83*n*3, 214
Belgium, wage subsidies in, 251
Bernard, A. B., 80
Bhagwati, Jagdish, 52*n*4
Bhattacharya, Rwitwika, 67, 277, 283
Bhavnani, R., 152
Blanchard, O., 186, 187, 190, 190*n*2
Blinder, A. S., 214
Botswana
  economic growth in, 125, 126*t*
  institutional framework in, 57
brain development, 222
Brazil
  economic growth in, 125, 126*t*
  exchange rate during global financial
  crisis, 210

Brazil (*continued*)
  foreign capital and trade in, 146
  infrastructure investments in, 138,
    139, 141n4
  middle-income trap in, 39, 40f
  reserve currency and, 211
  savings rate in, 3
burden of disease, 32
Burundi, education in, 222
Busse, M., 112

C

Calvert-Henderson Quality of Life
  Indicators, 17
Calvo, G. A., 185, 209
capacity building for innovation, 49, 74–77,
  75f, 76t
cap-and-trade programs, 260, 261
capital flows, 269–275
  to developing countries, 5, 6t,
    269–270, 270t
  global financial crisis and, 5, 6t, 7n1
  globalization and, 257–258, 269
  policy development and, 272–274
  quality of capital and, 265
capital insurance, 266
capital ratios, 264, 265–266
capital requirements, 266–267
Caprio, G., Jr., 113
carbon taxes, 260, 261
Cargill, 84n6
Caribbean. *See* Latin America and the
  Caribbean
catastrophes, risk management for,
  283–285
Celasun, O., 35n13, 148n4, 155
Center for Global Development, 147n1
Central Asia. *See* Europe and Central Asia
Chad, economic growth in, 4
"The Challenges of Growth, Employment
  and Social Cohesion" (ILO & IMF), 244
children
  malnutrition, 31–32, 127
  mortality rates, 32, 35n9
Chile, exchange rate during global financial
  crisis, 210
China
  alternative energy investments in, 262
  economic growth in, 45, 66, 125, 126t
  education in, 100–101, 100–101t
  foreign capital and trade in, 146
  hybrid and electric vehicles in, 92n6
  innovation capacity in, 76, 76t, 80

knowledge transfer to, 128
labor market in, 236, 243
poverty rate in, 35n4, 47
R&D spending in, 95, 96–97t
regional growth and, 56, 56f, 132
reserve currency and, 211
savings rate in, 3
trade policy in, 146, 215
urbanization in, 122n1, 242
USPTO patents granted to, 99, 99t
Christensen, C. M., 80
Clemens, M., 152
climate change, 257, 259–262, 279–280
cognitive development, 222
collective bargaining, 252–253
collective welfare paradigm, 189
college wage premium, 227, 242
Colombia, exchange rate during global
  financial crisis, 210
Commission on Growth and Development,
  125, 126
Commission on the Measurement of
  Economic Performance and Social
  Progress, 22n2
commodity prices, 5
Commonwealth of Independent States.
  See also Russian Federation
  insecure work arrangements in, 240
  trade impact of global financial crisis in,
    237, 237t
competitiveness, 159–164
  corporate social responsibility and,
    162–163
  economic growth and, 118, 119–120
  globalization and, 161
  health care policy and, 231
  innovation and, 81
  middle-income trap and, 40, 41f
  policy development for, 161–162
  regional development and, 160–161
conditional cash transfers, 228
corporate governance, 58–59
corporate social responsibility (CSR),
  162–163
credit markets, 61–62, 205–207, 267
CSR (corporate social responsibility),
  162–163

D

Darby, M. R., 81
Datang Telecom Technology, 83n2
Deaton, A., 221
deflation, 181

deleveraging, 62

Dell, M., 260

Dell'Ariccia, G., 186, 187, 190, 190*n*2

demographic shifts, 232, 236, 242. *See also* urbanization

dependency ratio, 232, 236

Deutscher, E., 156*n*3

devaluation risk, 137, 137*t*, 141*n*3

developing countries
  capital flows to, 5, 6*t*, 269–270, 270*t*
  economic situation in, 4–5, 4*t*
  education in, 226
  labor force in, 235–236
  standardized test scores in, 222–223

development. *See also* growth and development strategies
  challenges for, 61–66
  constraints on, 55–60
  defining and measuring, 9–24, 11–16*t*
  MDGs and, 28–29, 28*t*
  middle-income trap, 39–43, 40–41*f*
  paradigm shift for, 118–119, 143–149
  political framework and, 50–51, 67–70
  in postcrisis environment, 1–70
  poverty traps, 25–37, 26*t*
  private sector role in, 71–114
  strategies for, 45–53

disasters, risk management for, 283–285

Doha Round (WTO), 65

Dominican Republic, education in, 222

Dorn, David, 243

Dow Chemical, 84*n*6

E

Ease of Doing Business Database (World Bank), 112, 112*f*

East Asia and Pacific. *See also specific countries*
  education in, 100–101, 100–101*t*, 227
  infrastructure investments in, 139–140, 140*f*
  labor force participation rate in, 238, 238*t*
  middle-income trap in, 39, 41
  poverty in, 30, 147*n*2, 239
  trade policy in, 215–216

Easterlin, R. A., 18

Easterlin Paradox, 18

Easterly, W., 25, 26, 27, 51*n*1, 152, 167

Eastern Europe. *See* Europe and Central Asia

economic growth. *See also* growth and development strategies
  education and, 127, 219–220

globalization and, 125
  labor market trends and, 244–245
  poverty reduction and, 22*n*1, 46–47, 147*n*2
  regulatory framework and, 77, 105–106, 106*f*
  trade and, 49, 50

economics of happiness, 17

Ecuador, education in, 222

education
  access and quality, 225–229
  early childhood development and, 222–223
  economic growth and, 127, 219–220
  gender parity in, 30–31, 31*f*, 226
  innovation capacity and, 100–101, 100–101*t*
  labor market policies and, 247–248, 248*t*
  MDGs on, 30–31, 35*n*6, 226
  youth unemployment and, 241

Education for All (EFA), 225–226

Egypt, grassroots movements in, 69

electric vehicles, 92*n*6

elites and state capture, 68

emerging market economies
  growth of, 4–5, 4*t*, 66
  private capital flows to, 5, 6*t*, 269–270, 270*t*

entrepreneurship, 50, 79–80, 83*n*1, 102*n*2

Europe and Central Asia. *See also specific countries*
  informal sector in, 251
  infrastructure investments in, 139, 140, 140*f*

exchange rate regimes
  capital flows and, 209–211, 273
  competitiveness and, 128, 160, 272
  fiscal multipliers and, 202
  reserve currencies and, 66
  trade policies and, 215

F

Farrell, D., 107

FDI. *See* foreign direct investment

Federal Reserve (U.S.), 205

Feldstein, M., 203*n*1

financial crisis. *See* global financial crisis of 2008

financial regulation, 111–114, 206–207, 257, 265–266

financing
  for development, 5, 155–156
  of health care, 234

monetary policy and, 185–191
private sector role in infrastructure, 135–142, 136*f*, 136*t*, 138*f*, 139*t*, 140*f*
state intervention role in, 131–133
trade policy and, 213–216
urbanization and, 121–122, 171–177
growth paradigm, 45–50, 47*t*, 48*f*
Growth Report (World Bank), 225

H

Hallward-Driemeier, M., 112
Hanushek, E. A., 227
happiness measures, 17–22, 18–21*f*
Happy Planet Index, 22
Hargadon, A., 81
Hay Group, 83*n*5
health care policy, 127, 220, 225, 231–234
health insurance, 233
Heavily Indebted Poor Countries (HIPC) Initiative, 34
Heller, P., 231, 232, 234
Hellman, J., 58
high-income countries
happiness measures in, 18*f*, 19
total factor productivity as growth driver in, 47
HIPC (Heavily Indebted Poor Countries) Initiative, 34
HIV/AIDS, 32
Hong Kong SAR, China
economic growth in, 125, 126*t*
education in, 100–101, 100–101*t*
regional growth and, 56
Hsiao, W., 231, 232, 234
Huawei Technologies, 83*n*2
Hulten, C. R., 77*n*2
human development, 217–253
early childhood development, 221–224
education access and quality, 225–229
health care policy, 231–234
innovation capacity and, 100–101, 100–101*t*
labor market and, 235–253
Human Development Index, 22
Human Development Report (UN), 219
human rights, 219
Hungary
exchange rate during global financial crisis, 210
foreign capital and trade in, 146
Hunger, 31–32, 127, 221
hybrid vehicles, 92*n*6

I

ILO (International Labour Organization), 235, 244
Ilzetzki, E., 202, 203
IMF (International Monetary Fund), 6, 194, 205, 211, 244
income inequality, 20–22, 56, 227, 242
income taxes, 107
Independent Evaluation Group (World Bank), 278, 279
Index of Living Standards, 17
Index of Sustainable Economic Welfare/ Genuine Progress Indicators (ISEW/ GPI), 17
India
economic growth in, 45, 66
education in, 222
foreign capital and trade in, 146
grassroots movements in, 69
infrastructure investments in, 138, 139, 141*n*4
innovation capacity in, 76, 76*t*
labor market in, 236, 243
poverty rate in, 35*n*5, 47
reserve currency and, 211
savings rate in, 3
urbanization in, 242
Indonesia
competitiveness ranking for, 40, 41*f*
economic growth in, 125, 126*t*
education in, 100–101, 100*t*, 102*n*4
R&D spending in, 96–97*t*
regional growth and, 56
USPTO patents granted to, 99, 99*t*
industrialization, 49, 175, 245
industrial mix, 87–94, 90*f*
infant industry protection, 131
infant mortality, 32, 232
inflation rate, 5, 128, 180–181, 187, 278
informal sector
GDP and, 23*n*4
governance and, 59
labor market policies and, 251
regulatory framework and, 106–107, 108*f*, 109*n*1
state capture and, 68
youth in, 240
information asymmetry, 189, 232
information technology, 50, 91, 92*n*8, 174, 243
infrastructure
investments in, 41, 126, 148*n*8
natural disasters and, 283, 284

infrastructure (*continued*)
    poverty traps and, 34*n*2
    private sector role in, 7*n*3, 135–142,
        136*f,* 136*t,* 138*f,* 139*t,* 140*f*
    telecommunications, 137–138
    urbanization and, 172, 174
innovation
    in advanced materials, 92*n*5
    capacity building for, 49, 74–77, 75*f,* 76*t*
    education levels and, 225
    firms as source of, 79–85, 101–102
    human capital investments, 100–101,
        100–101*t*
    industrial mix and, 87–94, 90*f*
    offshoring and outsourcing jobs and,
        243–244
    patenting and, 98–99, 99*t*
    research intensity and, 87–94, 89*f*
    small businesses, role of, 82, 82*t*
    technological capacity, 95–96, 96–97*t*
    technology absorption and generation,
        96–98, 97–98*f*
    urbanization and, 176
insecure work arrangements, 240
institutional framework
    as development constraint, 56–57
    labor market policies and, 247–248,
        248*t,* 249–253
    natural disasters and, 283
    poverty traps and, 27
    property rights and, 167
insurance
    capital insurance, 266
    health insurance, 233
intellectual property rights, 42*n*1, 92*n*4, 261
International Conference on Financing for
    Development, 152
International Labour Organization (ILO),
    235, 244
International Monetary Fund (IMF), 6, 194,
    205, 211, 244
investment climate, 112, 112*f,* 247–248, 248*t*
Ireland, wage subsidies in, 251
Isaksson, A., 77*n*2

J

Jacoby, H., 223
Japan
    earthquake and tsunami (2011), 284
    economic growth in, 125, 126*t*
    education in, 100–101, 100–101*t,* 102*n*4
    innovation capacity in, 76, 76*t*
    investment rates in, 41

job-search assistance programs in, 250
    knowledge transfer to, 128
    manufacturing sector in, 91–92*n*2
    R&D spending in, 95, 96–97*t*
    regional growth and, 56, 56*f,* 120, 132
    trade impact of global financial crisis in,
        237, 237*t*
    USPTO patents granted to, 99, 99*t,* 102*n*1
Jensen, J. B., 80
job-search assistance, 250
job training, 249–250
Johnson, S., 27, 56, 57, 59
Jones, B., 260
Jones, C. I., 78*n*7
Jorgenson, D. W., 77*n*3

K

Kaminsky, G. L., 185
Keynesianism, 179–180, 190, 201
Kimko, D. D., 227
knowledge transfer, 128
Kojima, K., 55, 120
Korea, Republic of
    alternative energy investments in, 262
    competitiveness in, 119–120
    economic growth in, 125, 126*t*
    education in, 100–101, 100–101*t,* 102*n*4
    innovation capacity in, 76, 76*t,* 80
    investment rates in, 41
    job-search assistance programs in, 250
    middle-income trap in, 39, 40*f*
    R&D spending in, 95, 96–97*t*
    regional growth and, 56, 132
    reserve currency and, 211
    USPTO patents granted to, 99, 99*t*
Krishnan, P., 227
Krueger, Anne, 147, 148*n*10
Krugman, P., 185, 214
Krutikova, S., 227
Kuznets, Simon, 10

L

labor force participation rate (LFPR), 32,
    33*f,* 237–238, 238*t,* 240–241
labor market
    college wage premium, 242
    corporate profits and, 244
    economic growth and, 220
    gender parity in, 32, 33*f,* 237–238, 238*t*
    globalization and, 235–236, 236*t*
    information technology and, 243
    insecure work arrangements, 240
    institutional framework and, 249–253

Millennium Development Goals (MDGs)
(*continued*)
for human development, 219
for hunger, 31–32
as measure of development, 17
for poverty reduction, 27, 28–30, 28*t,* 30*f*
precrisis growth and, 29–31*f,* 29–34, 33*f*
Minsky, H. P., 188
monetary policy, 185–191
asset bubbles and, 273
credit market bubbles and, 205–206
financial regulation and, 267
financing for development and, 155
macroeconomic theory and, 181
Monterrey Consensus (2002), 152
mortgage markets, 61–62
Multidimensional Poverty Index, 147*n*2
Multilateral Debt Relief Initiative
(MDRI), 34

N

Nabeshima, K., 42
Nallari, Raj, 3, 55, 61, 67, 73, 105, 111, 117, 131,
159, 165, 179, 185, 201, 219, 221, 225, 231,
247, 257, 259, 263, 269, 283
natural disasters, 283–285
natural resources and land policy, 49,
120–121, 165–169, 166*f,* 168*t,* 174, 261
Netherlands, wage subsidies in, 251
net national disposable income (NNDI),
10, 23*n*6
net national income (NNI), 10, 23*n*6
Niger, education in, 222
NNDI (net national disposable income), 10,
23*n*6
NNI (net national income), 10, 23*n*6
North Africa. *See* Middle East and
North Africa
North, D. C., 57

O

OECD. *See* Organisation for Economic
Co-operation and Development
official development assistance (ODA),
33–34, 35*n*11, 144–145, 145*f,* 148*n*5
offshoring and outsourcing of jobs,
243–244
Olken, B., 260
Oman, economic growth in, 125, 126*t*
Organisation for Economic Co-operation
and Development (OECD)
on aid effectiveness, 153, 155
dashboard of indicators and, 17

organized labor, 252–253
Oviedo, A. M., 105
Oxford Poverty and Human Development
Initiative, 147*n*2

P

Pacific region. *See* East Asia and Pacific
Pages, C., 112
Palley, T., 214
"paradox of deleveraging," 62
Paris Declaration on Aid Effectiveness
(2005), 151, 154*f*
patents, 88, 98–99, 99*t,* 232
Paulson, Henry, 68
Paus, E., 42
Persson, T., 56
Philippines
competitiveness ranking for, 40, 41*f*
education in, 100–101, 100–101*t,* 102*n*4
middle-income trap in, 39, 40*f*
R&D spending in, 95, 96–97*t*
regional growth and, 56
USPTO patents granted to, 99, 99*t*
Poland
exchange rate during global financial
crisis, 210
foreign capital and trade in, 146
policy development
capital flows and, 272–274
for competitiveness, 161–162
for credit bubble prevention, 206–207
macroeconomic theory and, 179–183
trade policy, 213–216
urbanization and, 172
political framework
development and, 50–51, 67–70
income inequality as development
constraint for, 56
natural disasters and, 283
poverty traps and, 27
property rights and, 167–168
poverty reduction
early childhood development and, 221–222
economic growth and, 22*n*1, 46–47, 147*n*2
land policy and, 120
poverty traps, 25–37, 26*t*
PPI (private participation in
infrastructure), 135–142, 136*f,* 139*t*
prenatal care, 221
prices. *See also* asset prices
commodity prices, 5
food prices, 5, 278
health care rationing and, 233

Turkey
    exchange rate during global financial
        crisis, 210
    infrastructure investments in, 139

U

UNDESA (United Nations Department
    of Economic and Social Affairs),
    143–144, 145
unemployment rates, 236, 238–241,
    239t, 241t
UN-Habitat, 121
unionized labor, 252–253
United Nations Department of Economic
    and Social Affairs (UNDESA),
    143–144, 145
urbanization
    competitiveness and, 160–161, 173t
    fiscal sustainability of, 175
    geography of, 172–174
    as growth driver, 121–122
    industrialization and, 175
    innovation and, 176
    labor market trends and, 242
    land-use planning and zoning for, 174
    policy framework for, 172
    services delivery and, 175
    sustainability of, 174–175
U.S. Patent and Trademark Office
    (USPTO), 98–99, 99t

V

value-added taxes (VAT), 107
Vegh, C. A., 185, 202, 203
Vietnam
    economic growth in, 45
    middle-income trap in, 42
    R&D spending in, 95, 96–97t
    regional growth and, 56, 56f
    USPTO patents granted to, 99, 99t

Viotti, E. B., 77n5
vocational training, 241, 250
Vu, K. M., 77n3
vulnerable jobs, 240

W

wages
    college wage premium, 227, 242
    income inequality, 20–22, 56
    subsidies, 251
Walliser, J., 35n13, 148n4, 155
Washington Consensus, 143
water supply, 174–175
wealth inequality, 56
Weingast, B. R., 57
well-being measures, 17–22, 18–21f
wind energy, 262
Wolfers, J., 19–20, 21
women
    health of, 221
    labor force participation rate, 32,
        33f, 237–238, 238t
    property rights and, 120–121, 166
World Trade Organization (WTO), 65
Wu, H., 42n1

Y

youth
    malnutrition and, 31–32, 127
    mortality rates, 32, 35n9
    unemployment rates, 240–241,
        241t, 250
Yusuf, Shahid, 42, 45, 73, 79, 87,
    95, 117, 171

Z

Zambia, education in, 222
Zedillo, Ernesto, 65
Zhongxing Telecom, 83n2
Zucker, L. G., 81

ECO-AUDIT
Environmental Benefits Statement

The World Bank is committed to preserving endangered forests and natural resources. The Office of the Publisher has chosen to print *Frontiers in Development Policy* on recycled paper with 50 percent post-consumer waste, in accordance with the recommended standards for paper usage set by the Green Press Initiative, a nonprofit program supporting publishers in using fiber that is not sourced from endangered forests. For more information, visit www.greenpress initiative.org.

Saved:
- 4 trees
- 1 million British thermal units of total energy
- 417 pounds of net greenhouse gases
- 1,880 gallons of water
- 119 pounds of solid waste

green
press
INITIATIVE